**Successful
Outdoor
Writing**

Successful Outdoor Writing

By Jack Samson

Writer's Digest Books
Cincinnati, Ohio

Successful Outdoor Writing. Copyright© 1979 by Jack Samson. Printed in the United States of America. All rights reserved. No part of this book may be reproduced in any form or by any electronic or mechanical means including information storage and retrieval systems without permission in writing from the publisher, except by a reviewer who may quote brief passages in a review. Writer's Digest Books, 9933 Alliance Road, Cincinnati, Ohio 45242. **First Edition.**

Library of Congress Cataloging in Publication Data
Samson, Jack.
   Successful outdoor writing.
    1. Journalism, Outdoor. I. Title.
PN4784.O9S2   808'.025   79-11854
ISBN 0-911654-66-6

Book design by Barron Krody.

This book is fondly dedicated to all those outdoor writers who, over the years, have waited for the mailman.

Acknowledgements

The following articles and excerpts appear courtesy of *Field & Stream*, CBS Publications: "Just a Dog" by Corey Ford, copyright© 1952; "The One-Shot Antelope Hunt" by Jack Samson, copyright© 1973; "And I Do Not Walk Alone" by Bill Tarrant, copyright© 1974; "Hunting the Hard Country" by Jack Samson, copyright© 1975; "Day of the Elk" by Jack Samson, copyright© 1977; "Brown Dog" by Gene Hill, "9x9=Moral Decline" by George Reiger, "The Sweet and Sour of Diesel Power" by Bill Kilpatrick, "The Call" by Gary Sitton, "Low Rod" by Gene Hill, "Chart Your Way to Better Fishing" by F.M. Paulson, "Tarpon Madness" by Jack Samson, "Venison Treats" and "Wild Mushrooms" by Sylvia Bashline, and "Build Your Own Camp Kitchen" by Rick Webb, copyright© 1978; "The Mighty Mackerel" by Sylvia Bashline, and "Lure Yourself from the Winter Doldrums" by Coulman Wescott, copyright© 1979 by CBS Publications.

Excerpts from "The Black Marlin of Hawaii," "The Rockies: Timberline Trout," "Montauk: Days of the Striper," and "Iceland: Land of the Salmon" by Jack Samson were taken from *The Sportsman's World*, copyright© 1976 by Jack Samson and appear courtesy of the publisher, Holt, Rinehart and Winston.

Excerpts from "The Snook with the Faraway Look" by Clive Gammon from *Sports Illustrated*, copyright© 1978 by Time-Life, Inc.; "Boating Organizations You Should Know" by Joanne Fishman from *Sea* magazine, copyright© 1979 by CBS Publications; "Dixie's Forgotten Fighters" by Vic McLeran from *Southern Outdoors*, copyright© 1979 by B.A.S.S. Publications; "Born Again: An Arctic Spring" by Fred Bruemmer from *International Wildlife*, copyright© 1979 by the National Wildlife Federation; "Bones in the Bahamas" by Jack Samson from *Sportfishing* magazine, copyright© 1968 by Yachting Publishing Corp., appear by permission of the publishers.

Excerpts from *Wild, Wild Woman*, copyright© 1978 by Maggie Nichols, appear by permission of the author and the publisher, Berkley Publishing Corp.

Photo Credits: Opposite title page: courtesy Colorado Office of Tourism; opposite preface: courtesy Arkansas Department of Parks and Tourism; opposite Introduction: courtesy *Field & Stream*; opposite Chapter One: courtesy Idaho Division of Tourism; opposite Chapter Two: courtesy *Field & Stream*; opposite Chapter Three: Tennessee Department of Tourist Development; opposite Chapter Four: courtesy *Field & Stream*; opposite Chapter Five: Ken Stiebben; opposite Chapter Six: Pete Czura; opposite Chapter Seven: Bill McRae; opposite Chapter Eight: Bill McRae; opposite Chapter Nine: courtesy New York State Department of Commerce; opposite Chapter Ten: Tennessee Department of Tourist Development; opposite Chapter Eleven: Pete Czura; opposite Chapter Twelve: Jim Tallon; opposite Chapter Thirteen: courtesy *Field & Stream*; opposite Chapter Fourteen: courtesy West Virginia Department of Commerce; opposite Chapter Fifteen: courtesy Tennessee Department of Tourist Development; opposite Chapter Sixteen: courtesy Colorado Office of Tourism; opposite Chapter Seventeen: courtesy *Field & Stream*; opposite Chapter Eighteen: Doug Wilson; Page 41: courtesy *Field & Stream*; Page 75: courtesy *Field & Stream*; Page 145: courtesy *Field & Stream*; Page 153: Bill McRae; Page 183: Oregon State Travel Information Section; Page 197: courtesy *Field & Stream*.

Other Books by Jack Samson:

The Bear Book

The Pond

A Fine and Pleasant Misery

The Sportsman's World

The Worlds of Ernest Thompson Seton

Falconry Today

The Best of Corey Ford

Line Down! The Special World of Big Game Fishing

Contents

1 Preface
4 Foreword by Nelson Bryant
7 Introduction
13 1. So You Want to Be an Outdoor Writer
23 2. The Basic Requirement for Success
33 3. Writing the Basic News Story
43 4. How to Write the Basic Feature Story
55 5. Writing for Outdoor Magazines
67 6. How to Market and Package Your Magazine Story
75 7. Writing an Outdoor Column
85 8. The Importance of Photography to an Outdoor Writer
99 9. How to Write Outdoor Copy for Radio and Television
111 10. Writing Outdoor Books
121 11. The Fishing Writer
129 12. The Shooting Writer
137 13. The Conservation/Nature Writer
145 14. The Camping Writer
155 15. The Boating Writer

167 16. The Recreational Vehicle Writer
175 17. The Dog Writer
189 18. PR Careers for the Outdoor Writer
197 Appendixes
    198 1. Some Useful Feature Techniques
    202 2. Making Fishing Come Alive
    205 3. A How-To Feature
    211 4. The Short How-To
    215 5. Writing for Mood: A Hunting Story
    218 6. RV Writing: A Product Evaluation
    221 7. Outdoor Food Writing
    226 8. A Humorous Outdoor Column
    228 9. A Boating/Fishing Article
    231 10. An Outdoor PR Article
    234 11. A Man's World No Longer
    239 12. Nature Writing: A Conventional Treatment of a Classic Theme
    241 13. A Conservation Essay

Preface

You would not be reading this if you didn't love the outdoors. At some point (perhaps after that last long look at the darkening woods when it's time to head back) there is the realization that it would be such a pleasure to earn your living writing about the outdoors. It would give you the chance to work where you feel most at home and alive—and the chance never to return again to that deadening job. For most of us that desire came early in life. For others it comes after years of breathing stale air in the prison of office walls. This book will help you convert that desire into action.

I can cite any number of cases where writers succeeded in a matter of months and many, many others where it took years. The latter is more likely, but this book is being written to help the aspiring outdoor writer cut down the length of time it takes to be recognized and accepted in this very specialized field.

Because of the length of time it takes to be recognized, it may be impossible (for financial or other reasons) to devote yourself full time to outdoor writing. If this is so, don't give up. There remain excellent opportunities for converting your interest in the outdoors into articles, photos, and stories. In addition to the excitement of sharing your experiences (and what you have learned) with fellow sportsmen, writing can bring in extra income to finance more getaway trips or to purchase that handmade flyrod or super down bag you've eyed for so long.

This book was written to guide and advise the beginning outdoor writer.

If someone had written a book like this for me back in the mid-1940s—when I decided I wanted to be an outdoor writer—it would have saved me a lot of experimentation, rejection slips and heartbreak.

Writers like me kept at it until we sold more stories and finally earned a name. We did everything wrong so many times that doing it the right way was usually arrived at by the process of elimination. Looking back on it now, I don't know what possessed editors like Hugh Grey of *Field & Stream,* Bill Rae of *Outdoor Life* and Ted Kesting of *Sports Afield* to even use the photographs we took. They were, by today's standards, simply awful. But then black and white photos were all the outdoor magazines ran, and anything in focus must have been considered a bonus.

I only hope the many young people who have written me over the years—and to whom I have written a letter of encouragement only (because I did not have the time to write more)—will read this book. These are the people—youngsters for the most part—who write to the editors of large outdoor magazines. They usually write in longhand, in pencil. The note goes something like this:

> Dear Sir: I live in a small town and love to hunt and fish. I spend all my time out of school and on weekends either hunting and fishing or learning about animals and birds and fish. I read your magazine each month from cover to cover and think it's great, especially the hunting and fishing departments. I would like to write a story for your magazine about a really big bass I caught this spring. Can you tell me how I go about writing for your magazine?

I never take these letters lightly. I answer each one to the best of my ability in the limited time I have because I feel the eagerness and pathos in those letters. Only a professional outdoor writer or editor who has spent many years in small towns and cities trying to find out why an editor did not like a story that had just been returned with a rejection slip can really feel the need and know the hopelessness of trying to compete when one is not yet ready or qualified and doesn't even know the ground rules. And the frustrating thing for an editor is that he knows how many formidable obstacles there are in the way of success in this highly competitive field. Sometimes, when the handwriting is really bad and the letter full of grammatical errors and poor spelling, there is a temptation to tell the hopeful writer to forget it, but I don't. Because I look back and remember—when my three sons were little—more than twenty years ago. I was living on the outskirts of a city in the Southwest and writing seven outdoor columns a week for a wire service, two daily papers, three weeklies and a magazine. I received $5 a week for each column—$35 per week—$140 per month. That, for the mid-1950s, was not bad money. And—added to an occasional magazine article in a regional or national magazine—it gave me a good supplemental income to that of a journalist. I never met a rich newspaperman who lived on his salary.

In spite of a degree in journalism and a lot of writing experience, I didn't really know that much about outdoor writing then. I knew how to write an informative how-to-do-it outdoor column and a passable feature story. My photography was mediocre at best. Fortunately no editor ever wrote me and told me to try another career. They just sent me rejection slips until I, over the years, could have papered a barn over with them. If I had received a letter telling me to forget outdoor writing as a career—especially after a particularly long siege of rejection slips—I might just have chucked the whole thing. So I do not discourage anyone from trying this field.

I have written this book with the beginning outdoor writer in mind, to give him the benefit of what I have learned the hard way, and perhaps to save him from the common mistakes. It may also be of considerable use to the professional outdoor writer. There are a lot of outdoor writers today who are making a good living in the freelance field who could stand to sharpen their skills in certain areas. None of us is ever so good that we cannot learn from others.

Jack Samson

Editor, *Field & Stream*

Foreword

I wish this book had been around when I launched my career in outdoor writing—although *launched* is perhaps too forceful a word, implying a vigor and assurance that scarcely characterized my first obscure fumblings under the pines—because it would have saved me much cold tracking.

I ventured into the field about twenty-five years ago for economic reasons. I was the managing editor of a small New Hampshire daily and my salary wasn't sufficient to meet the mortgage payments on the lovely old farmhouse my wife and I had just bought.

"Never fear, my dear," I said. "I'll sell enough stories to the outdoor magazines to make up the difference."

Three months later with the bank snarling at my heels I made my first sale. The story involved chumming rainbow trout with cottage cheese, and I remember the trip vividly because as my companion and I started to catch fish I was attacked by a virus.

It got so bad I couldn't look through my camera's viewfinder for more than five seconds before heaving, and the sylvan silence of that lovely remote pond was shattered by my dreadful retching and the sympathetic howling of my pointer Argus on the shore.

I got at least half a dozen good color shots, however, and although I didn't know it at the time, that parlous day marked the beginning of what eventually became a full-time vocation.

There was, to be sure, a hiatus of more than a year between my managing editor's job and when I joined the *New York Times* as their outdoor columnist—fourteen months of building docks that all began to look the same—and I still nurture a fading dream that I will someday write a first-class narrative poem that reviewers will compare favorably with Hart Crane's song of love to the Brooklyn Bridge, but the world of outdoor writing has been good to me.

A reverence for the language is the first requisite for good writing in any field, and this must be backed by solid information and research.

Beyond this, and a clean, honest style, the various publications and radio and television stations have their own requirements, and understanding those requirements will save the aspiring writer a good deal of effort and heartache. The beginner in the field will find the answers to such questions in Jack Samson's book. Everything is covered, from writing to photography; from actual examples of what he regards as superior work to pitfalls to avoid when submitting a manuscript or making an inquiry about a story idea.

In the past decade, writing and photography in outdoor magazines has been steadily improving, and at its best it need not take a back seat to that produced for any other specialized market.

The competition is strong, but the growing environmental awareness, particularly among those under the age of thirty-five that manifests itself in camping, hiking, backpacking, canoeing, fishing, and, to a lesser degree, hunting, is producing a new group of readers whose interests will be given increasing coverage.

I can think of no man more qualified than Jack Samson to provide such guidance. A flyer for General Chennault in China in World War II, Samson returned home, received a journalism degree from the University of New Mexico, covered the Korean War for what was then The United Press; was awarded a Nieman fellowship at Harvard for the excellence of his reportage; went to work for The Associated Press, which included writing an outdoor column, contributed to the major outdoor magazines and joined *Field & Stream* as managing editor in 1970.

He is a hard-nosed, talented newsman of broad experience doing what he likes best and willing to share what he has learned.

Nelson Bryant
Outdoor Editor, *New York Times*
December 24, 1978

Introduction

Just what is an outdoor writer? There are times I wish we could drop the term "outdoor writer" in favor of a better one, but I cannot think of a substitute. You might say an outdoor writer is simply a writer who chooses to write on outdoor subjects, or that an outdoor writer is no different—in principle—from a technical writer who writes for industry; a writer who turns out plays or poetry or a writer who specializes in novels or short stories. You could argue that a writer is a writer no matter what the subject—there's a fair degree of truth to that.

I know several fine novelists—one a nationally known mystery writer—who write an occasional fishing story for magazines. But that does not make them outdoor writers.

An outdoor writer, if asked, would say he is a hunter, or fisherman, or backpacker, who writes about the sport he loves. Writing is a means for the outdoor writer, not an end. The outdoor writer concerns himself with activities generally considered "outdoor sports." This does not include spectator sports, nor such urban games as golf or tennis.

In the words of outdoor writer Maggie Nichols:

> Outdoor sports are highly personal activities, involving no rigid schedules or complex game plans, requiring no company, and ambiguous in the way success is measured. They can be done alone, with a partner, or with a group. . . . Some can be enjoyed for just part of a day; others need sizeable commitments of time. Some can take place minutes from home; some call for major expeditions. Most involve a certain amount of physical exertion, although this is very much a matter of degree, since sitting still is sometimes the main requirement.

For our purposes outdoor sports do have two essential characteristics. They are dependent upon a wild (or at the very least non-urban) setting, and they derive either wholly or in part from man's earliest efforts to sustain himself and his family. These are the few remaining areas where modern man can reaffirm his primal connection to the natural world, and through this challenge enrich his life. They include fishing, hunting, camping, trapping, boating, backpacking, and training and handling dogs.

Since the days shortly after World War II the outdoor field—or what has come to be known as the outdoor leisure market—has undergone tremendous expansion and diversification. No longer is the outdoors the exclusive realm of the Boy Scout and the hardcore woodsman. Outdoor activities became immensely popular—and even fashionable in the mid-1960s—perhaps because they fit well into the "back to the earth" and fitness movements.

Suddenly the outdoor image became widely attractive to people in all walks of life. People who wouldn't walk across the street on a sunny day outfitted themselves in hiking boots and mountain parkas. Outdoors was in. This, combined with the enormous increase in leisure time, contributed greatly to the growth of outdoor interests.

Dramatic, too, have been the results of the application of modern technology and materials to outdoor equipment. Lightweight, durable materials beginning with aluminum and fiberglass have made boats, trailers, campers and packframes more portable. Ultralight rods and reels, dehydrated foods, and improved fabrics and insulation for tents, sleeping bags and clothing have enabled the average outdoorsman to reach with ease areas formerly accessible only to the wealthy sportsman. The development of such efficient and mobile equipment as the chain saw, the all-terrain vehicle, the four-wheel drive vehicle, the houseboat and the motor home have not only made life easier for the outdoorsman but allowed him to take his family with him on trips.

The days of mountain men are gone forever. No more must men lug canned goods and sacks of beans and flour high into the mountains. Gone also are the huge, heavy canvas tents (except those still used by professional outfitters for elk hunts or trail rides). Modern gear has made much of this physical labor unnecessary.

Small outboard motors may now be carried with one hand where years ago it took two men to carry an outboard motor down to a dock. Electric trolling motors and electronic depth finders have come along to make the motorized fisherman not only silent, but all-seeing. Mountain or rockclimbing gear has become virtually space-age oriented. The outdoor field—gearwise—is a whole new ball game.

On the other hand, there are things that never change. The awe of nature's elements, the grandeur of mountains, plains and the sea will always enchant man. Nature and its creatures are a mystery which—while much of it has been explained—will remain mysterious and fascinating forever. A leaping salmon or a soaring eagle are as moving today as they were to the first man who saw them.

Technological advances have not always been beneficial to the environment. The snowmobile, dune buggy and trailbike have brought down the wrath of those concerned with habitat destruction. Highly efficient commercial fishing methods have depleted many species of sport fish. New dams enlarge recreational facilities at the cost of siltation and other environmental deterioration. Agricultural pesticides have diminished game and songbird species alike. Disposable containers and packaging clutter waterways and landscapes and pose a hazard to wildlife.

If one is to be an outdoor writer in the 1980s it is important to know that attitudes as well as equipment have changed. More Americans live in cities today than ever before (75 percent in 1978 versus 56 percent in 1940). This has resulted in great numbers of people having no first-hand knowledge about nature and its creatures.

In the past several decades there have sprung up many organizations and individuals—loosely known as "protectionists"—who decry the killing of wild creatures for any reason—food or sport. Their attitudes reflect a number of factors, but especially the fact that they were urban raised. A generation grew up that had seldom or never seen a wild creature outside of a zoo and had never observed life on a farm. And at the same time, many Americans continued to hunt and fish as they had for generations. There was an inevitable clash of ideas and opinions. The anti- and pro-hunting forces divided into warring camps, and the ideological battle is still going on. Up until these attacks on their favorite sports, hunters and fishermen had mainly been organized into local groups. But this new threat organized them nationally as never before.

By 1978, a number of national organizations—such as The National Wildlife Federation, National Wildlife Institute, Izaak Walton League, Ducks Unlimited, National Shooting Sports Foundation, National Rifle Association and others—had rallied behind the sportsman on a national level. Established conservation organizations the calibre of The Audubon Society, World Wildlife Fund, and Sierra Club took the stand that hunting was a necessary and valuable wildlife management tool.

The anti-hunting and fishing forces stayed away from the subject of meat-eating, which would have led them into a maze of contradictions. Anyone who eats meat (or even owns a cat or dog and feeds these animals anything except vegetable matter) deprives himself or herself of the only philosophically defensible argument against killing animals. For that matter, if they wear leather in any form they do the same thing.

Men, deer, fish, birds and insects all live and die. To try to escape complicity in death on this earth, one would have to stop walking on the ground to avoid killing insects or to stop mowing lawns. Mowing a lawn, says Gene Lyons in an article in *Harper's,* eliminates habitat for small mammals and birds. Draining swamps in order to rid an area of mosquitoes reduces the number of ducks, muskrats, otters, turtles and fish.

Fortunately, the general public is beginning to recognize that the protectionist and the outdoor sportsman have a common goal: the preservation of habitat. For decades, sportsmen's money has gone to establish sanctuaries, game parks, national parks, wilderness areas and preserves. It is inevitable that, while managing these areas for the betterment of game species, non-game species benefit. Only thirty-five species of animals are legally hunted in the United States; more than eight hundred are not. While more than seven hundred species of birds benefit from these areas purchased and maintained by funds charged and contributed voluntarily by hunters and fishermen, seventy-four species only are legally hunted. No endangered species is legally hunted, and The National Wildlife Federation says no species was ever put on the endangered list by sport hunting in America in the twentieth century. On the other side of the ledger, many species have been brought back from the brink of extinction by wildlife management that was almost completely financed by fees and taxes on hunters and fishermen.

It is obvious to those who have spent a career in the outdoor field that the most serious threat to all of us who love nature and its creatures is the indiscriminate developer and polluter; the great industries of mining, livestock, timber, oil, farming, commercial fishing, and whaling; plus the relentless pressure of our population growth. There is a great need today for the type of investigative writing that revealed Watergate or the GAO scandals in the general news area. There are many Watergates in the environmental field that should be exposed by concerned outdoor writers. There are constant attempts to "land grab" on the part of developers and special-interest groups. There are giant conglomerates that can and will continue to pollute our lakes, streams and seas and pave over our land. There is waste, ineptitude and greed in many plans of the federal government for our natural resources. The Army Corp of Engineers alone, if allowed to complete all the plans on their drawing board, could dam every free-flowing river in America.

Investigative outdoor writing is only one niche in the field, though extremely rewarding and certainly vital to the preservation of our land and wild creatures. However, there are many other areas that will be discussed later in the book: humor, food, photography, camping, backpacking, boating, recreational vehicles, hunting dogs and the traditional hunting and fishing fields available to the outdoor writer.

An outdoor writer is merely a good newspaper reporter, magazine writer, or radio or TV writer who has the good fortune to live and work most of the time in the great outdoors. In my many years with the wire services and radio and television news writing, I covered wars, politics, accidents, crime, science, sports, religion, and heaven knows how many other subjects. The outdoor writer has no less a wide field to choose from—he just has more fun.

So You Want to Be an Outdoor Writer

1.

Well, that's about half of what you need to make it—the most important half. You must be driven enough to sacrifice creature comforts for some time before becoming a success in this field. It is not a field (compared to certain other professions) in which making money should be the primary motivation. It is doubtful that an outdoor writer will ever strike it rich, if by being rich one is talking about money and material things.

But to spend one's life in the outdoors and not have to punch a timeclock or spend eight hours a day at a desk is rich by my standards. Being close to nature and its creatures can be very satisfying.

On the other hand, there is no reason an outdoor writer should have to live on the scent of salt spray or the sight of desert sunrises. A good living can be made by writing in this field once the writer has mastered the basics of the trade. Many outdoor writers enjoy the freedom of full-time freelancing and live comfortably.

At *Field & Stream*, our department editors live in various parts of the country and never come near the home office in New York. All average $11,000-$20,000 a year writing one story or column for this magazine per month, and that does not include what they make with other magazines and by writing books. Naturally, not all aspiring outdoor writers are going to wind up on the staff of *Field & Stream*, but in addition to the major national outdoor sporting magazines there are now scores of smaller regional camping, backpacking, fishing and hunting publications that appear each month, including those put out by state game and fish departments. And, for the nature photographer, there are magazines such as *Audubon, National Wildlife,* and a host of others. Knowing what I know today about this field I would have no fear of moving to Idaho or British Columbia to freelance stories on the outdoors. If I could not net a five-figure income, I would be ashamed of myself. I doubt that I'd have to work a five-day week, either.

It depends on what sort of outdoor writing one does, of course.

There are thousands of writers writing today for the outdoor field. *Writer's Market,* a huge and invaluable book published annually by Writer's Digest Books, divides the outdoor markets roughly into the animal; automotive and motorcycle; nature, conservation, and ecology; and sport and outdoor publications. The 1979 *Writer's Market* lists 4,500 places to sell articles, books, short stories, novels, fillers, plays, poetry, jokes, and more. Not all of these are obvious outlets for the writer who wants to specialize in the outdoor field, but there are at least 150 markets listed by *Writer's Market* for the outdoor writer in 1979. These are magazines; there are also newspapers, radio, television, wire services, and book publishers—all of which pay for outdoor stories.

The 1979 *Photographer's Market* lists over 250 periodicals that use wildlife and scenic photography. A freelance photographer can also sell shots of wild animals and nature through stock photo agencies or to audiovisual firms; book publishers; and companies that produce posters, prints, brochures, calendars, and postcards.

As I noted in the Introduction, the outdoor recreation field is tremendously expanded and diversified today. When I first began writing outdoor columns on hunting and fishing there were very few bowhunters, and these few seemed a select group, not often seen or heard from. The same was true of black-powder aficionados. Today many states have special seasons for these two types of hobbyists, and their numbers are legion. An example from the world of fishing: What was just another fish—the bass—has become a widespread cult, endlessly refining its equipment and techniques.

It is best to specialize in this day and age. The day is gone when a writer could say he or she made a living writing general stories on the entire outdoors. A general outdoor freelance writer does not usually sell as regularly as one who is well known as an expert in one or two fields. Special-interest magazines are the rule, serving specialized audiences. Even on the remaining general outdoor magazines, the nonspecialist columnist is usually a well-established, longtime outdoor personality. The amount of knowledge required to make you expert in any one field is immense. To attempt a broad range of expertise today may be impossible; not to mention the tremendous competition the writer faces in the general outdoor writing markets, competing even with people who are not primarily outdoor writers at all.

We are in an age of specialization. And this extends even to outdoor writing. A writer who is a recreational vehicle editor for a magazine, newspaper, or wire service need not write about much else. The same can be true of a boating editor, a camping editor, or a travel editor. Specialized fields that are a bit wider are, for example, the outdoor editor or the hunting and fishing editor. He or she has a lot more room in which to branch out.

So you know it is best to specialize. The next step is to take a close look at yourself and decide which area you are most suited to writing about. Some of the questions you should consider are: Where does my widest experience lie? Which sport am I most skilled at? Which do I have the most equipment for? Which do I have the most friends and relatives engaged in (to give me a wider pool of experience to dip from)? Which do I find it easiest to express myself about? Which have I done the most reading in? Which is the one that I *care* the most about?

Once you have narrowed down the area or areas that you might wish to specialize in, the next, and just as important thing to do is sound out that particular market. In the case of bowhunting, for example, a bit of research would reveal that:

1. 80 percent of the bowhunters in your state also hunt big game with a rifle. In fact, 30 percent of the bowhunters in a recent national survey belong to the National Rifle Association (NRA). 55 percent of the bowhunters also hunt birds with a shotgun, and 79 percent hunt small game.
2. In a recent market research study eight of ten big game rifle hunters said they want to try bowhunting. As urbanization increases and habitat shrinks, the limited range of the bow can be expected to

result in increased numbers of bowhunters in the future.
3. 64 percent of the bowhunters are over 30 years of age, 36 percent are under 30.
4. Only 7 percent of America's bowhunters hunt only with a bow.
5. 57 percent of the bowhunters have attended college, 18 percent have graduated.
6. 16 percent of the big-game hunters in America today are bowhunters (that's one out of six).
7. 2 percent of the big-game hunters use black powder weapons.
8. 78 percent of the bowhunters are also campers.
9. 70 percent of the bowhunters are married.
10. Twelve states permit a deer to be taken in bowhunting season and another in rifle season. Five more states have such a law under consideration. One state permits two deer per license and two states have no limit on deer during the season beyond one deer per day.
11. Bow seasons range from 18 days to 165 days per year, with five states permitting year-round bowhunting.
12. Thirty-nine states have spring turkey bowhunting seasons and twenty-eight have fall turkey bowhunting seasons.
13. 56 percent of the states report that they expect the total number of hunters to *increase* by 1980. Most others expect the number to stay about the same.
14. 96 percent of the 1-1/2 million American bowhunters are male. That means there are about 60,000 women bowhunters.
15. Eighteen states now offer late bowhunting seasons, after rifle season, in addition to their early bowhunting season. Increased recreation is the result in addition to maximum utilization of available public lands, with a minimum effect upon wildlife.
16. A wildlife chief in one of our largest states recently commented: "During rifle season it seems like the guys that get the real big bucks are the ones who bowhunted beforehand and had them spotted and figured out before rifle season opened."
17. The cost of recreation is always a factor. Not only are introductory costs usually lower in bowhunting, but arrows are recoverable, bullets are not. This adds up for the practicing bowhunter. A present rifle hunter can take up bowhunting at a lower cost then he might suspect.
18. Bowhunting is easy to learn. Who has not shot a bow and arrow when young? The skill almost seems to come naturally. Certainly, the conscientious new bowhunter will practice beforehand and hunt

only with hunting heads that are sharpened daily, and after every shot.
19. Bowhunting has a minimum effect upon wildlife. It is a recreational sport. It is estimated that only about 5 percent of the bowhunters harvest game in any given year. In bowhunting the quality of the hunt counts much.
20. Most bowhunters hunt with a relative or friend. It is an excellent way to introduce sons and daughters to hunting while there are few people in the woods.
21. Federal matching funds are available for the local construction of new American Archery Council ranges for municipal parks.
22. Related to No. 21 above, over $12 million has been provided in 11 percent federal excise tax funds from the sale of archery equipment since the manufacturer supported tax went into effect in 1975. These funds may be used by the states for hunter safety training, public target ranges and wildlife restoration projects.

[Facts on bowhunting for the year 1978, courtesy of the American Archery Council, 200 Castlewood Road, North Palm Beach, FL 33408.]

A close look at this example will show a number of things about the field: the size of the audience, who they are and where they are located, whether or not the sport is growing, and the many overlapping interests they have in other outdoor sports. All of this information will eventually be vital to the development of a column or article and to the slant you might give to the subject.

A second important step in your research must now be done. Survey the existing treatment of your field: Are there already numerous books, articles and magazines devoted to it? Who are the established experts? What kinds of articles seem to appear most consistently? Does much of the information cover the same ground? Is there a need (and here look to yourself and others you know involved in the sport) for more diverse or specialized information?

The example we have just considered deals with a relatively small and specialized outdoor field. But it does show the value of obtaining research on a field before entering it. The research material available on a subject like camping alone is mind boggling.

A few places to check for statistics and trends are clubs and national associations, manufacturers, trade associations, state and national governmental agencies (fish and game departments, for instance), and the outdoor editor of your local newspaper and regional outdoor magazines. These sources will show the beginning writer what the market is like and will also give an idea of the size and specific characteristics of the audience. That is important. A writer who can demonstrate to a daily metropolitan newspaper, regional or national magazine, television station or book publisher that the audience is there and in specific numbers has a distinct advantage over a beginner who cannot.

There are some areas of the outdoors that are not only overcrowded, but require a tremendous amount of very specialized knowledge in order to compete successfully. Take the job of shooting editor as an example. One does not just decide to become a gun editor or shooting editor and move into that slot overnight. The late Warren Page, shooting editor of *Field & Stream,* and Jack O'Connor, shooting editor of *Outdoor Life,* had both amassed a staggering knowledge of their trades during the many years they worked for these two magazines. In addition to traveling over most of the world in pursuit of birds and big game, these two men were experts on the handling of rifles, shotguns, and handguns. They were gunsmiths, ballistic experts, truly fine shots, photographers, and highly professional writers. The men who have come along to fill their shoes in the last few years—Bob Brister of *Field & Stream,* Jim Carmaichael of *Outdoor Life,* Grits Gresham of *Sports Afield,* and professionals the calibre of John Wooters, Col. Charles Adkins, Elmer Keith, and John Amber of the "vertical" or specialized gun magazines and catalogues, have spent lifetimes learning their trade. There are good, young gun writers coming up today— the Rick Jamisons and Jim Woods of the gun world—who show signs of becoming very successful. But it is a tough business and competitive to the point of excluding all but the best. This is also true for persons specializing in such fields as gundogs and recreational vehicles.

The fishing field also tends to be overcrowded. However, this field allows more writers to enter it, because it is not quite as technically restrictive as the gun writer category, and fortunately, fishing is probably the nation's largest participation sport. There are at least sixty million fishermen in America today, counting the youngsters who do not need a license until age fourteen, the senior citizens who are not required to buy a license after age sixty-five, and the many saltwater fishermen. The interest in fishing grows each year, and there is still room for a fishing writer.

You by no means have to restrict yourself to hunting and fishing in the outdoor field—although perhaps the greatest percentage of outdoor writers work in those areas. We have seen the rise in travel editors in the bigger magazines, and travel writing can be outdoor writing. All three of the largest outdoor magazines have reflected the rapid increase of interest in harvesting and eating wild plants and cooking fish and game. It has become the subject of popular columns and features in larger newspapers and of a number of best-selling and excellent books.

Nature and conservation is a field that is experiencing rapid growth. This is the area for writers interested in and concerned about the welfare of our lakes, streams, rivers, oceans, deserts, wetlands, mountains, and our wild creatures in general. Nature and conservation writers the calibre of Les Line of *Audubon* magazine, George Harrison and George Reiger are typical of the many who expose and help to eliminate many of the destructive forces acting upon our natural environment. All these men have excellent backgrounds in the biological sciences. This is one outdoor writing area in which academic training is almost essential. You are going to have to be able to deal with highly complex and sophisticated issues, problems and questions.

* * *

Choosing your field is a very personal decision, in which many factors must be carefully weighed. At the basis of the decision is a deep, personal involvement with a sport. In these days of increasing regulation and vanishing wilderness, outdoor writing is much more than a mere outlet for this love and concern. It is a means by which your feelings about the outdoors, through the print or broadcast media, can influence and educate the public, and perhaps help to turn the tide.

A Thumbnail Guide to Research

Once you have chosen your field, you will want to give yourself a good grounding in it. (Or you may want further information for marketing purposes, as described earlier in this Chapter). As important as direct experience is to the outdoor writer, the more you have read on your subject the better off you will be. The following is a short, general guide to basic research.

Research is fairly easy if you have access to a library and are familiar with some standard reference tools and with library procedure. Don't worry if your library is very small. Most libraries now belong to networks that allow them to borrow any book you could ever want from other libraries. And if you are close to a college or university library, so much the better. Even if you are not a student they will usually allow you to use their facilities.

If you know nothing at all about a subject a good place to start is an encyclopedia. This will give you a quick overview of your topic before you set about after greater detail. (Be sure to read the how-to-use-it section in the front before you use an encyclopedia or, for that matter, any reference book; this will save you much fumbling around.)

Next, go to your library's card catalog. This lists all the books they have in three ways: by author, title and subject. The *Subject Guide to Books in Print,* issued yearly, lists all the books currently available on your subject and should be on your library's reference shelf. If you have read a good book by some author, the edition of *Books in Print* that lists books by author will show you what else he has written, whether any of his books are in paperback, and if anything he has written is due to come out soon. And if you find something interesting that your library doesn't have, look it up in *Book Review Digest* before you ask them to order it. These books contain all book reviews written since 1905 and will tell you at a glance if the book is what you are looking for.

Some worthwhile and even classic books in your field may have gone out of print and will not be listed. To find these you need to look for bibliographies. You might have noticed a bibliography (list of books for further reference) in a book you've already read. This is an excellent source of additional material. Other bibliographies are available from clubs and national associations. There may even be a formal bibliography available for your subject; your librarian would know about it.

After you have digested all the books, we can move over to the magazines. To locate magazines in your field, the first place to look is the *Reader's Guide to Periodical Literature.* This is an index by subject, author and title of 130 magazines. It is updated twice a month and goes all the way back to 1900; it should keep you busy for awhile.

There are also a number of specialized periodical indexes. One which should interest the nature/conservation writer is the *Biological and Agricultural Index.* The special indexes cover many more periodicals than the *Reader's Guide.* Two other books you should look at are *Ulrich's Periodicals Directory* and the *Standard Periodicals Directory.*

These two volumes list all periodicals in the United States and Canada by subject. They are important not only for research but for getting to know your market. Another marketing aid is *N. W. Ayer's Directory of Newspapers and Periodicals.* This is a listing of every newspaper and magazine in the country. Should you want to go worldwide, *Ulrich's International Periodicals Directory* is a comprehensive two-volume reference.

Sounds like a lot of reading for an outdoorsman, doesn't it? I cannot stress strongly enough that the more you know about your subject, the better off you will be. You don't have to stumble from book to book by yourself. Your librarian is a highly trained professional and is there to help you, not just to check out books.

There is one other thing you can begin doing right now: Start building a file of stories from magazines and newspapers on your favorite subject in the outdoor field. You never know when the wealth of material you can compile yourself may come in handy. Don't stop at clipping stories from the major national and specialty magazines, either. Years ago, I wrote to the public relations directors of all the fifty state game and fish departments and asked to be put on the mailing lists for their monthly magazines and newsletters. Most of them began to send me literature for free. A few charged me for it and I paid, figuring the information the publications contained would be valuable to me in time—and it has been. A subject file of stories arranged alphabetically (just as you might arrange the photos you keep in stock) can grow over the years into an invaluable collection of information in your special field.

The Basic Requirements for Success

2.

For the outdoor writer it is difficult to say which is more important: the ability to write or a technical knowledge of your chosen field.

Just how good a writer do you have to be to be an outdoor writer? It will help if you have a sound background in grammar and composition. You need not have graduated from high school, but it certainly will help if your favorite subject was English and you have natural ability and a desire to write. This is a book on how to be a successful outdoor writer, but don't look here for a creative writing course. Anyone who can write a clear, concise sentence can be an outdoor writer—given drive, ambition and, most important, direct hands-on knowledge of the subject. I've just said you must be able to write clearly and concisely, and many times just that and no more will do the job. However, it is experience and expertise in a specialized outdoor field that counts. If you haven't done what you are writing about it won't matter how good a writer you are. There is no room for bluffing in outdoor writing. Your readers have been through it all and know it—and you had better know it, too.

The first step is learning to type. It is almost a necessity that today's writer be able to type, and in many cases the job calls for an ability to use a teletype machine or one of its new computerized equivalents. This may sound elementary, but if I had one bit of advice to give to an aspiring outdoor writer—and only one—I would advise him to learn to type first. If you are working in a print medium and can't type, you will be hampered and slowed every step of the way. It is not necessary to know professional touch-typing, but it certainly is an advantage. Like many older reporters I type with two fingers and am able to type ninety words a minute (Much to the surprise of secretaries who watch me for the first time). But there are obvious disadvantages to my system: While I can take dictation over the phone very well without looking at the keys, I have never been able to glance over at a sheet of numbers and type them without looking back to the keys for the appropriate figure.

The outdoor writer, like the newspaperman, needs only a few basic tools. The typewriter must be considered the most important. It can be either a standard or a portable. I have one of each: the standard for writing at home and the portable for work while traveling.

The outdoor writer must have a working knowledge of photography. One need not be a professional photographer, but it is necessary to be able to take a clear photograph of an event or object both under natural light conditions and with flash equipment. Most 35mm SLR cameras today are able to do both, with the advent of extremely "fast" films. We will discuss this in detail in Chapter Eight.

The outdoor writer must have a sound background in natural history. In today's world of "protectionist" versus outdoor sportsman, environmentalist versus industry, it is essential that the outdoor writer understand the natural sciences. He must have a working knowledge of such diverse subjects as wildlife management and pollution in all its forms. He must be an expert on energy and its various effects on the environment. He must understand the complicated balance of nature and the dynamics of ecosystems.

There is no substitute for experience plus a tremendous amount of reading and research.

In many of the heated discussions of the day, scientific truth is hard to come by and subtle of interpretation. When one realizes that "a sound background in natural sciences" may mean a PhD in the case of specialized areas of ornithology or zoology, one knows that it is no easy task for an outdoor writer to be an expert.

This doesn't mean you have to avoid every complex or highly technical subject. If you don't have a PhD yourself, find someone who has. Experts are often more than willing to assist the lay writer interested in their area. Who knows, there might be articles or even a book in this type of collaboration—your skill in transmitting the outdoor experience and his expert knowledge.

The conservation writer has one of the most demanding jobs in outdoor writing today. He or she is subject to both praise and attack on all fronts. Any treatment of this important topic in today's complex, ecology-minded world can stir up strong resentment. The writer must strive to stay completely honest and must under no circumstances be inhibited by the advertisers that buy space in the newspaper or magazine for which he writes. It is not only difficult but embarrassing when a conservation editor must expose a large advertiser as a major polluter or exploiter of the environment.

Much of industry is making a strong effort today to operate in harmony with the environment, and the conservation editor should tell this side of the story as well as expose the polluters and overdevelopers. By doing so, the conservation editor is constantly irritating one side or the other—sometimes both. It takes an extremely knowledgeable person to handle this job on a large publication today, but at the same time it may be the most important of all the outdoor writing jobs. For if we do not preserve our habitat—whether it be lake, stream, forest or ocean—and our wildlife for future generations, we will have failed in an awesome responsibility.

An outdoor writer must command respect in his field. If his outdoor column is full of factual errors he will not remain in the job long. Those who know the outdoors can spot a sloppy or uninformed outdoor writer very quickly. A magazine the age and size of *Field & Stream* has become a bible to many outdoorsmen. It is always amusing (and instructive) to me to see how fast our readers will pick up a mistake. The accidental misnaming of a local species of fish will bring hundreds of letters, most of them gleefully pointing out the mistake and adding some reference to the "city slickers" who edit outdoor magazines. Far from annoying me (except at the copy editor who made the error) it makes me realize all the more how avidly people read our magazine and what a huge audience we have.

The outdoor writer is being judged by his peers in each column or story he writes. He must show a thorough knowledge of equipment and its use. He must be reliable in reporting new developments in his chosen field and be fluent in its "language."

Fortunately, most outdoor writers and editors who work in the hunting and fishing fields as a career grew up participating in these two sports. It is in that case less difficult for the individual to keep up with new developments in tackle and techniques, guns, ammunition and related equipment. Even if he hunts or fishes often, however, there is such a mass of new developments each year that the outdoor editor is hard pressed to keep up. He must read constantly and attend the many local and national trade shows, such as the biannual National Sporting Goods Association (NSGA) shows; the American Fishing Tackle Association (AFTA) annual meeting; the National Rifle Association (NRA) conventions, Outdoor Writers Association of America (OWAA) convention; and a host of other professional and equipment shows. In addition he must be on the mailing lists of all the gun, ammunition and tackle companies in order to receive their latest catalogues. This is also true of camping, boating, clothing, backpacking, photography and many other companies that produce outdoor equipment. Since an outdoor writer is constantly traveling and is often in the company of other outdoor people, he must not only be able to discuss outdoor equipment knowledgeably, he must be able to use it well. If this sounds easy or routine, remember that this means becoming proficient, in the case of the fishing writer, in the use of fly rods for both fresh and salt water, flies, and the many categories of lines. Then there is spin fishing, spin-casting, bait-casting or the use of a level-winding reel and rod in both fresh and salt water. Surf-casting alone takes years to master. Big-game fishing not only takes years to learn but is one of the most expensive sports today. And unless a writer has caught a marlin or tuna, for example, he is hardly qualified to speak on the subject of sportfishing boats, big-game rods and reels, terminal tackle, or the methods and techniques of catching the big blue-water game fish. The same is true with subjects such as trap and skeet shooting and the hunting of upland game birds. The outdoor writer who has never snow-camped will not keep the attention of a young reader who has backpacked into the Adirondacks with his aluminum backpack frame, snowshoes, dehydrated food, portable tent, tiny pocket stove and ultra-light sleeping bag to spend a few days ice fishing or hunting snowshoe rabbits.

Those who raise dogs for a living will know quickly if the dog editor knows what he or she is talking about. Dog writers have a vocabulary all their own—as do dog lovers. The person who has spent a great deal of time and money on one of today's four-wheeled recreational vehicles will read an RV writer only once if he doesn't tell the RV owner something the owner wants to know and sound like he knows what he's talking about.

An outdoor writer must be deeply involved in his subject before considering it as a career. It is possible to learn, and expand your knowledge, as you go along; but whatever your level of expertise, never pretend that you know more than you do. If you're an old spin-fishing hand making your first flycasting expedition, make it clear that this is the case. If you're doing a column on your first bowhunting trip, say this is a first-time experience. Your bowhunting reader will identify with you and not only appreciate the coverage his sport is getting but will respect you for your honesty. And he will be more likely to forgive your technical errors than if you wrote as a self-proclaimed expert.

The outdoor writer must be honest. We have noted that honesty is indispensable in a conservation writer. Honesty should prevail in all outdoor writing. Every outdoor writer must be scrupulous in the reporting of facts in stories, the evaluation of merchandise, the attribution of quotes, and the balance of conflicting opinions.

There have been abuses over the years that have given the outdoor writer a bad name in some areas. "Freebies" have been handed out to freelance and staff outdoor writers as long as I have been in this field. Most airlines once made it possible for the outdoor writer to get where he needed to go for a story simply because the airline public relations man realized it would benefit the airline. If a good story is printed in a national magazine, book, or large newspaper about an area served by the airline, it usually means more people will want to go there. It has been customary—but not required—that the airline on which the writer traveled be mentioned in the story. But because of a number of unscrupulous "outdoor writers" of the past few decades most airlines are now reluctant to issue free tickets—even to legitimate staff writers of major publications. This reluctance came about because many writers simply took the free rides for personal reasons, often taking along spouses, children or friends with no intention of doing a story. Many places of lodging around the world that once afforded the outdoor writer free accommodations—hunting and fishing lodges and plush resorts alike—have been burned by dishonest outdoor writers so many times that they are now requiring payment (usually at a discount) or a guarantee of publication before giving free accommodations. They have every right to do so.

Many sporting goods manufacturers, which years ago sent guns and tackle to outdoor writers "on consignment" with no need for the equipment to be returned, now insist on prepayment (with discount, of course). Years ago the company could be reasonably sure the product would be tested and written about. Today, however, they can be sure of neither a return of the product nor even a mention in print. The OWAA has insisted on rigid standards of honesty and behavior for its more than three-thousand members. Word travels quickly around the outdoor field that a writer is "on the take," and usually that writer does not last long. We constantly receive complaints at the home office of *Field & Stream* from airlines, resorts and tourist divisions of states and foreign countries about persons representing themselves as staff writers of this magazine. We advise the companies and agencies to check credentials carefully before issuing free tickets or giving free accommodations.

Recently someone claiming to be the publisher of *Field & Stream* ran up a large hotel bill in a major southwestern city. Then he "rented" a four-wheel-drive recreational vehicle from a firm in that same city and rode off into the sunset. He had not been apprehended the last time I inquired!

An Outdoor Writer Must Find His Own Writing Style. A prospective outdoor writer should strive for his or her own writing style. A good rule of thumb is to learn to say things simply, and in the fewest possible words. Newspaper or wire service training can be valuable. Some of the best outdoor writers being published today learned their writing in the news field. Avoid long and cumbersome words. No editor is impressed with words that only a professor of English literature would know.

But effective outdoor writing goes beyond a clean and uncluttered style. I don't think I could explain this any better than others have already done. Rudolph Flesch wrote in *The Art of Readable Writing*:

> In one way or another your language differs from that of anybody else. It's part of your own unique personality. It has traces of the family you grew up in, the place where you came from, the people you have associated with, the jobs you have had, the schools you went to, the books you have read, your hobbies, your sports, your philosophy, your religion,

your politics, your prejudices, your memories, your ambitions, your dreams, and your love life. The way you form your sentences shows your outlook on life; the words you choose show your temperament and your aspirations.

And Thomas H. Cain wrote in *Common Sense About Writing:*

> The essence of your style is you—your individuality, your particular voice, your unique way of thinking, and speaking. But this cannot be taught. For better or worse, it is you, and you are it. If your writing were entirely you, however, the rest of us could not understand it . . . . But if you don't allow your own voice to come through, you may be clear but not worth reading . . . . If there were a master rule about style it would be this: *sound like yourself; let your own voice and personality come through* [italics mine].

An Outdoor Writer Must Be Disciplined. Writing is hard work. Good writing is even harder. There is all sorts of sage advice on how to be a good writer, but "applying the seat of the pants to the seat of the chair" is about the best I know. A writer who wants to sell stories in the outdoor field is going to have to be very, very productive. You are going to have to write and write and write. You will not sell a lot of stories at first, but if you follow basic guidelines I have outlined in this book you will begin to sell. After that it is research, marketing, photography and packaging that will make you a successful outdoor writer. Earlier in this chapter I said that anyone who can write a clear, concise sentence can sell. True, but only if he or she puts a lot of hard work and thought into the project.

I took a writing course at Harvard in 1960, the year I was awarded a Nieman Fellowship. Nieman Fellows are chosen each year—about a dozen from the United States—and allowed to take the courses of their choice for a full year at Harvard, all expenses paid. I was working for The Associated Press at the time and AP gave me a leave of absence. I took a number of great courses, but my favorite was the writing course, taught by Professor Theodore Morrison. Among the things that left an indelible impression on me about Ted Morrison (besides the fact that he thought "The Owl and the Pussycat" and passages from the Book of Ruth in the Bible were two of the great pieces of writing) was an expression he had. "If you wait for the muse to muse," he said, "you will write very little in this world." He was so right. There are thousands of frustrated writers sitting hunched over typewriters in walk-up, cold-water flats and suburban split-levels, elegant brownstones and country cabins, waiting for the muse to come along and produce that Great American Novel!

In the wire services, which I still consider one of the greatest training grounds for writers, we wrote steadily for eight-hour shifts. Whether we had any interest in politics, crime, art, science, horse racing or medicine made no difference. We wrote about whatever was news five days a week, year in and year out. As if that wasn't discipline enough, a wire service staffer must learn to write the same story twice in the same eight-hour shift. The first time it is written it will be either for afternoon or morning newspapers around the world, depending on what shift the reporter works. But during that time the story must be rewritten for the papers that will be on deadline when the next staffer comes on duty. This means that—even though the story has been done once—it must be written again as though it were a new story with a different lead, new facts that have become available, and an updated version that sounds fresh to the readers of the new publishing cycle. Believe me, after one has done that for years, sitting down to writing a magazine story or a newspaper column is pure pleasure! The wire services teach you that no matter how tired you are, no matter how badly you may feel physically or emotionally, no matter what personal problems you have, you write and you *keep* writing because somewhere, all around the world, some paper is going to press in the next few minutes and needs the story *you* are writing.

Outdoor writing is not a career to be taken lightly. Just learning the skills is rigorous and demanding. But over and above acquiring the knowledge and mastering the techniques, you must be persistent. It is the ability to press on in the face of risks, obstacles and disappointments, this clarity of purpose and willingness to go the extra mile, that separates the successful outdoor writer from those who only yearn and dream.

* * *

These are basic requirements and tools necessary for you to become an outdoor writer. We will discuss individual categories of outdoor writing (and their individual requirements) in following chapters.

Outdoor writing is not a career to be taken lightly. It is demanding and requires considerable skills, honesty and integrity.

It will also call for the mastery of certain (depending on your field) basic forms and techniques. In the next chapter we will learn one of the most widely applicable: how to write a basic news story.

Writing the Basic News Story

3.

I have chosen to discuss the basic news story first because it has been the cornerstone of many outdoor writing careers.

Years ago, it was almost axiomatic that the most successful magazine writers came from the ranks of newspapermen. Many of the most gifted writers in America—Mark Twain, John O'Hara, Bret Harte, O. Henry, Sinclair Lewis, John Hersey, and Ernest Hemingway, as examples—were newspapermen who began writing news and moved into writing what is called "news features." From there they developed feature writing styles which fitted well into the magazine format and—expanded—into the short story and novel forms.

Some of you may intend to write for daily or weekly newspapers. You may have your sights set on writing for magazines in your chosen outdoor field. You may even decide to enter broadcast journalism. Whatever medium you choose, knowing how to write a basic news story can do nothing but help your career.

Whether you tend to be a hunting, fishing, boating, camping, travel, recreational vehicle, or environmental writer, there is sure to be a need for a news approach now and then in your work.

Several hundred years ago, back in our colonial days, newspaper style was considerably different from what it is today. A news story was written along the lines of a direct narrative, as though the writer was talking to the reader. Take an example from the Tuesday, February 3, 1863, issue of the *New York Times.* A front page news story began like this, without a dateline (place, such as a city) to tell the reader where the story originated.

> Mr. A.D. Boileau, of the *Philadelphia Evening Journal,* who was arrested and committed to Fort McHenry, at Baltimore, by order of Gen. Schenck, has written a conservative and loyal letter to the General, disavowing his knowledge of any objectional editorial being in the *Journal* until after its publication, and cordially disapproving said editorial, which referred to Jeff Davis' and President Lincoln's messages. He denies any design of injuring the Government, but claims being for the Union and crushing out the rebellion. The letter is said to be dignified and conciliatory in its character, and has had the effect to obtain his release.

While the article does get around to telling what happened, eventually, it is a long "lead" paragraph by modern news standards. Most news stories began that way in the days of the colonial newspaper, produced on a handpress with type hand-set by a printer. There was very little reporting as we know it today. The printer took what came into his shop from other publications or word of mouth and ran it. The papers were rarely larger than four 8½x11 pages, and there was no attempt to "structure" the story since it was assumed the reader was going to read the entire newspaper.

Even with the introduction of iron presses and new and more legible typefaces in the first half of the nineteenth century, news stories continued to be long and rambling. What changed all that was Mr. Samuel F.B. Morse's invention of the telegraph in 1844. As newspapers began linking up with the telegraph, the shape of the news story began changing. In most newspapers of that era, the telegraph news was printed in "bulletin" form and was set aside from the rest of the news, usually in a separate column. As a result, the lead sentences became shorter as editors began to "boil down" news into a lead sentence or first paragraph. The story, in news circles, is that the concise news lead began during the Civil War when the first war correspondents began vying for a "beat," or time advantage, over their rival correspondents. Supposedly, the harried telegraph operators of the day—besieged by savagely competing correspondents and not wishing to be accused of favoritism—allowed each war correspondent to send one paragraph only, on a rotation basis. They would then let the reporters send subsequent paragraphs on the same rotation. This resulted in the correspondents' trying to get as much news as possible into the beginning paragraph and saw the beginning of what was called the "inverted pyramid" news story. Each paragraph, after the first, held news of decreasing importance. No matter where the correspondent's story was cut, whether by a break in telecommunication or by an editor with little space to devote to the story, the story would still be a comprehensible whole. The inverted pyramid is still the basic ingredient of news stories. It has been referred to in other ways, such as getting the five Ws into the first paragraph—Who, What, When, Where and Why. It amounts to the same thing and is still being taught in journalism schools today.

> Washington, Nov. 18—James T. McIntyre, Jr., the Budget Director, is reported to favor a rollback in President Carter's plans for a 3 percent increase in military spending next year so that $1 billion to $2 billion more would be available for domestic social programs already hit hard by budget cuts.

That just about says it all. The story goes on for columns, but the reader already knows the essence of the news story and, if interested, may go on to read more details about it.

This, basically, is what you will have to do with whatever news comes up in your chosen outdoor field. In writing wire service stories for UPI and AP, I wrote thousands of news leads on outdoor subjects. They covered news on hunting and fishing and countless other categories, but they all had one thing in common: They had the news in the first paragraph. For example:

> Seoul, Korea, Oct. 21 (UP)—Park Sung Yee, Defense Minister, said today that the vast demilitarized zone extending across the width of the penninsula between North and South Korea had become a vast game preserve since human habitation had been prevented in it for such a long time.

> Tokyo, Feb. 6 (AP)—The Japanese government announced today the capture of two more South Korean fishing boats it said had entered Japanese fishing grounds in violation of a law passed by the Diet six months ago.

> Santa Fe, N.M., Aug. 16 (AP)—The State Game and Fish Commission today set season dates and bag limits for small game, bird, and big game for the coming fall and added that good rainfall this spring and summer had provided excellent habitat for most of the state's game animals and birds.
>
> Albuquerque, N.M., Oct. 1 (AP)—An alliance of big ranchers, cattlemen, and members of the oil and gas industry have banded together in a massive attempt at a "land grab" which will deny the state's sportsmen access to thousands of acres of prime hunting and fishing land now under state control.
>
> New York, Sept. 3 (AP)—In what many fisheries biologists consider a move of reverse logic, the Department of Environmental Protection announced today that, instead of appropriating more funds to combat stream pollution, it would close down a number of its trout hatcheries.

You see the point. The method works the same way for any outdoor subject. A boating writer could have a lead which runs:

> Akron, Oh., Feb. 1—The Evinrude Company today brought out its new motors for 1979, dispelling any rumors in the boating industry that they had planned to reduce the horsepower of new outboard motors.

A camping writer might have a lead which goes:

> San Rafael, Calif., May 3—Two young campers, stranded for 48 hours on the sheer north face of Capulin Mountain, were rescued by Park Service helicopter early today after ropes were lowered to the ledge where they had weathered a two-day storm.

A travel writer might turn the following lead in to his local newspaper:

> Acapulco, Mexico, Aug. 3—The Global Hotel chain, which owns resort hotels from the Caribbean to Hawaii, today opened its newest plush resort hotel here in an effort to attract both big game fishermen and sun worshippers.

And an environmental investigative reporter could easily turn out the following lead for his or her news story:

> Atlantic City, N.J., March 24—Caesar's Forum, the multimillion-dollar development firm building three hotels in this coastal gambling city, was told by a federal judge today that it is violating the state's Tidelands Bill by draining a saltwater marsh in order to build an 18-hole golf course.

The basic concept of getting most if not all of the news into the first part of the story applies also to radio and television—media which had a slow but considerable effect on the treatment of news. Readers of newspapers, who heard the tragic Hindenburg zeppelin disaster "live" from Lakehurst, New Jersey, and who later listened to Edward R. Murrow's nightly broadcasts about the London bombing raids during World War II, gradually came to expect more than the telegraph-style news story from print media. News had suddenly become global. It was not as important for the writer to get all the Ws into the lead of the story as it was for him to be sure and get the *why* into it. With the advent of electronic-age journalism, the why supplied meaning and context to the news. It led to modern "interpretation" by newscasters and commentators. This news-analysis and in-depth reporting had a defect (and still does) in that it sometimes allowed announcers with excellent on-air and on-camera voices to offer opinions rather than fact. It was not always easy to find a good news reporter who could write scripts for these anchormen, or anchorpersons, as they came to be called on the distaff side. Most experienced reporters and news editors had neither the trained voices for radio or television nor (certainly not among the hundreds of reporters I have known during my career) the necessary glamorous looks!

The situation has changed now that the journalism schools are turning out trained news people who are entering broadcast journalism, although a few of the "rip 'n read" types are still around. This term originated with the ex-announcer who never covered a news story in his or her life but simply ripped off wire service radio news from a teleprinter and read it over the air when it came time for the news broadcasts.

For those of you who intend to enter broadcast journalism in the outdoor field, we will devote an upcoming chapter to how to write for radio and television. It differs in some ways from print media, but basically there is still the same need for accuracy of facts, honesty in reporting, and getting as much news as possible in a limited space—in this case, a time frame.

Writing concise, correct leads may sound easy at first, but it takes considerable practice. I may have made it sound simple, as I have written thousands of them. What I did not mention was that the most difficult part of writing a lead is to take a vast accumulation of facts—everything that happened—and come up with the shortest and most accurate way of saying it. This is hard to do. One can attend a convention or cover a state legislature session where many issues are discussed and much action is taken, and it is easy to miss the real news if one is not careful.

An extreme example might be the reporter who was sent out by his sports editor to cover the passage of an important conservation measure by the state senate. When he did not call in his story by press time, the editor began making phone calls and found the reporter, finally, in a favorite bar.

"What happened to the conservation bill and why the hell didn't you file a story?" the editor shouted into the phone.

"There was no story," said the reporter. "The bill never came up. There was a shooting in a hearing room and the state senator who introduced it was killed."

Granted, this is a little on the extreme side as an example, but take my word for it, I have seen many almost as blatant examples of reporters' missing the boat!

The art of writing a lead for a news story is this process of distilling, from the mass of facts and figures and quotations, the single statement that says what really happened. It is not as easy as it sounds, but there are a few rules of the road that will make it easier.

Early in school, most students learn English composition. The first thing you should do before attempting to write a news story lead is forget all you were ever taught about English composition. Unlike the first sentence of a theme in English composition, the news story lead is not a preface. It does not *lead up to* the story. It *is* the story—in capsule form. This is the most difficult adjustment a beginning writer faces in learning how to write a news story.

Not only is this sentence the story, but it should be the story expressed in as effective and emphatic a way as possible. The three key elements that make up a good news story lead are: voice, verb selection, and subordination. By voice I mean describing activity with the use of active verbs rather than passive ones. For example it is far better to say:

> A section of rock cliff *crashed* into a valley today, *demolishing* two cabins and a ski tow tower before coming to a halt at the bottom,

than it is to say:

> Two cabins and a ski tow tower *were damaged* today when a portion

of rock cliff slid to the bottom of the valley.

A strong verb can breathe life into a news lead, while no adjective or adverb can inject emphasis. Here is an example of what I mean by trying to use a modifier when a strong verb would have been better:

> A huge forest fire, fought by hundreds of Hopi Indian firefighters, *was totally* out of control for three days, before finally being extinguished.

It would have been far better to have written:

> A huge forest fire, fought by hundreds of Hopi Indian firefighters, *raged* out of control for three days before being extinguished.

By subordination I mean putting the "angle" or substance of the news into the main clause of the sentence, not into the lesser subordinate clause. An example:

> State Game and Fish Director Homer Gulliver today accused Gov. Frank Chavez of favoritism and racism in appointing members of the Game Commission, before resigning in anger.

If the reader didn't get to the end of the sentence, he would never have found out that the director had resigned. It would have been far stronger and more sensible to have written:

> State Game Director Homer Gulliver *resigned in anger* today after accusing Gov. Frank Chavez of favoritism and racism in the appointment of game commissioners.

Obviously, after the lead paragraph, the story should go on to tell the details of what happened. I could devote pages to "developing the news story," but it really is simply a matter of gathering all your information and quotes, arranging them (after doing the lead paragraph) into what you think is the order of importance, and then telling the story in a specific and concrete manner that can be easily understood by the average reader. Read news stories in a good newspaper if you have any questions about how this is done. It is not so difficult. Writing the lead is the only really difficult part of writing a good news story. In telling the rest of the story, with as much detail as possible, use the minimum number of words, avoid the use of long and cumbersome words, stick strictly to facts and exact quotes, and maintain journalistic integrity (which is just another way of saying be honest).

Honesty is a primary responsibility of the reporter. Your job is getting the news to the public. Don't feed them a bunch of opinions (yours or anyone else's) unless they are clearly labeled as such. No matter how you feel about the latest outrage by a land developer, when you sit down to write your story, leave those feelings behind. Keep the opinions on the editorial pages (or save them for your in-depth feature story).

An old newsroom cliche is that names make news. This is still true, and reporters should include as many names as possible in their stories. In doing so, you must keep identification in mind. People must be clearly and *correctly* identified to avoid embarrassment and possible lawsuits.

Identifying the source of information is always a vital part of a news story. The reporter is the middleman in the news delivery process. He must make it clear where his information came from. Attribution should be used with every direct quotation and whenever a reporter gets information from a source.

Speaking of long and cumbersome words, in your attribution, stick to "he said" or "she said." "Expostulated," "explained," "suggested," "intoned," etc., are what I call "garbage words." Also, using "pointed out" instead of "said" has an air of editorializing. It sounds as though the person is pointing out an obvious fact. Too many broadcast journalists use it. Try to avoid jargon or highly technical terms. Stay away from such unnecessary adverbs as "totally" destroyed. It is redundant. How else can you be destroyed but totally? The same goes for "completely," as in "completely baffled," "completely exhausted," etc.

Another example of silly use of a word is: "taken to the hospital where he was said to be *critical.*" Nonsense. Was he critical of the food? the service? Say what you mean: "He was taken to a hospital where he was said to be in critical *condition.*"

There may be cases where it is necessary for you to phone in a news story. Dictation may be done after the story is written, but there are occasions—such as on a fast-developing story concerning the outdoors—when dictation must be done from notes. Composing a story while dictating is very difficult. I have done it all through my career, covering plane crashes, politics, and wars, and I can only say I like nothing less than to have to dictate a news story from notes. It takes practice and an ability to see the spoken word as though it were on paper—grammar, punctuation, and all. It is far better, if at all possi-

WRITING THE BASIC NEWS STORY 41

ble, to type out our story then read it over the phone. I cannot tell you how to master dictation any other way than by practicing it. Dictation style is somewhat complicated, but it really is just common sense. You simply have to remember that the person taking down your story over the phone is not seeing it. He is hearing it for the first time, so you must tell him everything. For example, here is how the story would look on paper:

> Atlanta, Ga., July 26—Two persons were killed and another seriously injured here today when a motorboat spun out of control and raced wildly around a lake full of swimmers and fishermen. It finally ran aground on a small island where it flipped over.
> Killed were Edward J. Grove, 16, and Mary B. Hughes, 15, both of Atlanta. Injured and taken to Mercy Hospital (where he was said to be in "satisfactory condition") was Gordon Z. Brown, 22, of Janesville.
> "It was a frightening moment for a while there," said Deputy Sheriff Blaisdale Zimmerman. "We could have lost a lot of people!"

Here is how the same story would have to be dictated over the phone to make it easy for the rewrite person to type it properly:

> Dateline: Atlanta, Ga., July 26—Two persons were killed and another seriously injured here today when a motorboat spun out of control and raced wildly around a lake full of swimmers and fishermen. Period. It finally ran aground on a small island where it flipped over. Period. New graph.
> Killed were Edward J., as in Jacob, Grove (spell out last name), comma, sixteen, one-six, comma, and Mary B., as in baby, Hughes (spell out last name), comma, fifteen, one-five, comma, both of Atlanta. Injured and taken to Mercy Hospital, bracket, where he was said to be in, quote, satisfactory condition, end quote and unbracket, was Gordon Z., as in zebra, Brown, (spell out last name), comma, twenty-two, two-two, comma, of Janesville. New graph.
> Quote. It was a frightening moment for a while there, comma, end quote, said Deputy Sheriff Blaisdale Zimmerman (spell out first and last names). Period. Quote. We could have lost a lot of people, exclamation point, end quote.

Looks hard? It is. But then everything is, until you master it. The next chapter, for those of you who neither plan to get into the news area nor expect to work for newspapers, will be on writing the feature story. This opens up the field to writing for magazines and books.

How to Write the Basic Feature Story

4.

When I went to journalism school (AB Journalism, University of New Mexico, 1949) distinguishing between a feature story and a news story was fairly simple. Anything that was not "hard news" (crime, disaster, war, politics, etc.) came under the loose heading of "features." Since I was primarily interested in newspaper work, the only feature writing I expected to do was what was called "news features." They were the human interest stories the city editor liked to put on page one or wherever he had space between hard news stories. Generally, they were about the little old lady who was discovered, after years of running a sidewalk newsstand, to have $500,000 in small bills tucked away in her dingy mattress.

You have read them many times. They are still on the front pages of your local, daily, and weekly papers, and they are an integral part of journalism. They generally make people feel better, and perhaps that is why the news feature story has lasted so long. People read so much about death and violence in the news that they need a little breather now and then.

My mother never understood why anyone would want to be a newspaperman. She had married my father when he was an editorial writer on the *Providence Journal*. He had graduated from Brown University and, like me, had come back from a world war and finished college. I know she never really understood the news business because, even in her seventies, she would ask me: "Why don't you ever write about anything *nice*? All you ever write about is people getting killed and horrible things like that." The feature story was probably invented for people like my mother.

In those days the news feature story was usually entertaining. But, with the advent of electronic journalism and the strident 1960s, the news feature story evolved into what many news people called "in-depth" reporting. The feature story began to take its place as a legitimate form of news.

For example, in the early 1950s the story of the little old newsstand lady probably would have begun with such a lead paragraph:

> Dayton, Oh., March 2—Everyone loved Sally Brown, the 78-year-old owner of Brown's Sidewalk Newsstand. But nobody knew that Sally Brown was a half millionairess.

Today, a news feature lead paragraph from the November 26, 1978, issue of the *New York Times* reads like this:

> Atlanta, Nov. 25—Thousands of confidential memorandums and other internal documents of the Army Corps of Engineers indicate a continuing practice of accounting manipulation, guesswork and misleading statements to Congress to justify construction of the $2 billion Tennessee-Tombigbee Waterway through Mississippi and Alabama.

There is no need to get the old five Ws of the news lead into this feature lead either, because the story goes on in great length to examine the background and present status of the situation. This is the modern, in-depth, interpretive reporting written for newspapers and news magazines today that not only tells the public all the facts, but *what the facts mean*. This does pose some problems in that not all investigative or interpretive reporters are qualified to decide just what the facts *do* mean, but it does illustrate the style of the news feature.

What distinguishes the good feature story from all other forms of news writing is that the feature story is an organic whole, unlike the news story, which is written in successively more expendable paragraph units. Just as the news story's first paragraph attempts to be the story in capsule form, the whole feature story—however long—is the story.

By its very nature a feature story is going to be longer than the average news story. This is axiomatic, because the average news story is going to be chopped from the bottom up by an editor no matter how short it already is—unless it happens to be one of the most important news stories of the day (and even then it probably will be cut).

One of the difficulties in writing feature stories—if one has been writing news stories for any length of time—is adjusting to the fact that getting the news as high up in the story as possible is no longer important. What *is* important is the choice of words to set mood and handle description.

Also, to maintain the story's organic wholeness, transitions are far more important in feature stories than in news stories, where they may be purely mechanical—perhaps just one word. Because of the internal threads running through the whole of a feature story, transitions are critical and may be paragraph length.

A successful feature-story writer must be a skilled writer. News will sometimes carry itself because of its news value. Feature writing depends upon the skill of a writer to get the reader interested.

The writer of newspaper features, magazine stories and books must remember that today's readers are also watchers of television and are accustomed to getting their news and in-depth features replete with pictures. As a result, there is hardly a newspaper and very few magazines today that would consider running a feature story without accompanying photos or illustrative art. But a writer cannot hope to succeed in keeping a reader's attention on the basis of photos and art. The writing must be good enough to ensure that the reader hears, feels and is in touch with the subject. While the television commentator has the advantage of good photographic "props" (a picture is worth ten thousand words), the feature writer has to depend upon forceful writing to maintain the strength of his story. After all, *words* are all a writer has to use as tools of his trade. They must be very strong tools. However, I cannot say often enough that it is not necessary to string adjectives together in order to achieve good descriptions. In my experience as an editor, the best writing has been that in which the writer uses the fewest, and not necessarily the longest, possible words. The *exact* word—not the word that's just okay or workable—is the secret of good feature writing. In Appendix One, you will find a discussion of some techniques I have found useful in my feature writing.

It is important to first think of a theme or centralized idea to give order and unity to a feature story. This is more difficult than it sounds.

You don't have a clear-cut pattern like the inverted pyramid of a news story. And the time element, which helps to structure a news story, is in the feature usually unimportant or even irrelevant. The writer must depend upon an angle on which to structure his or her approach to the feature story.

I can best illustrate this by example. In the December, 1978, issue of *Natural History* magazine, there was a story on the tree snail of Hawaii being threatened by everything from human pressures to carnivorous relatives. The author, Alan D. Hart, got into his story with a neat angle by tying into Darwin's *Origin of Species*. He began:

> Had Charles Darwin visited Hawaii, he would have found in the archipelago another natural laboratory that vividly demonstrated his theory of evolution. The islands are the most geographically isolated in the world, separated from the nearest continent or large island group by more than 2,000 miles of Pacific Ocean. Isolation, time and habitat diversity have produced a most distinctive land bioata. More than 97 percent of Hawaii's native flowering plants, nonmigratory land birds, insects, and land snails occur naturally nowhere else on earth.

Hart then went on to describe how the snail's restriction to the islands for millions of years had resulted in the kind of adaptive changes first recorded by Darwin.

Some writers call the process of picking an angle around which to structure a feature story "walking around the story." This is a good expression. It describes the process of looking at the facts you have gathered, sifting through them, and seeing what the interesting parts are. Then, you consider the interesting parts, turning them around in your mind, looking for links and playing with slants. This winnowing process goes on until all the important pieces fall together and you are left with your angle; an angle that ties together the interesting aspects. If you bring your basic writer's instinct to bear, the important angle will finally surface.

Profiles are feature stories, and writing a profile of anyone requires a good angle. You cannot start out by saying, "John Clymer was born seventy-two years ago. He went to school when he was six years old." Oh, you *can* start a profile that way but it is doubtful that you will sell it to anyone. Take the way Erwin (Joe) Bauer, one of this country's best outdoor writers and photographers, handled a profile on John Clymer in the December/January issue of *National Wildlife* magazine:

> It is winter on the open plains of what is now western Wyoming. A

soft snow covers the Wind River Valley and faintly in the distance looms Crowheart Butte, for ages a landmark of the Crow Indians. In the foreground a sudden, savage drama is taking place.

Three mounted Crow hunters have isolated a small band of bison from a much larger herd. They are attempting to kill as many as possible, because the hunters are even more dependent on the bison for survival than on their long-haired half-wild horses. One brave, wrapped in a woolen trade blanket coat, draws a short bow. Another thrusts a spear into the loin of a buffalo as his horse lunges. But, the third Indian has been ripped from his pony by a crazed bull. Even if the man survives, he may never hunt again.

The drama is only a rendering on canvas, but it is so real that a viewer shares the desperation of the hunters and almost hears the heavy crunch of hoofs and bodies on the snowpack. In all of its vivid authenticity, this painting is typical of the highly acclaimed work of a shy Wyoming artist named John Clymer. Best known for his renderings of the Old West, Clymer is also a premier wildlife painter who concentrates his formidable talents on the majestic mammals of the Rocky Mountains.

Now, there is no doubt in anybody's mind what this magazine story is going to be about. It is going to be about a magnificent wildlife artist, his life and his work. But the way Bauer got into his story was unique and very professional. It would have been difficult for any editor to have turned down that feature story profile—especially when it came complete with samples of Clymer's marvelous art. What Bauer did, and what all good feature writers should strive to do in writing a feature story, is to capture the attention of the reader at the earliest possible time. This applies to writing a feature story for a newspaper as well as for a magazine. It is true also of presenting feature material in any form of media, whether it be radio, TV, or books. A lead should be provocative and even aggressive, of which the following is an example. Here, in six breezy sentences from *Sports Illustrated,* the author has made you want to know more about a professional golfer who is also a sportsman and a strong personality:

> Andy Bean likes to fish. He also likes to hunt, wrestle alligators, bite covers off golf balls, drive cars like Burt Reynolds, have a good laugh, collect guns, argue with fools and "wimmen" and play golf like a son of a gun. He's good ol' Andy. His father told him never to hit a hook or trust a Yankee, and his dream is to win the U.S. Open and to outrun the local fuzz in the soft sand of the Florida orange groves. Every so often there is another entry in "The Next Jack Nicklaus Sweepstakes." Well, shucks. Andy Bean is the next Andy Bean.

When it comes to getting a reader's attention, there are few writers who can match David Newell, one of the best outdoor writers in America and a former editor of *Field & Stream* back during World War II days. The first paragraph of *The Trouble of It Is,* a fine book about his childhood in western Florida, reads:

> My name is Billy Driggers of the Withlocoochee River Driggerses, nephew to Winton Zebulon Epps who busted the mold when they made him. I reckon that's a good thing for the world because even his own folks couldn't of stood two of him.

Now if that doesn't make a reader want to go on and find out what kind of a man Winton Epps was, I don't know what would!

Though a bit convoluted, this lead could work well for a magazine story lead. I doubt if it would work as well for a newspaper, mostly because of its length.

The first paragraph of a story picked as the best outdoor story for the year 1977 went:

> In October, when the bright gold leaves of the aspens have fallen from the stands of trees in the header canyons of the high country, the wind blows chill and clear down from the snow-clad peaks across the line in Colorado. And it is then that the elk hunting is at its best in the tall spruce-and-ponderosa-covered mountains of northern New Mexico—where the herds start feeling the urge to move down to winter range before the first heavy snows blast through the passes on the wings of blizzards that can blanket a mountain range in hours.

Who am I to argue with *Best Sports Stories 1977,* published by E. P. Dutton, even if I did write that lead for a story called "Elk Hunting the High Lonesome" for *Field & Stream.*

The lead for a story doesn't have to be long or descriptive to get the reader into it. One of the greatest one-sentence leads I have ever read was written by Norman Maclean, who wrote a book on fly fishing in Montana, called *A River Runs Through It, and Other Stories* (University of Chicago Press). Maclean's father was a minister and a trout fisherman. The story began:

> In our family there was no clear line between religion and fly fishing.

The book was nominated for a Pulitzer Prize. No Wonder!

Direct quotes sometimes get the reader's attention quickly in a feature story.

"What they should do is blow up the Alaska Pipeline and that would prevent any oil spill in the ocean!"

That was the first suggestion made by Joe Glotz, vice president of Friends of Animals, as a panel was held in Anchorage, Alaska, in an effort to find ways to insure that such spills will not occur.

Bits of literature can often be used to get into a story. In a story entitled "Ice Fishing, the Moronic Sport" from the book *Silent Seasons*, edited and illustrated by Russell Chatham (E. P. Dutton, New York) writer Jim Harrison starts out with this verse:

> There are strange things done 'neath the midnight sun.
> —Bob Service

That quote was used as a subtitle. Then his lead paragraph went:

> We're not actually *that* far north. Yes, a small church in the Upper Peninsula had a blessing of snowmobiles, and not a trace of irony was noticed. But the sense of the Arctic does pull on us: days shorten, men mumble, the euchre games at the tavern grow extended and violent. There is much talk in December and January of just when the bay will freeze over.

That quote was an effective gimmick to grab attention.

Earlier in this chapter I stressed that a feature story is an organic structure. Thus, unlike the news story, which may be chopped from the bottom up without hurting its meaning, the *end* of a feature story is every bit as important as the beginning.

I cannot think of a better example to show that the end of a feature story is as important as the beginning, than to quote a story written by the late Corey Ford. Corey, who died of cancer in 1969, wrote for the *New Yorker,* the *Saturday Evening Post* and other magazines, was the author of a number of fine books. He also wrote a monthly column for *Field & Stream* for sixteen years. It was called "The Lower Forty" and was one of the most-read outdoor columns in America. In one of Corey's last columns, one of his characters, Judge Parker, wrote a letter to a newborn grandson. The letter began:

> To My Grandson:
> This letter will be yours on December 2, 1977, your sixteenth birthday. If I am alive then, I will read it to you. If I have checked out before that date, please go off by yourself, alone, and read it aloud.

The letter then went on to tell of all the gifts of life the grandfather had willed to the baby. And the letter ended:

> All these things and more I leave to you, my beloved grandson. Perhaps I will live long enough to be at your side when they become your memories, too. But, if I do not, I raise my glass to you across the years.

The true role of the ending of a feature story is to *restate* the approach the writer has taken to his subject matter. Two examples of this "restatement" follow. The first is from Clive Gammon's very funny story "The Snook with the Faraway Look" (*Sports Illustrated*, January 16, 1978):

> Forever lost is the name of the passenger who ordered the last champagne cocktail before the *Titanic* hit the ice. But I am nearly certain that I can close the file on a historical parallel. Late on the afternoon of Thursday, Nov. 10, 1977, I believe I was the last man to pay the full price for a fishing rod at Abercrombie & Fitch before that august sporting goods emporium gurgled beneath the waters of insolvency.
>
> I'd just arrived home, and I was unwrapping the rod with half an ear tuned to the six o'clock news when the tidings came. A bitter moment that became even more bitter when I realized that I would miss A&F's closing sale. I am probably the only angler in New York City who did not head down to 45th and Madison for some cut-price tackle the following week. When they opened the doors to the throng, I was 3,600 miles away, dangling a cube of filet mignon, medium rare, into the murky waters of a tributary of the Amazon and hoping for a piranha or two.
>
> * * *
>
> Several catfish later, he called me over again. He had something for me. An enormous speckled shrimp. A mastershrimp he had just netted. Unforgivably, for a moment I thought he wanted to sell it. But no. "Robalo!" he said, gesturing for my hook. He mounted the tail section and indicated the water. I cast.
>
> Mr. Abercrombie, Mr. Fitch, I have a happy ending for you, as you pace above the clouds in your heavenly safari suits. Your rod caught me a robalo. I will not say how large it was, but it certainly had a faraway look when I slid it gently back into the lagoon. After all, that little fish had a place in history. The first snook to be caught on the last rod with a full A&F price tag. Or I am almost sure it was.

The second is from a story of mine, "Hunting the Hard Country," from *Field & Stream:*

> It's been said that everything grows bigger in Texas, and there's not

much to argue about in that statement if you've ever hunted the Big Thicket Country west of San Antonio.

For the good Lord not only made everything big, He made it rough, tough, hard, prickly, sharp, hot, cold, wet, dry, and full of things that bite, sting, stab, gouge, and hang on till the last minute. But most of all, He made it beautiful.

* * *

And beyond that same ridge, and a dozen more like it, the hard land ran on to towns where the lights were being turned on against the darkness sliding over the big thicket ever so slowly from the east, towns like Eagle Pass and Uvalde—home of former Vice President of the United States John Nance Garner. "Cactus Jack," who grew up in the hard country, lived to his nineties, rocking on the front porch of his board house and spitting tobacco juice into the front yard. Some say the old man never gave a hoot what anybody thought of him and had a sneaking suspicion that everybody in Washington was a damned fool. It's probably no wonder. When you spend ninety years in the Big Thicket everything else seems kind of small and unimportant.

Restatement, properly done, will make a reader remember a story a long time after reading it.

Interviews are another key to hard-to-forget feature stories. Handling an interview can be difficult or easy, depending upon a writer's ability to ask questions. I learned to interview the hard way—by constantly doing it. I have interviewed kings, presidents, generals, statesmen, criminals and "show-biz" types. I have interviewed them in English and many times through an interpreter. If one likes interviewing and plans to do a lot of it, I would advise taking a course in shorthand. Before I became a reporter, I was able to write letters in handwriting. Now, because of years of taking notes at top speed at everything from a political convention to a meeting of a state legislature, not only can no one else read my handwriting, but I have difficulty making it out myself! Fortunately for the feature writer starting out today, the small, lightweight and highly efficient tape recorders available on the market for reasonable prices make notetaking unnecessary most of the time.

Several years ago I flew to Admiralty Island in Alaska to fish with the late Bing Crosby. We stayed five days and caught some fine coho salmon, searun brook trout and Dolly Varden trout—all on fly rods. I had brought along a small tape recorder and—while sitting around the dinner table at night—I asked Bing about his life. He was a relaxed man, a marvelous talker and he spoke of his youth in the Northwest, his beginnings in show business and his many hunting and fishing trips all over the world. That tape recorder enabled me to later write the story of his outdoor career for *Field & Stream*. It never hurts to carry one wherever you go. You never know whom you might meet!

Humor is a special form of feature writing, and it is probably the most difficult (at least for me) to write. In humorous writing the approach or slant of your piece is the most important part of the story—you might even say it *is* the story. Seeing the humor in situations is the first step toward expressing it. One has to have that peculiar sense of what *is* funny to be able to put it down on paper. I think that even the best humor writers in the field might have a hard time teaching someone to write it. Here's a good example to illustrate humor in the outdoor field. Ed Zern's book review of *Lady Chatterley's Lover* has become a classic. He wrote it for *Field & Stream* in 1959, and it is still being used as an example of low-key, tongue-in-cheek humor:

> Although written many years ago, *Lady Chatterley's Lover* has just been reissued by Grove Press, and this fictional account of the day-by-day life of an English gamekeeper is still of considerable interest to outdoor-minded readers, as it contains many passages on pheasant raising, the apprehending of poachers, ways to control vermin, and other chores and duties of the professional gamekeeper. Unfortunately one is obliged to wade through many pages of extraneous material in order to discover and savor these sidelights on the management of a Midlands shooting estate, and in this reviewer's opinion, this book cannot take the place of J. R. Miller's *Practical Gamekeeping*.

As funny as the review was, the magazine received hundreds of letters telling the editor that Zern had completely misunderstood *Lady Chatterley's Lover!*

Patrick F. McManus also is a very funny man, and yet his style is very different from that of Ed Zern. Pat exaggerates and enlivens the ordinary in his writing in a way that only another example will illustrate. In a great book entitled *A Fine and Pleasant Misery* (Holt, Rinehart & Winston, New York), Pat devotes one chapter to "Great Outdoor Gadgets Nobody Ever Invented."

> There are a number of life preservers for use by stream fishermen on the market now, but like so many other inventions designed for the outdoorperson, their creators have stopped short of the mark. The basic

idea of these life preservers is that if you fall into the water they can be inflated by blowing into a tube. With the kind of water I generally fall into, I don't want to waste any time blowing on some dumb tube. On some of the falls I've taken, I probably could have blown up a seven-man life raft by the time I hit the water if mere floating had been my chief concern. To hell with floating—what I need in the way of a life preserver is something that really *preserves* my life. As I see it, this would be a recording device installed in fishing vests. While I was contemplating whether to cross a peeled sapling over a sixty-foot-deep river gorge or make a running leap to land on some moss-covered rock in the middle of some rapids, the life preserver would activate automatically and shout through two stereo loudspeakers set at full volume, "DON'T TRY IT, YOU FOOL, DON'T TRY IT!"

See what I mean? Unless you think that way to begin with, it is going to be a tough job writing humor.

Writing for Outdoor Magazines

5.

For the writer who knows and loves the outdoors the magazine world is filled with possibilities.

More than sixty magazines are directly devoted to the outdoor field. There are three large national outdoor magazines devoted primarily to fishing and hunting: *Field & Stream, Outdoor Life,* and *Sports Afield*—the "Big Three." Other national magazines are specialized to one degree or another such as *B.A.S.S. Magazine, American Shotgunner,* and *Camping Journal.* The number of regional magazines is increasing each year; these include such publications as *Western Outdoors, Southern Outdoors* and *New England Outdoors.* These sixty or more magazines are published in addition to the magazines put out each month by game and fish departments of the fifty states.

So far we have only considered those magazines which are primarily oriented toward hunting and fishing or camping. For the outdoor writer who is more interested in ecology and the environment, or what is loosely termed "nature writing," there are many fine magazines published which cover that field. To name but a few, there are *Natural History, American Outdoors, Nature, Audubon,* and the publications put out by environmental groups such as The Sierra Club.

The "Big Three" have been around a long time—eighty years or more. They are not difficult to sell to if a writer takes time to study each magazine's style and learn its needs. Naturally these three outdoor magazines pay the best—with the possible exception of *Sports Illustrated,* a Time-Life-owned magazine that concentrates on the so-called jock sports—football, baseball, basketball, hockey, boxing, etc. But *Sports Illustrated* frequently runs articles on fishing, mountain climbing, backpacking, whitewater canoeing, hunting, or conservation. Many of the stories are assigned to staff writers, but the magazine also takes an occasional freelance story. The pay is excellent. (See the current *Writer's Market* for the latest rates of this and other magazines.)

Pay for a story in the "Big Three" outdoor magazines today runs from approximately $700 for a beginning or first-time acceptance to $800-$1,500 for well-known and frequent contributors. A payment of $1,500 or more for a twenty-five hundred word story with photos is not at all uncommon for "name" outdoor writers, such as Fred Bear, the well-known archer and head of Bear Archery Company.

The smaller regional and specialized magazines pay less—probably starting about $250 for twenty-five hundred words and running up to $500. Their photo requirements are not nearly as stringent, and the literary quality need not be as good. However, it has been my experience that it is best to write as well as one can for small regional and special-interest magazines as for the national ones. The editor may not have the same manuscript budget as the editor on a national magazine, but he or she probably knows and appreciates good writing just as much and is more liable to buy a piece that clearly shows that the writer has worked carefully on it.

Pay for the outdoor writer has come a long way since the days when writers of my age and experience started in the field. I sold my first story to a national outdoor magazine—*Field & Stream,* as a matter of fact—in June, 1948, for the then-unheard-of price of $75. Since I was attending college on the G.I. Bill of Rights at the time and was being paid $75 per month by the government to attend school, that story represented a whole month's pay! Peter Barrett, senior editor of *Field & Stream* today and former outdoor editor of *True* and editor of *True's Hunting Annuals* for many years, says he received $50 for a story in *Field & Stream* in 1947, and he considered that excellent pay. Remember that these were stories in the twenty-five hundred to three thousand-word class with black and white photos. Then-editor Hugh Grey did not use color often. In other words, pay for a standard-length story in the national outdoor magazines has risen in the past thirty years from an average of $50 to $75 per story to a current average of about $700.

The magazines published each month by the various departments of game and fish are usually staff written and produced. Most do not pay freelance writers, but I have seen instances where they accept stories from people outside the department if the editor felt there was useful information in it. They usually carry no advertising and are devoted to scientific game and fish management and/or natural history. They represent no real market for the would-be outdoor writer except, perhaps, as an initial experience in being published.

There are several considerations to keep in mind in your initial approach to the outdoor magazine market. You can aim high at first—hoping for the larger sums of money paid by the big-circulation magazines—or you can start off by writing for the smaller regional magazines. You will be paid less by the regionals but you will gain valuable experience. A good writer who knows his subject can begin by selling to these magazines on a regular basis in order to become known in the field.

And, although the rate of pay is not as high from the smaller magazines, simple arithmetic will show you that selling four stories to small magazines for $250 each is the same as selling one to a larger national magazine for $1,000. There are some other advantages to selling to the smaller magazines: The stories may be shorter; not as many photos may be needed; the magazine might want black and white photos rather than color; and the competition may not be as steep. Hundreds of manuscripts a week arrive at *Field & Stream*. Out of that batch assistant editors, associate editors, senior and managing editors read and return two-thirds of them. The remaining one-third winds up on my desk for a final decision. Of that third, I would estimate that about five stories are purchased. Not all of these are stories that go into what we call the "front of the book" or the editorial well, for which we pay our highest rates. Many of them are how-it's-dones for which we pay $250 each, or stories for our regional section for which we pay $350 each. You can see that chances for any one manuscript to be accepted are quite low on a national outdoor magazine.

Most national outdoor magazines are thinking about putting out regional editions or are already doing so. *Outdoor Life* and *Field & Stream* now have regional sections twelve months of the year. In the case of *Field & Stream,* a different (for example, eight-page) section—made up of regionally slanted hunting or fishing feature stories—goes to the East, South, Midwest, West, and Far West. Each of these regions contain approximately one-quarter million subscribers of *Field & Stream.* This move to regionalization was made to help the national magazines compete with the growing numbers of regional hunting and fishing magazines for readership and advertisers.

I doubt if the editor of a regional hunting or fishing magazine receives anywhere near one hundred manuscripts a week. That makes his or her decision to buy or reject much easier. So, ask for a copy of every small magazine in the outdoor field and read it carefully.

The outdoor field is a big one—with sixty million people fishing and twenty million hunting, just to name the two biggest areas—but it is also a small field in that most writers and photographers either know each other personally or know *of* each other. Most of us read each magazine that comes out, whether it is a weekly such as *Sports Illustrated,* a monthly such as *Western Outdoors,* or bimonthly, like *Gray's Sporting Journal* and others.

I cannot think of a "name" writer writing for the bigger magazines today who did not start out by writing for the smaller regionals or the specialized magazines. By specialized magazines, I mean publications such as *Guns, Guns & Ammo,* and Petersen's *Hunting* magazine, all published by the Petersen Publishing Company of Los Angeles, California. In the publishing field, these magazines are known as "vertical gun books," meaning they contain nothing else but gun information. *Fly Fishing* and *Salt Water Sportsman* would be considered vertical fishing magazines.

By reading these regional and specialized magazines each month, editors and writers begin to notice the bylines of writers who sell on a consistent basis. If an editor of a national special-interest magazine has become familiar with a writer's byline from local or specialized magazines, he is far more apt to answer a query letter with a go-ahead than if the name were new to him. Many of the staffers of *Field & Stream,* as well as of the other large outdoor magazines, began by writing for these magazines. I know I did—selling outdoor stories to state magazines such as *New Mexico Magazine, New Mexico Stockman, Guns and Hunting, Sportfishing, Salt Water Sportsman, Fly Fisherman,*

Rod & Gun, American Sportsman, and a host of others, some still published.

We have already noted the number of magazines available to you as an outdoor writer. Don't expect to find all of them on the newsstand—*Natural History* and *Audubon* won't be, for example. The best system that I know of ensuring yourself a sample of each magazine you want for your files is to look up the magazine in this year's *Writer's Market*. There you will find the address of the publication, the name of the editor, and many more specifics which we will be concerned with later in this chapter. I would write the editor, saying you would like to submit stories to the magazine and ask for a copy. You may not get the current issue, but you are almost certain to get a copy of the magazine. That will allow you to read it from cover to cover to find out what it *is*. Each magazine has a personality all its own, as does a newspaper.

As outdoor writers you are going to be writing for a specialized field; fortunately, I might add, since most of the general-circulation magazines have gone out of business. Magazines exist today in a special-interest world, and that works to the advantage of the outdoor writer. It is easier to study a special-interest magazine and find out its needs than a general-interest one. What do you look for in the magazine? Obviously, you would look at the stories, their titles, subheads, and the story itself to find out what the editor and his readers like to read. And the format, photographs, illustrations, types and lengths of captions. But there are other areas to watch. For instance, reading the editorials can tell you how the editor views his magazine, his readers, and the field in which he works.

The columns or departments of a magazine will tell what kind of features the staff writers are assigned. Read what's been written in the various departments and by associate editors on the magazine staff to determine what writing styles the editor likes. Pay particular attention to the how-to material and humor. That is important, since you may not only want to write for the magazine, you may also want to work for it someday.

The "letters-to-the-editor" page will give a good idea of how the readers react to specific stories and what they like and dislike. Don't overlook reading even the ads of a magazine. You can learn a lot about the kind of readers a magazine has by what advertisers appear in that magazine.

Before attempting to submit a story to the editor of *any* magazine, the writer should get some important information. For example, what length of story is preferred? How many words does the average story in that magazine run? You can count the words if necessary, but it is easier to write the magazine. The editors will send you what is known in the industry as "specs"—guidelines to the length of stories, the editorial slant or approach preferred, the form in which the manuscript should be submitted (usually with a self-addressed return envelope with the necessary postage on it), the type and number of photographs desired, the categories of outdoor sports it carries, and the rates of payment. Knowing this saves a lot of experimenting (and rejection slips). This information can also be found in *Writer's Market*.

The writer should then find out how much lead time the editor works with. "Lead time" is the number of months an editor plans his magazine prior to the publication date. Most editors of the larger national monthly outdoor magazines work four to five months ahead. In other words, the editor is planning his October issue in June. He is finished with the June issue, which has already been mailed to subscribers by the middle of May or is going on the newsstand for sale in late May. The editor has also put together the issues for July, August and September. These magazines have gone from the editor's office to the art department to the production editors. Now the editor is thinking October. The editor of a national outdoor magazine must always live, professionally, almost half a year ahead. That is why it is vitally important that the budding outdoor writer know what the editor needs at any given time of the year. The editor has an editorial budget that allows him just so much money to spend on purchasing stories each year, just as he has a yearly art budget and a yearly photo budget. If he receives a story in June about the best ways to fish for trout in the spring—even though the story may be well-written and have excellent photographs accompanying it—he probably will return it. He may tell the writer the story was well done and suggest that he submit it again in, say, January when he will be planning his spring issues; if he is a nice guy and has time to tell the writer, that is.

On the other hand if the writer, knowing about lead time, submitted to the same editor in June a well-done story on how to take trout in the fall months, the chances are he would sell it easily. It is amazing how many outdoor writers today, including many who submit and sell stories regularly to large outdoor magazines, still do not fully understand the importance of timing. I constantly return well-written stories with good photographs to professional outdoor writers simply because the timing of the story is all wrong. If I purchased the piece, it would probably remain in inventory for half a year before being used, and I would be tying up budgeted funds I need for current stories. I suspect the reason most outdoor writers continue to submit material at the wrong time is that there is an overwhelming temptation to send in a good story of a trip the writer has just made. He or she has the story fresh in mind, the photos came out well, and the writer just can't resist mailing it right off—either not knowing or not caring that the editor is, literally, thinking four months from the time the manuscript arrives. Far better to write the story while it is still fresh in mind and then put it away in the files to be submitted at the appropriate time.

Many smart and successful outdoor writers make appointments to come to New York and visit the editorial offices of *Field & Stream*. (They are only encouraged to do so, however, after they are firmly established as professionals.) Not only do they find out what the lead time of the magazine is, but they personally meet the editors who will buy and edit their stories in the future. The face and personality of the writer is then known to the editorial staff, and that always helps. Many of the regular contributors are also savvy enough to ask *what stories will be needed in the months to come*. That is using one's head. Many times the editor will have an adequate inventory of stories in almost all categories—trout fishing, bass fishing, saltwater fishing, upland game bird hunting, conservation, big-game hunting—but perhaps he is short on waterfowl hunting.

The editor probably will receive a number of waterfowl-hunting stories in the mail in the next few months—many by competent and experienced outdoor writers—but if this particular writer notices that such a story is needed and requests to do it, the chances are very good he will get the assignment. Editors (like most people) are impressed with common sense and initiative. A beginning writer must learn to satisfy the needs and requirements of a magazine and its readers—as well as to learn to write well.

After you have formed an opinion of the magazine, its editors and readers, and think you know what kind of story they like, it's time to write it.

If you have come up with an idea you think might sell, write the editor a query letter (discussed in Chapter Six) and hope for a go-ahead. If you receive a green light, study the magazine again (paying particular attention to the last six months' issues) to see if anyone else has written a story along the same line. If you find one take notes on style. slant, the writer's use of statistics or quotes, whether it is written in the first, second or third person, and what kind of photos or art are used to illustrate it. This information will help you select a suitable but unique angle or approach for your story.

I sold a story in about 1969 to *American Sportsman* on marlin fishing off North Key Largo, Florida. I had been reading big-game fishing stories for years, and I found that they generally tended to play up the successful catch. I had just come back from a trip where I had spent eight brutal hours fighting a blue marlin on twenty-pound line—only to lose the fish to a shark after dark right below the transom of the boat. I wrote a story about how it feels to lose a great game fish, and the editors thought it was an interesting departure from the standard big-game fishing story. It was called "Marlin By Moonlight" and brought quite a bit of complimentary reader mail, according to then-editor Bob Elman.

I mentioned in Chapter One that it is a good idea to clip everything you can concerning your chosen outdoor field. Clip things from newspapers, magazines, and old books, and take notes about things you hear on radio and television. You may not use it today or this month, but someday that fact is going to come in handy. My outdoor files over the years are the size of a modest library, and almost all of this information has been useful along the way.

And don't worry if the fact, subject or idea appears to be a bit offbeat. Sometimes it turns out to be just the slant an editor is looking for. Take an example: Years ago I had been doing some big-game fishing using kites. The system was developed by a number of outdoor types—captains like Tommy Gifford, Johnny Harms, Allen Self, Al Pfleuger and others. Allen Self used to run a boat out of North Key Largo, Florida, and he refined the system of kite fishing by fastening kites to helium-filled balloons on days when there was not enough wind to keep them aloft. Kite fishing was a fascinating kind of angling and not too well known outside of the Florida and Caribbean area, although it had been originally invented by the Polynesians centuries ago.

At any rate, I was sitting on a New Jersey beach a few years later when a friend of mine wondered aloud why nobody had invented a way to get live bait out to schools of stripers feeding just beyond the breaking surf. They were too deep to wade to and too far to cast to. The fishing kite! Why not?

I sent a query to the editor of *Field & Stream* (this was back in the late 1960s) and got a go-ahead. I looked carefully at how he liked his how-it's-done stories; then I got a nice series of action photos of the kite flying, some shots of fighting fish, and a closeup of a nice striper. He not only bought the story for the front of the magazine and paid me very well, but cover-lined the story! The magazine later received hundreds of letters from surf fishermen the country over asking how they could make or where they could buy the fishing kites.

For many years it was difficult to tell the outdoor magazines apart. Their covers all featured paintings by outdoor artists, and just about every story in them sounded just like every other. There were exceptions, of course. There were the great writers of years back—Havilah Babcock, Nash Buckingham, Hemingway, Corey Ford, Zane Grey, Earle Stanley Gardner, Phillip Wyle and a lot of others. These writers had their own distinctive styles, but they were in the minority. Most of the pieces bought from freelance writers were what we today call the "Me 'n Joe" story. This type of story usually starts out with something like:

> It was cold and dark when Joe Glotz, my hunting buddy, knocked on the front door and I knew it was time to climb out of the warm bed and get into my hunting clothes. After a warm breakfast of ham and eggs we stepped out into the freezing air of the yard and picked up our decoys which we had stacked on the porch the night before. . . .

From there the story went right into the hunting and fishing trip. It's not that it wasn't interesting. I grew up reading about so-and-so and Joe hunting and fishing all over the world. As a matter of fact, I wrote my share of such stories in my early career, and sold them too. Anyone who loves to fish or hunt can enjoy the stories and share the vicarious thrill. It was just that—after decades of reading the same type of story—*editors* got tired of the continuous narrative and started looking for something else.

Then there developed what I can only call the "formula" system of outdoor writing. That lasted for a number of years and finally everybody grew as weary of the formula as they had of "Me 'n Joe." It, too, was rather simple. It began with a lot of action, and then flashed back to old "Me 'n Joe" all over again. Sample:

> With a bellow of pain the mountain lion sprang from the top of the cedar tree where it had been putting up a valiant fight against five leaping dogs. I threw up my 30-30 carbine as the big cat, yellow eyes blazing, bounded straight at me.
>
> Look out! I dimly heard my hunting pal, Joe, call out as the giant cat

bore down on me. This is it, I thought as I raised the rifle.

It had all begun two days ago when Joe called me on the phone one night. "What do you think about trying to catch that big lion that has been killing cattle over on the Bar X Ranch?" he asked [etc.].

Eventually editors began to realize that there is very little difference between writing for an outdoor magazine and for any other magazine—whether it be the *New Yorker, Atlantic,* or *Field & Stream.*

Some of the finest writing I know today is being done by writers who say things in a fresh, unique manner. It's their thing, and more power to them. It is hard for an editor to turn down a story such as one by Russ Chatham on Pacific salmon fishing, which began:

> Salmon and steelhead forage widely on the open ocean in a dining room bound only by the continents, and this vastness implies perfectly the breadth of spirit these noble fish embody. To understand the salmon, it has been said, would be to crack the universe.

That is writing at its best.

Take an opening paragraph that Gene Hill wrote for one of the chapters of his *A Hunter's Fireside Book* and which appeared as a column in *Sports Afield:*

> November is almost at the end of the road. You start out where it's warm and still in the lingering pause of summer, go through the part where the leaves that are left are seared orange and look down into the valley where November lies.

That's about as far from "Me 'n Joe" as one can get.

But in this day and age of specialized magazines, or "special-interest magazines" as they are now called, we must consider a number of other factors besides *how* to write a story for a particular magazine. The term marketing—selling—has come to mean much more in the writing field than it once did. The competition is much greater than it once was, and editors are being swamped with manuscripts. In order to deliver to an editor a story that is likely to catch his eye and imagination, a writer must combine marketing and packaging. Packaging is not new; industries spend almost as much time and money on packaging many of their products today as they do in producing the product.

The next chapter will be devoted to the mechanics of packaging stories for magazines.

How to Market and Package Your Magazine Story

6.

A story is like any other product on today's market. It will sell better if it is attractively packaged. This does not mean you should etch your manuscript on alligator hide or scent the paper with the aroma of pine needles, but there are a number of ways in which a writer can make his manuscript package more appealing to an editor.

Photographs are very important today to the editor of an outdoor magazine—any type of outdoor magazine. We will devote a later chapter to cameras, their use, and such important matters as lenses, filters, film and the rest, but for now it will suffice to say the serious outdoor writer should learn how to take good photos—preferably with a good camera and in color. Color photos can be converted to black and white if that's what an editor wants—while, obviously, black and white cannot be made into color. Most editors also prefer color transparencies, either 35mm or 2¼x2¼, to color prints. It is easy to determine sharpness by putting them on a light box or by looking at them with a viewer, and they can be enlarged as much as one wants if they are sharp enough.

But if it's an unusual shot or subject, a good high-contrast black and white print may be used, even by the larger national magazines.

Every editor I know likes a wide selection of photos to pick from with a story. A variety of shots showing the terrain, some action photos, and some sharp, close-up photos of the type of game or fish sought will usually do nicely. Outdoor magazines have come a long way in the last decade from the days when the hunter or fisherman was photographed either standing over or holding up his bloody trophy. It is the opinion of most thoughtful outdoor editors today that readers would far rather see their favorite game or fish alive, in an attractive pose or in action, than dead—and especially dead and bloody. Those who love to hunt and fish know the kill is necessary. But most outdoor editors no longer belong to the Teddy Roosevelt and Robert Ruark school where blood and gore were rampant in the story. I would like to think I had a great deal to do with this trend since I began it with *Field & Stream* in 1972, and other magazines have followed suit.

A writer who sends in a batch of good photographs with a story may want those not chosen for publication returned to him as soon as possible for some other use in a related story or book. The writer should request that these photos be returned as soon as he receives word that the story has been purchased; otherwise, they could remain with the magazine until the story is published—which could be half a year or more. The editor will gladly return the photos he doesn't use if he knows the writer needs them back. A lot of editors, like me, have been freelance professional outdoor writers, and we know what it is like to have photos tied up.

There has been a lot of discussion in the outdoor magazine field about whether it is best to query an editor before sending in a story or whether the story has a better chance to sell if it shows up complete. The solution to this dilemma falls into the category of catering to the likes and dislikes of individual editors, and I would suggest a writer contact the editor and ask which the editor prefers. There are advantages and disadvantages to both systems.

On the plus side, it is far easier for an editor to read a short query—submitted with a few good sample photos—than it is for him to read the entire story. Most editors are very busy and appreciate anything that saves them time. Also, it is easier, cheaper, and less time-consuming for an outdoor writer to submit a query and a few photos than it is to submit a completely typed manuscript and a large selection of photos. If he or she gets a go-ahead on the query, then the story can be written and typed. Some editors prefer queries—in fact, many editors do. But don't make the mistake of querying an editor on the phone. The chances are that the phone call will reach him at just the wrong time and do the writer far more harm than good. The editor could have just had an argument with the publisher or ad director, or he could be snowed under with work, and the last thing he wants to discuss is a prospective story with some freelance writer.

On the minus side, an editor really cannot tell much from a query, other than that the writer can write a literate query and take a few photographs, either well or badly. Even if he does give a go-ahead for the story, the editor will have to read it eventually to see if it is any good. Many times the finished story turns out to be below standard, and the editor has to reject it after giving the author the green light. This does not make writers happy, and justifiably so. I am in agreement with Gene Hill, associate editor of *Field & Stream*, one of the best outdoor writers in America and one-time executive editor of *Sports Afield*. He feels that if a writer is enthusiastic enough to write a query and send in sample photos he just as easily can write the story and submit it. This also saves having to encourage a writer to write, based upon a query, and then reject the final story. Even though it takes more time to read it I would rather see a story come in, complete with pictures, "out of the blue" so to speak. If it is good there is no question about it, and if it is not the writer is not given false hope from the query go-ahead.

Query or not, sooner or later the story must be written. After the first draft, go back over it, checking carefully for possible errors, and revise it before having it professionally typed.

The first rule in writing outdoor magazine stories is to be clear and concise, and grammatically correct. No writer need soar to literary heights for the editor of an outdoor magazine, but never submit a story that is poorly written, badly typed, or written by hand. Nothing will spoil your polished prose more than a grammatical error—especially early in the story.

Right here is an excellent time to talk about packaging your manuscript. It should arrive on the editor's desk in as neat and professional a form as possible. There is nothing that turns off an editor more quickly than a handwritten or sloppy manuscript, unless it is photos not properly mounted that fall out of the envelope when it is opened. You'll have an almost certain rejection coming. If you are going to be a professional outdoor writer you must turn in professional manuscripts.

Obviously you are going to need a good workable typewriter, with new ribbons in it and clean type faces, not dirty or worn down by age. (If your typewriter keys are dirty, there is good gum type cleaner on the market that is easy to use.)

The paper you use is important. Because I wrote for years as a newspaperman I do my first drafts on the yellow, pulp-type paper we called "second sheets" in the wire services. However, the paper on which you type your finished manuscript should be 8½x11 white bond. Forget erasable papers. They're slippery, hard to handle, and *too* erasable—a slip of the pencil, and vital copy may be gone forever.

On the first page, in the upper left-hand corner, type your name, address, and phone number. In the upper right-hand corner type in the estimated length (in words) of your story. Writers count differently, but I estimate that the average 8½x11 page of double-spaced type, with the proper wide margins, contains about two-hundred fifty words. That means that two pages equal five hundred words; four pages one thousand words, and a ten-page story should be just about twenty-five hundred words. Since most magazine editors prefer stories in the twenty-five hundred to three thousand-word range, we are talking about ten to twelve pages of double-spaced type.

If you wish the editor to know what rights you intend to sell him (or retain for yourself) you can type that in below the word-count. I have to admit I'm a little turned off by a writer who types the rights he expects to sell on the manuscript. I figure if the writer is the least bit professional he would have looked up *Field & Stream* in the current *Writer's Market* to find what rights the magazine buys on accepted material. It strikes me as a bit arrogant on the part of the writer to think I might not *know* what rights I was going to buy. It gives me a negative attitude toward the writer—which may or may not matter—depending on how well-done the story is.

Center the title of the story in capital letters halfway down the page. Below that type your name, then move down about three lines and begin typing your story. Indent each paragraph five spaces. It is smart to number each page in the upper left hand corner and add a key word from your title; this prevents lost pages. Always double space your stories and double space between paragraphs. Margins should be one and one-half inches on all four sides of the page, using standard elite type. Since nobody in the world can trust the mails, always either use carbon paper when typing a manuscript or photocopy your finished manuscript so that you have a copy for your files.

Mail your manuscript in a 9x12 envelope with several cardboard "stiffeners" to make sure the manuscript and accompanying photos are not creased. Enclose another folded 9x12 envelope inside complete with your return address and the necessary postage on it. There are many ways to submit photos but, in the case of *Field & Stream*, I prefer 35mm transparencies or 2¼x2¼ transparencies inserted in plastic holders. These are 10x11½ plastic sheets and hold—in the case of 35mm—twenty slides in each one. They can be viewed quickly under a glass and do not slide about inside the mailing envelope. Do not staple manuscript pages; mail them loose. First-class mail is best for most manuscripts. It costs more than the fourth-class manuscript rate, but at least you are reasonably sure of its arrival, and what's more the post office is not required to return fourth class in case it cannot be delivered. When valuable photographs are enclosed, a manuscript can be sent registered mail.

What are the prime "don'ts" that a freelance writer should know before submitting a manucript to an editor? Here are a few I think the beginning writer should keep in mind:

Don't send an editor any samples of unpublished work. You may list a few published titles if you wish.

Don't send in multiple queries. Writers have sent me several pages of queries with spaces to check whether I want them or not. Usually I turn them all down. I feel this is "shotgunning" an editor. Be specific and positive. Show him you've done your homework.

Find out from *Writer's Market* who the editor is. Nothing annoys an editor more than to receive a query or manuscript addressed to an editor who has not been with the magazine for years! This makes me think that the writer hasn't read my magazine recently and doesn't know our current needs.

Don't phone an editor with a story idea. Either write the story and send it in, or send a query letter. The chances are good that the editor will have just spilled a cup of coffee all over his desk about the time your call comes in—or he's due in five minutes at the budget review. If so, you don't have a chance!

Don't send a manuscript or photos in one of those blasted padded envelopes, full of grey, fuzzy material that spills all over a desk or clothing.

Don't dress up manuscripts in bright colors or fancy strings or bows. Editors are not art critics. They are only interested in the writing and photos.

Don't submit a manuscript that has been read and turned down by several other magazines, and it looks it. Have it retyped, even if it does take time and money. An editor can tell when a manuscript has been well-thumbed, and, usually, he will figure that if another editor didn't buy it, why should he?

Don't forget the self-addressed return envelope with the necessary postage on it. Some magazines will not return manuscripts without them.

Don't send prints of photos unless that is all you have or the editor or magazine specifies black and white photos. Most editors today prefer color transparencies. Read *Writer's Market* to find out which the magazine prefers.

Don't write long, involved query letters. The editor may never get to the part where you describe your story idea. Write a short, simple query, like this:

Dear Sir:

    Would you be interested in a 2,500-3,000 word story on how to arrange decoy sets for various species of ducks and geese? I have 75-80 sharp 35mm Kodachrome color transparencies to illustrate the story. I can have it to you within a few days of your reply.

                             Sincerely yours,

                             John Down

Dear Sir:

    I have just completed six months studying the nesting, raising, hunting and feeding habits of the Great Horned Owl. I have some excellent color transparencies of the life cycle of this bird. I think your readers would find the story of great interest and I can send it to you (3,000 words) at your request.

                             Sincerely yours,

                             Cythnia Hoot

Don't send in a query that starts out with the first page of a story, then winds up by saying something like: "and that, in essence, is what my story is about. I can send the rest if you would like to see it." The editor, if he is anything like me, is going to wonder why in hell he or she didn't send the whole thing instead of just the first page.

Don't ask an editor what sort of approach he or she would like you to take with a story. The editor expects you to know that.

Don't ever say to an editor: "If you do not want this, please let me know as soon as you can because I am sure I can peddle it somewhere else very quickly!" (Not nearly as quickly as I would like him to!)

Don't ever tell an editor, "I think you should be doing more of this sort of thing in your magazine." That's what the editor is getting paid for—deciding just what should run in the magazine—and the last thing the editor wants from you is advice.

Writing an Outdoor Column

7.

An outdoor column is sort of the bread and butter of the outdoor writing business. It is where a writer is hired on a salary basis to write x number of outdoor columns per week or month. They could be for a newspaper or a magazine. The security of a job—versus freelance writing—is what appeals to many outdoor writers. There is also a sense of talking to readers who are familiar with your work—those who buy the newspaper or magazine regularly. I must have written more than a thousand columns for newspapers. When you consider I did one a week for The Associated Press for nine years, that alone equals almost five hundred. In addition, I wrote for other weekly and daily papers that were not members of the AP.

All this does not tell you how to be an outdoor writer for a daily or weekly newspaper or for a wire service, so let me get to the specifics. One good way of beginning: Decide first in what field you wish to specialize. I wrote a general hunting, fishing, nature-type column which, in a way, is specializing. Let us suppose you want to be a recreational vehicle writer. You may already have considerable knowledge about the subject. If you do not, but you simply find the topic interesting, I would suggest you first give yourself a good general grounding in your chosen field, as I outlined at the end of Chapter One.

Warren Page, the late great gun editor of *Field & Stream*, applied to this publication in 1948, to then-editor Hugh Grey, for the position of fishing editor. Hugh said he had just hired a young man named A. J. McClane for this job, but he needed someone to write a column on guns and shooting. Warren replied that he had been a gunnery instructor in the Navy during World War II and while he didn't think he knew enough to qualify as a gun editor, he would try if Hugh gave him the chance. Hugh told me years ago that Warren, in learning the intricacies of his trade, fell asleep nights for months, with books of ballistic tables spread across his chest. There is no substitute for deep-seated desire.

Have your local librarian supply you with an index of publications pertinent to your field. Then start reading all you can in these technical journals. They may seem rather complicated at first, but you will eventually begin to understand them. A beginning outdoor writer does not have to be an all-round expert on his chosen topic, but he must have *some* facts. If you have a general familiarity with your subject and you can write in an interesting style, readers will identify with and enjoy your columns. You could write a fascinating story on catfishing, for example, if you happened to be an expert at catching catfish. You need not know every area of fishing equally well, and you may never have caught anything except catfish in your life.

Start out with the things you know and systematically expand your knowledge and experience. Find out who the experts are. Write letters asking their opinion on something. Get quotes from them and then write back and ask them to confirm the quotes for a column or story you are doing. It will not be long before the authorities know who you are, and this is certainly a good start. Human nature being what it is, most authorities are flattered to have somebody ask their opinions—particularly on specialized subjects that require considerable experience or knowledge. You might even send a column or story to an expert for checking before submitting it to an editor. It would not be out of line to *say* it had been read and verified by the authoriy. Editors are impressed with thoroughness.

How do you go about convincing the editor of a newspaper that he needs a daily, weekly, or monthly column on the outdoors? First of all, he may already have one. Particularly if your subject is specialized (such as black powder shooting as opposed to a general hunting and fishing column), it is foolish to attempt to compete with an established column on the same subject in the same geographical area.

If the editor does not have an outdoor column, your success will depend upon where the newspaper is published. Obviously, you are not going to induce the editor of the *Village Voice* in Greenwich Village, New York, to run a column on hunting. This is not the only city where you would expect anti-hunting sentiment to run high. The same is true for much of Los Angeles, San Francisco, and Washington, DC. These regions are urban, liberal, and populated for the most part by people who not only know very little about hunting, but dislike it on general principles. Polls have proven this to be true. The reverse can be said of such cities as Atlanta, Georgia; Dallas, Texas; Denver, Colorado; Detroit, Michigan; and Bangor, Maine.

On the other hand the editor of the *Daily Oklahoman*—in hunting country—may be very interested. He may have overlooked the possibility of such a column because nobody ever insisted on one—or even suggested it. Coming up with the number of hunters in his readership area, plus what they spend each year for guns, ammunition, food, beverages, camping and boating gear, motels, recreational vehicles, etc., could very well win him over. Jim Bashline, who writes the outdoor column for the *Philadelphia Inquirer,* had no problem persuading his editors that they needed him. Pennsylvania sells more deer hunting licenses each year than any other state in the Union—*including* Texas!

Again, it would be difficult to convince the editors of various daily newspapers in and around Los Angeles that they should have a hunting column. However, they certainly do run a lot of columns devoted to fishing, camping, and backpacking. On the other hand, neither Bob Brister nor Tom Opre, outdoor writers on the *Houston Chronicle* and the *Detroit Free Press,* respectively, had much trouble convincing his editor of the need for a hunting column. Both men are in prime hunting as well as fishing territory. Florida newspapers too are fertile ground for fishing stories, as are New England, Midwestern, Southern, and Rocky Mountain papers. The West Coast papers are ripe for columns on recreational vehicles, camping, and backpacking.

Two periodicals you might want to look up at the beginning of your career as an outdoor writer are *Editor & Publisher,* available in most good bookstores or from 850 Third Avenue, New York, N.Y. 10022, and the directory of the Outdoor Writers Association of America.

OWAA has over three thousand members, and all of them had to be professionals in order to join. If you are not now qualified to join because you have not had enough material published, try to join as soon as possible.

Just knowing other OWAA members can help you a great deal, especially if they are in the same field as you are, or a related one. While you cannot regularly receive copies of the annual OWAA directory unless you are a member, you can ask around and see if a member lives near you. A member may have an outdated directory that he or she would be kind enough to give you. It may be a year or more old, but members do not move all that much. You can use the directory to contact writers in your field. Most of the outdoor editors I know are fine people always happy to help a novice break into the trade. In addition, the OWAA organization holds annual conventions at which recognized experts conduct valuable workshops and panels on outdoor writing.

Naturally, the pay varies for writers of newspaper columns—depending upon the size of the paper and its readership. I can tell you that a handful of outdoor columnists I know well on the big daily papers—Jim Hardie on the *Miami Herald*; Jim Bashline on the *Philadelphia Inquirer*; Lefty Kreh on the *Baltimore Sun*; Bob Brister on the *Houston Chronicle*; Tom McNally on the *Chicago Tribune*; Tom Opre on the *Detroit Free Press*; Roger Latham on the *Pittsburgh Press*; Jerry Meyers on the *Atlanta Constitution*; Nelson Bryant on the *New York Times*; Jerry Kenny on the *New York Daily News*; Bob Salie on the *Denver Post*; and a number of others—not only make good salaries but are highly respected in the outdoor field.

Once you have been given the go-ahead on a column, and are glorying in your editorial forum, you will quickly find out one thing: How long your column sticks around depends solely on its popularity. After all, an editor wants to win readers and sell more papers or magazines. He will judge your column's popularity by reader response, usually in the form of letters to the editor.

Here are a couple of tips that may help.

Humor and controversy are two of the very best ways to build readership. If you can, always try to include some humorous aspects. You should also strive for variety—but not to the point of writing about things you know nothing about. Two things to avoid, as they can be counted on to prompt a flow of nasty letters, are pictures of dead animals and pictures of lots of fish taken rather than a few.

Columns should always be seasonal. This is not a problem with a newspaper where the deadline is only days or a week from printing, but it must be kept in mind with a magazine where the deadline runs two to three months ahead of publication.

Outside of pleasing the editor and the readers, the column is all yours to say exactly what you want to say, in the way you want to say it.

What do newspaper readers want to know about in the outdoor field? It has been my experience that they both read and react to everything. I have won Press Association awards, while writing outdoor columns for The Associated Press, on everything from politics to nature. Outdoor writing covers a broad field, and I have never had trouble finding a topic to discuss. Again, it pays to read constantly and to clip as much as possible for your files. Consider the following samples of outdoor column leads I have done over the years, and you will see the spread of coverage in subject matter:

By Jack Samson, Associated Press Staff Writer

Members of the sole surviving flock of whooping cranes are about to start their risky flight from Canada to Texas again this year.

And the Fish and Wildlife Service, as well as a lot of conservationists and nature lovers, are worried sick about it.

General? Of course it is general—and appealing to a lot of people.

By Jack Samson, Associated Press Staff Writer

It's a good thing Izaak Walton isn't alive today.

The chances are he would cut his throat or drown himself in the nearest lake if he knew what they were using for bait in this day and age.

Cheese, That's what. And such un-fishy goodies as marshmallows.

The (ugh) baits being used now are apparently the invention of companies that had a surplus of stock and asked themselves the obvious question:

"Who can we get to buy the stuff we have left over?"

The answer (as anyone knows):

Fishermen. They will buy anything if they can just be sold on the idea it will catch fish.

There are times when the outdoor columnist gets himself, or herself, on the front page of the newspaper. Take the following, run under a three-column banner headline in the *Albuquerque Journal* a few years back:

By Jack Samson, Associated Press Staff Writer

The New Mexico Land Resources Assn., a powerfully backed group of stockmen, bankers and mining men, has run up against its first substantial opposition to a plan for disposal of federal land in New Mexico.

Coming out strongly against what he termed a "land grab" was Rep. Lee Metcalf (D-Mont), the National Wildlife Institute, and the multi-million-dollar Pack Foundation headed by Arthur Pack of Tucson, Ariz.

This would fall under the heading of investigative reporting in the outdoor field.

Humor is a fine way to get the reader into an outdoor column. Take, for example, this approach which appeared under a two-column head reading "A Few Eating Hints for Lost Hunters":

By Jack Samson, Associated Press Staff Writer

The Forest Service has been delving into the problem of what to eat when lost.

Their studies in the West have come up with a few startling facts.

One of the things the Forest Service found passable was eating black moss that hangs from pine trees. You simply pluck it from the branches, roll it into a ball and begin chewing.

"You have to acquire a taste for this morsel," says Gail Thomas, a forester for the Western Pine Assn., in what may be the understatement of the year.

Even people who didn't hunt and fish, but simply liked the outdoors, wrote letters about that column.

Most outdoor columns run about five hundred words—roughly two double-spaced typewritten pages. Occasionally, if the story is very important, it may run much longer. The column begins with a news lead or it may have a feature opening. Except for "breaking" or fast developing stories on some outdoor subject, most outdoor columns are written in a feature style.

Take, for example, the beginning of an outdoor column which Nelson Bryant, outdoor editor of the *New York Times*, did one time after we had hunted together in Texas:

By Nelson Bryant, special to *The New York Times*

Eagle Pass, Tex.—Seeming to writhe through the dense mist rising from the water before us, the skeletons of drowned, stunted oaks were the first objects to materialize as the day grew brighter.

Jack Samson and I were in a blind on the Farias Ranch in southwest Texas waiting for ducks to come to the two dozen decoys we had set out before us. The area we were hunting was a so-called tank, a man-made pool with a dam at its lower end designed to catch rainfall and runoff for livestock and wild birds and animals. "Tank" is actually a misnomer, for the lake before us was more than a mile long and a half-mile wide.

This is certainly no news lead, but it does set the atmosphere.

Another good gimmick is to let letters to the editor run alone:

By Jack Samson, Associated Press Staff Writer

Sometimes in an outdoor column it is better to let a letter speak for itself. A lot of them are from "cranks" or someone with a personal bone to pick. But again many are from conscientious sportsmen who have something important to say. This, we think, is such a one.

"Dear Sir: This letter has been building for several years . . . ."

It is an attention-getter and is why so many people read the letters to the editor columns in newspapers and magazines.

I have found that challenging an established policy or a so-called truth is a good way to get attention in an outdoor column. Take these two as examples:

By Jack Samson, Associated Press Staff Writer

About this time every year—when all of us can hardly wait for spring to arrive—somebody calls us about sighting the first robin.

What people don't know is that in most areas of the United States all robins don't migrate south for the winter. Many of them stay right where they have been all year. They move to swamp bottoms where the cover is thick; their plumage color changes a bit to gray to blend with their surroundings; and they don't sing as they do in spring or summer. But they stay all year and few people but naturalists and birdwatchers know they are there.

Or:

By Jack Samson, Associated Press Staff Writer

Those thousands and thousands of acres of frontier lands in the West—bought by our country at three cents an acre in 1803—were settled because of a hat.

That's right, a hat. It was a fancy one and referred to as the "D'Orsay"—a stylish bit of headgear worn by men of fashion in those days and made from the fine, clipped inner pelt of the beaver. It was even supposed to restore a man's hearing if worn long enough.

There have been a lot of reasons advanced for the settling of the great American West—gold in California, the lush Oregon country, or just the lure of adventure. 'Taint so, say the historians and conservation men. The million-dollar beaver-trapping industry was the real reason.

You can see that the style of writing is really not as important as what you write *about*. Being a good storyteller is the secret. Jack London was one of the greatest. He was also one of our first outdoor writers. So was Hemingway with his *Old Man and the Sea*. Outdoor writing covers a vast expanse of territory.

Of course, it would be nice to be syndicated—as is Jack Anderson—in a great many papers across the country. I don't personally know many writers—at least not writers whose columns clearly fall into the outdoor category—who are syndicated.

Syndicates sell stories to publishers on a commission basis, with the author receiving 40 to 60 percent of the gross proceeds. On the other hand, there are syndicates that pay a writer or columnist a salary or a minimum guarantee. One problem with syndication in the outdoor field is that the writer has to be sure his material does not compete with that of others in an already crowded field. This is difficult in as specialized a field as outdoor writing.

Another factor is the need to choose a syndicate that will properly promote the writer's column; this is not always easy to find. The larger syndicates, as *Writer's Market* suggests, usually promote their writers best. A list of the syndicates, and all the titles of the columns and features they handle, appears in the *Editor and Publisher Syndicate Directory,* available for five dollars from 850 Third Avenue, New York, NY 10022. Some writers have managed to syndicate their own material, but in this case they must bear the cost of soliciting their clients. Though they receive 100 percent of the proceeds, they are also responsible for mailing and reproducing their columns and for billing. It can become very complicated and quite expensive. I suggest you start out with writing a column for a single newspaper first—and establish yourself as a successful outdoor columnist—before you concern yourself with the problems of syndication.

A writer has to be very good to be syndicated. Bob Considine was just such an exceptional columnist. He was also an outdoor enthusiast, and I am grateful I knew him as a friend. Let me give an example of his fine feature style when he wrote of the death of the journalist Cornelius Ryan, author of *The Longest Day* and *A Bridge Too Far*. "Connie" Ryan was a marvelous man—fisherman, storyteller, and ex-foreign correspondent. Bob Considine wrote this syndicated column shortly before his own death. It appeared in many papers, but I quote from a copy of the *San Francisco Examiner* of Friday, November 29, 1974:

> There was this night in Eindhoven, Holland. Last September. The public square was immersed in light, smothered in sound. The Dutch people of the area had come to the place to be part of the 30th anniversary of their liberation from the Nazis by American paratroops.
>
> Prince Bernhard, resplendent in his General's (Field Marshal's?) uniform, marched briskly to his place in the reviewing stand. Dozens of groups ranging from old Dutch resistance fighters to children so young they had probably never heard of Hitler or Von Rundstedt, or Maxwell Taylor or Jim Gavin, entered the square with spit-and-polish precision.
>
> On the scene was one who didn't walk so good. He needed the help of a stout cane and the arm of his unswervingly wonderful wife, Kathy. It took him a terribly long time to make it across the rapidly filling square to a seat in the reviewing place.
>
> It was Connie Ryan, making what turned out to be his last public appearance. A friend in the stands wept quietly.

Ben Wright, the former publisher of *Field & Stream*, and a friend of both Connie and Bob, told me who the friend was who wept. It was Bob Considine. Bob was a sports and "outdoor writer." That term covers a lot. He could convey a very personal involvement (read: enthusiasm, excitement, knowledge, curiosity) in a subject without his ego getting in the way.

If I wish you beginners anything, it is that you write a column that well.

8. The Importance of Photography to an Outdoor Writer

Today the camera is as important to an outdoor writer as is the typewriter. If you intend to be a professional, and successful outdoor writer, you must learn to use a camera. Most magazine and daily newspaper editors not only expect their outdoor writers to supply quality photographs, but will always think twice before buying a story without pictures. I sometimes purchase stories for *Field & Stream* from writers who do not supply photos, but usually only in cases where the writer is well known. Most editors prefer, as I do, that a writer submit a dozen or so 35mm or 2¼x2¼ color transparencies. On rare occasions, I may purchase a good story from a writer who includes in his query letter an apology for having no photos, explaining that his camera malfunctioned or his film got damaged or whatever. At least I am prepared and can make plans to use shots from our own files. However, ordinarily I will not buy a story without pictures unless it is exceptionally well written, on an extraordinary subject, or I feel that illustration would be better than photos.

Professional outdoor writers the caliber of Byron Dalrymple,

Charley Dickey, Irwin Bauer, Charles Farmer, Norman Strung, Charles Waterman, Gil Drake, Jr., and many others can be counted upon to send in dozens of excellent photographs from which to choose for each story. Some of these writers, for instance Norm Strung, learned photography well while selling stories to magazines such as *Field & Stream.* I can remember lengthy discussions of photographic problems with Norm when he was first developing a style as an outdoor writer in the early 1970s. Most outdoor magazine editors, if asked, will take the time to tell a beginning photographer or writer what is wrong with his material.

I also buy photographs of wildlife and scenery from photographers who write very little. Professional wildlife photographers such as Bill McRae, Bill Browning, Perry Shankle, and numerous others can be counted on to submit top-notch photographs on a regular basis. Years ago I began buying these photographs whenever they came in—knowing I would be running a story later in the year on the animal, bird, or fish in the photo. My purchases paid off many times, because often a good story on a hunting or fishing trip would arrive months later but the photos would be below standard. Our pay rate is $150 per color photo and $50 for black and white. If the photo is used as a two-page spread, we send the photographer another $150. If the photo turns out to be good for a cover, the pay is $500. We buy all photo rights in order to build up a current color file.

Most outdoor magazines will purchase photographs for their files. Send a sample of your work, twenty to twenty-five transparencies, in a plastic slide page. Suit the subjects to the magazine, and choose the slides carefully to show the range of your abilities and techniques. Send along a simple, direct letter telling a little about yourself (keep it short—editors are often pressed for time). The tone of your letter should be "keep me in mind."

The big outdoor magazines are not the only places where a photographer can sell outdoor photographs. To get an idea of the incredibly wide spread of markets available to today's photographer, look at the current *Photographer's Market,* published annually by Writer's Digest Books. Since the title of this work is *Successful Outdoor Writing,* I am not going to attempt to tell you how to become a successful professional photographer. Nor do I intend to explain every technique and technicality of outdoor photography. Not only would I not be so presumptuous (although I have won OWAA photo awards and have been paid for decades for my outdoor photography), but this topic in itself would more than fill this book. There are a great many fine texts on the subject, and your library has a few. I found *Camera Afield,* by Sid Latham, Stackpole Books, 1978, to be a good one, and I can highly recommend it to the novice outdoor writer/photographer.

It is simply not necessary to be all that proficient in order to take good outdoor photos. Making a living as a studio or an industrial photographer or one specializing in fashion would require much intensive and specialized training, and would call for diverse, bulky, and specialized equipment.

One prerequisite of outdoor photography is that the equipment be as portable as possible. Fortunately—thanks to space-age metals and design—the modern outdoor photographer is easily able to carry equipment to the tops of mountains, where years ago it would have taken horses to pack the comparable gear. I can remember climbing all day to the top of Wheeler Peak in New Mexico with the late Harold Walters of Santa Fe. Harold was known for his marvelous photos of mountains. He carried a huge 8x10 plate camera and tripod while I toted his film packs and other gear. I shudder to think of having to make that climb today carrying those twelve to fourteen pounds of equipment.

I will probably get all sorts of arguments from outdoor photographers on what constitutes sufficient photographic equipment for an outdoor writer. I have never yet had a discussion with an outdoor photographer that didn't end up in a disagreement about which is the best camera, lens, filter, tripod, carrying case, etc. There is such an abundance of fine, lightweight equipment on the market today—especially Japanese-made equipment—that disagreements are probably inevitable. I will try to avoid mentioning too many brand names, but this will be difficult in some areas—particularly in film. When you talk about the best equipment for outdoor photography, you have to bear in mind what your individual needs are. You may simply want to photograph scenics and situations—people fishing, hunting, backpacking, camping, or boating—or you might wish to focus on birds or wildlife. First let us discuss the bare necessities. After that—depending upon what sort of outdoor photography you have in mind—you can read about some handy accessories used in specialized photography.

I feel that the most useful camera on the market for the outdoor photographer is the single-lens reflex (SLR) 35mm camera. It is capable of taking black and white photos and both color transparencies and color prints in rolls of twenty and thirty-six exposures. It is lightweight, compact, easy to carry, versatile, and especially good for taking action pictures. It can utilize a complete system of specialized, interchangeable lenses, ranging all the way from standard and wide-angle to close-up and telephoto lenses. Another advantage of SLR cameras is that they allow you to see the object you are focusing on through the lens itself, as opposed to the old system of looking through a viewfinder placed on top of the camera. Moderately priced SLR cameras are now available with built-in light meters that allow the photographer to focus and select his proper exposure while looking through the lens.

If you can afford only one lens, I recommend the "normal" or "standard" lens that comes with an SLR. It will be somewhere from 48mm to 58mm and preferably should have a lens speed of f1.4. This lens is adequate for most outdoor jobs.

There are those photographers who claim they get sharper pictures by enlarging 2¼x2¼ negatives than they do with 35mm film. I am not here to argue the merits of each. If you prefer a 2¼x2¼ camera, fine. They are heavier for the most part and that is why I carry 35mm cameras, but it is up to the individual.

A skylight (ultraviolet) filter is almost a necessity for daylight color film to eliminate the bluish tones one occasionally sees in prints and slides. This filter makes color transparencies "warmer" and more natural-looking. It also protects the expensive lens against scratches and does not change your exposure readings even though it fits over the lens.

There are two options in outdoor photography for shooting pictures in near darkness: available-light photography or flash. We can now do available-light photography under conditions unheard of years ago, thanks to new color films with incredibly fast emulsion speeds. When I first began outdoor photography, about the only fast film was Kodak Tri-X Pan for black and white prints. It has a speed (or ASA) of 200. There was no such thing as high-speed color film. Today there are excellent color transparency films in speeds of up to 400 (for example, Ektachrome professional film) which can be purchased at any camera store.

Many of us do available-light photography with fast films because flash units tend to be bulky and add weight to our cameras. However, there are many times when flash equipment is an absolute necessity, such as when it is completely dark. Flash units are not expensive anymore and can easily be carried in a camera case. They are attached directly to the SLR camera and are synchronized electronically with the shutter. They may also be used in bright sunlight to "fill in" shadows.

The last piece of bare-necessity equipment is a carrying bag or case. Make sure it has strong straps, and plenty of room inside for extra film, filters, lenses, and other accessories. For outdoor photographic work, it had better be waterproof, too! It is essential to have a bag that will keep out driving rain (or water—in case the bag falls in). I solved the hazard of water damage by purchasing an aluminum case that snaps shut and locks. Also, because it is polished aluminum, it does not absorb heat from direct sunlight. Excessive heat will cause film to "fog." Many an outdoor photographer's trip was spoiled because he or she carried film in a black camera case in a hot climate.

You can pick up a good basic outfit, as described, for about $350. It can be added to in time. Meanwhile, you can be a perfectly good outdoor photographer, using this basic camera system.

A lens shade may not really fall under the category of bare necessities, but you might want one, since much of your photography will be done outdoors in bright sunlight. A lens shade either snaps or screws onto the lens. One feature of lens shades which should be kept in mind is that while they are fine for keeping sunlight and glare off standard and telephoto lenses, they will sometimes not work well with wide-angle lenses. If you plan to use a lens shade with a wide-angle lens, be sure to get a compatible shade. The wrong shade will cause your photos to "vignette," that is, it will interfere with the area your lens "sees" and will cut off the edges of your pictures.

Eventually you are going to want to extend your photo-capability, and I would suggest you next consider purchasing a good telephoto lens. There are all sorts of opinions on this, but I personally prefer a 70mm to 210mm f3.5 macro-focusing auto-zoom. With this lens, I am able to take good long-distance telephoto shots and close-up photos of objects not more than a few inches from the lens. At last I am freed from years of using the separate macro lens that had to be installed each time I wanted an extreme close-up. A 300mm telephoto lens is about as long as you should go at first. This is just about the longest lens you can use and still hand-hold the camera. Even then, it is best to steady the camera on a solid surface such as a rock or tree limb. A small, lightweight, and collapsible tripod should be purchased next. It is always best to use the tripod with the telephoto lens if time permits.

This enables better focusing and results in sharper pictures.

In much outdoor photography, it is necessary to encompass a great deal in one picture. For this reason, you should next acquire a wide-angle lens—either a 24mm or a 28mm lens will do very well. I use mine constantly, particularly on boats where it is a problem to get angler, fish, and much of the boat into the same picture. A wide-angle lens is very important for photographing scenery and groups of people. With the equipment listed thus far, there is almost no outdoor situation you cannot cope with from a photographic standpoint.

The film you use will make a great deal of difference. As a general rule, the slower the film speed (ASA), the sharper and less "grainy" the transparency will be. Hence, a film such as Kodak's Kodachrome 25 (with an ASA of 25), a very slow film, should yield a sharper picture than a high-speed film—given all the correct lighting conditions and shutter openings. The choice of film speed, at least in my case, depends upon the amount of light available. I like to use the slow fine-grain film when I am shooting in extremely bright sunlight, such as that found in the Rockies or on the white beaches of the Bahamas. I prefer to go to Kodachrome 64 (ASA 64) when there is not quite so much light or when it is slightly cloudy. For overcast-day, early-morning, and late-afternoon light conditions, I switch to Ektachrome (ASA 200) professional film.

A number of outdoor writers I know, especially those on the bigger newspapers, shoot in black and white because newspapers use black and white almost exclusively. On the other hand, such outdoor columnists as Jim Bashline on the *Philadelphia Inquirer* and Bob Brister on the *Houston Chronicle* shoot 35mm color transparencies in order to give themselves color slides for their files. Newspapers can convert color transparencies into black and white photos. Most newspaper outdoor columnists write stories for outdoor magazines also. Since magazines use mainly color shots, it makes more sense to take color pictures that can be converted to black and white when necessary.

As I said earlier, 35mm color film comes in rolls of both twenty and thirty-six exposures. Always use the thirty-six-exposure rolls when going on a job or into the field. Professional outdoor photographers can regale you for days with tales of the great shots they missed because they exposed the last frame on the twenty-exposure roll just before that great shot presented itself. Obviously, if you plan to take only a few pictures at home for a specific purpose, the twenty-exposure rolls are more practical.

I began shooting Nikon cameras in the 1960s and have stayed with them—not necessarily because they are the best, but because I have grown so accustomed to this particular camera and its controls that I can operate it almost without thinking. There are several excellent SLR cameras in roughly the same price range, such as Pentax, Canon, Olympus, and many others.

Over the years I have learned to carry two camera bodies (the camera minus lens) whenever I went on a story. I learned this from Sid Latham, who has not only written books on outdoor photography but has had a long and distinguished career as a professional photographer. With the best camera in the world, Latham told me, there will occasionally be that tiny bit of sand or dust causing a slight malfunction that will throw off the shutter speed. The light meter will cease to function, or a dozen other "gremlins" may appear to plague a photographer. This is less important when one is shooting a story at home or close to a camera repair shop. But when it happens on safari in Africa or while mountain climbing, it is a serious matter. The second or back-up camera has saved many a picture story for me.

I am quite enthusiastic about using a polarizing filter, as are a number of other outdoor photographers who take pictures close to water. This filter works the same way as do polarized glasses—allowing one to see down through water by cutting the glare. Like the sky-light filter, it is screwed onto the regular lens and can be rotated with the fingers until the glare is removed. One word of caution: when the glare is gone and you are ready to take the picture, make a last-minute check of your light meter reading. Rotating the polarizing filter changes the light reaching the meter, and you may have an incorrect setting. Polarizing filters are very effective for photographing fish in streams and lakes and are essential for photographing big game fish beneath the surface of the sea.

I became interested in underwater photography a number of years ago. This is a highly specialized field which calls for sophisticated equipment. You need either an underwater camera, such as the Nikonos, or a watertight plastic housing for your SLR. Some other necessities are special filters and an underwater light meter. Underwater photography is a field full of challenges, and one that requires some study. There are a number of fine basic books on the subject. An excellent one is Flip Schulke's *Underwater Photography for Everyone*, published by Prentice-Hall.

Have your cameras checked regularly by a reputable camera repair shop. Moisture, dust, dirt, and even fungus can invade the camera and cause malfunctions. Check and replace light meter batteries every few months. They don't cost much and are a critical factor in getting a correct light reading.

For very important pictures which *must* turn out correctly, use another light meter as a backup. I use either my spare camera body—interchanging the lenses to make sure I get the same reading on both meters—or a small, sensitive, hand-held light meter.

I experimented for years with a variety of small flash units that snapped onto my cameras. They were light and stowed easily but, after having some trouble with them all, I finally switched to using a heavy battery-powered strobe. Although it weighs several pounds, it does not often fail me. I carry the power pack over a shoulder when I go on assignments which I know will require a lot of flash pictures. The strobe is capable of taking literally thousands of flash photos with the same flashtube.

I have discovered that there are many good telephoto lenses on the market, manufactured by a different company than makes my cameras. Telephoto and zoom lenses are very costly. The less expensive ones made by companies with a not-so-internationally-known name can save one a good deal of money. They can be made to fit your camera with inexpensive adapter rings.

You can also buy a 2x auto-teleconverter. It is quite inexpensive and magnifies (in the case of mine, which is made by the Asanuma Company and is adaptable to my Nikons) by two. In other words, I can snap a Vivitar 300mm telephoto lens on my Nikon with a teleconverter between the camera and the lens, and I have a 600mm lens. While this system saves one from having to buy costly high-powered telephoto lenses for specialized photography, it does have a few drawbacks. Teleconverters will not work on zoom telephoto lenses, and it is necessary to open up your lens several "stops" or slow your shutter speed to compensate for the loss of light.

There is a class of telephoto lenses which I call "short teles." One I particularly like and have used for years is a 43mm to 86mm auto-zoom. It has some interesting applications for outdoor photographers. Many times one does not want the person being photographed to be conscious that a picture is being taken. Snapping on one of these medium-range telephoto lenses allows the photographer to work from a short distance away. The lens is not heavy, nor is it as cumbersome as the long lenses. It is also good for pictorials and for photographing

THE IMPORTANCE OF PHOTOGRAPHY 93

people—fishermen, hikers, canoeists, etc. Mountain scenery magnified by four—which is about what a 200mm tele does—is beautiful to see.

When you get up to the 200mm telephotos, it is best never to shoot a picture at any shutter speed less than 1/125. When you get to 300mm and up, never try it at less than 1/250 unless the camera is on a tripod. Even a breath or a heartbeat will cause blurring at that magnification. Another fact to remember is that modern film can be shot at a higher ASA than is stated on the box the film comes in. In cases of very little light, an entire roll of ASA 200 Ektachrome can be shot by changing the ASA setting on the camera to 400. The Kodak laboratory will charge you a bit more for processing, but having that hard-to-get picture is well worth the extra cost. Just be sure to mark the film roll when you remove it from the camera and to advise the lab of your ASA settings.

The question arises as to where to take your film for processing. Three factors enter into this decision: quality of developing, cost, and service. Kodachrome, no matter where it is taken, winds up at a Kodak lab. Ektachrome can be processed by any lab, but here is where quality of developing comes in. The only way to find out about processing labs (say through drugstores or camera shops) is to try them. Do not entrust them with your precious roll of snow leopard shots; use something you can bear to lose.

Another option is prepaid mailers. Kodak sells prepaid developing mailers for its color films. These enable you to mail an exposed roll to a Kodak lab from wherever you happen to be. Kodak will develop the film and send it to your home or anywhere else you specify. This way you are not carrying around exposed film. Film manufacturers stress that exposed film should be processed as soon as possible. This is especially important for color print films, where you actually lose color balance in time. Transparencies, which are what you will be using most, are not that critical, but don't let an exposed roll sit in the glove box of your jeep for three weeks.

Vibration can damage shutters, which are extremely delicate. To prevent this, I suggest you line your carrying case with soft rubber foam and cut out spaces for cameras, lenses, and flash equipment. Vibration is particularly prevalent in small aircraft and on boats running in choppy seas.

Nelson Bryant, outdoor editor of the *New York Times*, effectively solved the problem of protecting cameras. Instead of worrying about bad weather, he bought a Nikonos underwater camera. It has an f2.5 lens, and the only drawback is that it has to be manually rather than visually focused. It has no light meter, but Nelson uses it so much that he can almost tell what his exposure should be just by glancing at the sky. Since it has a wide-angle lens, he always has plenty of depth of field. It has a battered grape jelly jar lid for a lens cover, but the camera has survived dunkings in countless rivers and he always comes back with good, high-contrast photos.

One of your camera's worst enemies is salt water. This doesn't just mean don't drop your camera in the ocean. Corrosive saltwater spray can work its way into your camera's vitals. An easy way to protect your camera from it—and from windblown sand too—is to put your camera in a plastic bag. Fasten the bag with rubber bands and cut a hole for the lens, making sure that the bag is loose enough for you to operate the camera. After a day's shooting in such conditions, it is a good idea to carefully clean your lens and camera according to the specifications in your owner's manual (which, incidentally, you should have along on any field trip). An outdoor photographer's camera is exposed to so many harmful substances—dust, dirt, sweat (which is, after all, salt water)—that a thorough cleaning at the end of the day is wise insurance.

Always take along more film than you think you will need. It is ridiculous to save money on film and then find out—after jet fare and all sorts of expenses halfway around the world—that you don't have enough film for the job.

No matter what the airlines tell you, X-ray machines *will* damage film. Camera stores sell lead-lined bags in which to carry film. I always put mine in these bags and ship them with luggage. When my camera gear is put through X-ray or fluoroscope equipment at airport security gates, there is no film in either my cameras or my camera case.

As far as the actual taking of outdoor photographs is concerned, it is all a matter of practice makes perfect. One vital bit of advice I would give the novice outdoor photographer: learn how to "frame" photographs, whether they be of objects or scenes. Framing gives dimension to a photograph and literally a frame of reference.

With today's highly efficient cameras, it is easy to purchase one which will have shutter speeds of up to at least 1/500 of a second if not 1/1000 or higher. With 1/500 and 1/1000, you will be able to stop most action. I am able to take clear photos of running game, flying birds, and leaping fish at 1/500 and seldom find it necessary to go to 1/1000. If you want to shoot at such high speeds, make sure your lens openings will allow it. Many times a shutter is capable of very high speeds but the lens cannot be opened wide enough to admit sufficient light. This can be a problem when using telephoto lenses too.

From the back of an elephant in India once, I photographed a huge tigress. I was using a 70mm to 210mm auto-zoom telephoto lens with a speed of f3.5—not a very fast lens. The tigress was lying half in and half out of early-morning sunlight, and it was difficult to make the elephant remain motionless. I took a dozen shots of the tigress before she leisurely got up and walked away. By the time I had opened the lens up all the way to f3.5, I had to cut down my shutter speed from 1/250 to 1/90 of a second. Since the camera was being hand-held, many of the shots were just slightly blurred at that low speed. I did manage to get two excellent ones, but if that lens had been capable of opening to f2.8 or f1.4, I would have had some very sharp photos despite bad light conditions.

There is a new generation of what I call "smart" cameras on the market. They may someday be the ultimate solution to an outdoor photographer's problems. They are small, sturdy, lightweight, and have built-in flash units operated by pencil (AA) batteries. This eliminates carrying separate flash units. The one I have now is fully automatic. I need only point it and click the shutter. It is automatically set for 1/250, and if there is not enough light present to allow the camera to take a good photo at that speed, the camera automatically drops the shutter speed down to 1/125. It has an f2.8 lens, which is fast enough for most work, and uses conventional 35mm film. I carry it in a fishing vest or hunting jacket and use it as a back-up camera. To my surprise, over the past year it has taken several better pictures than my larger cameras. I have blown up pictures from this camera, and they were so sharp that my art director at *Field & Stream* was able to use them for a double-page spread.

There is another camera on the market today which automatically loads and winds itself as it is being used. One of these days, the manufacturers are going to develop these "smart" cameras to the point where it will be almost impossible for an outdoor photographer to make a mistake. I could certainly have saved a lot of money and disappointment if such cameras had been available about twenty-five years ago!

* * *

In this chapter, I have tried to stress that outdoor photography can be learned by doing. After six months of experimenting, you can expect to be an adequate photographer. After a year or so of taking pictures and keeping up with developments in the photographic world, you should be a capable outdoor photographer.

I have never considered myself a professional photographer, though I have won awards and had my photos published in more national magazines than I ever dreamed. The technical aspects of photography may seem forbidding at first, but in time photography will be a natural and almost unconscious part of the outdoor writer's job.

TIPS:

1. Try to remember to either have a companion or yourself wear brightly colored shirts or jackets, and perhaps hats, for an outdoor photo story. For years, every hunter and fisherman wore his old Army, Navy, or Marine Corps khakis (and some still do), but very little contrast results when wearing such clothing. Red, yellow, or orange is best.

2. After you photograph your friend in his orange hunting togs, have him sign a model release. Whenever a photo used for commercial purposes has in it a recognizable likeness of a person, you must have a release. For complete information and sample release, see *Photographer's Market*.

3. A common cause of lost photo sales is improper exposure. To avoid the heartbreak of an underexposed photo of Bigfoot, bracket your exposures.

4. Besides being protected from rain and other water, cameras should be protected from the direct rays of the sun to prevent their heating up. Heat "fogs" film. I usually either cover my cameras with a white towel in the field or in a boat or keep them in an aluminum carrying case which reflects the sun. When planning to photograph subjects in extreme cold—such as the Arctic—you should take your cameras to a camera shop and have the oil replaced with powdered graphite which will not freeze in extreme cold.

5. There is a clever device (one popular version is called a "Kuban-Hitch") made for outdoor photographers. It is an elastic harness that holds your camera or binoculars firmly against your chest. This solves the problem of cameras dangling on straps and snagging or knocking against things. It also leaves your hands free for other purposes.

6. Available on the market are several types of rifle stock camera mounts. These are very good for photographing flying birds and running game. The camera is fastened to the stock, and the trigger of the rifle sets off a cable release—a device which activates the shutter. With cameras using speeds of from 1/500 to 1/1000 of a second, these stocks make it far easier to "swing" along with a moving object—producing the best actions hots in wildlife photography.

7. Silhouette shots can be achieved by making sure the object you want to photograph is either against a very light background or light sky. Then set the light meter reading to the proper setting to photograph the bright areas behind the subject. The subject will then be underexposed and will appear as a silhouette.

8. "How-to" close-up shots can best be done with a macro or close-up lens. These can be purchased separately or, in many cases, are incorporated into telephoto lenses.

9. Series shots (and this is for the photographer who has progressed far into buying specialized equipment for the outdoor field) can best be taken with the aid of a motor drive. This machine is attached to the camera and, when the shutter is activated, will take a series of photos. The speed at which the drive operates can be preset. A motor drive is heavy to carry, but it increases the likelihood of good action shots.

How to Write Outdoor Copy for Radio and Television 9.

One bit of advice I can give to the outdoor writer who is considering the radio or television field: Broadcast writing is writing for the ear—not the eye. Listeners do not have the luxury of going back and "rehearing" what they may have missed—as does the reader in print journalism. It is essential that broadcast writing be as simple as possible and as clear as crystal.

It is unlikely that a great many of you will end up writing outdoor stories for radio. Radio is essentially a news medium. The four radio networks (ABC, CBS, NBC, and Mutual) feed their affiliates a steady diet of news. There is some commentary and public-service programming done by the networks, but the local-station format is primarily talk shows or music, fitting around news. Independently owned radio stations tend to emphasize local programming more than do network-affiliated radio stations. It is possible that a local radio station owner, news director, or program director would be interested enough in the outdoor or environmental field to want to carry such a program. I would like to see more of this done. The vast captive audience of automobile drivers represents a large segment of the population, and I am sure that many of them would find the subject of great interest.

While the backbone of the local radio station is still news, there is considerable room for public-service programming, and this is where the outdoor show comes in. Chances are that it would fit best close to the local news slot. The same is true for television. I have seen excellent outdoor radio and television programs in many large and medium-sized cities in this country over the last dozen years. Most of them have been devoted to local hunting and fishing, but a growing number of these shows devote time to conservation matters—particularly controversial ones. Regard for our environment has spread so rapidly in the past few years that it is taking up an increasing amount of space in magazines, newspapers, radio, and television. And well it should. We have only so much land, and our population (220 million) is growing at an alarming rate. If we do not make a concerted effort to save what land, lakes, streams, oceans, wildlife, and wildlife habitat remain, there will be little left for our grandchildren.

When I was a news director of both NBC and CBS affiliate stations, the demand for outdoor shows came from a variety of sources. I worked in a part of the country (the Southwest) where there was a lot of hunting and fishing. There was also a great deal of interest in conservation and environmental issues. The public would not only write letters to the station but would also call the sports director and demand more outdoor material. It was not too difficult to provide more on radio. We simply assigned an outdoor man to do a five-minute segment on hunting, fishing, and related subjects, to fit at the end of the regular evening sports news. We had no trouble finding a sponsor either.

On television, it was almost impossible to supply more outdoor material. The network fed us a constant supply of what is referred to as "jock" sports news each day: football, baseball, basketball, hockey, boxing, and the like. There was far more to choose from than the sports director needed for his fifteen minute segment. Network has never (as of this writing) felt much need to include outdoor sports in the regular sports programming. What little outdoor sports has been done on television has fallen into the entertainment category—such as ABC's "American Sportsman" or such fishing shows as "Gadabout Gaddis." Other outdoor programs, such as "Wild Kingdom" and "Last of the Wild," were shows devoted primarily to protectionist and nature themes.

What our television viewers wanted was information on hunting and fishing, and they wanted it visually. The trouble was that we were limited in the number of cameramen we could assign to cover an outdoor sports event. All stations face this problem. Opening day of trout season is usually an interesting feature story in every state where trout abound. We could have done an admirable job on this subject if our cameramen had not been tied up with local political stories, crime, traffic accidents, etc. If the cameramen covered any local sports at all, they were local jock sports. So, as usual, the outdoor field took a back seat.

This still happens today—especially on large metropolitan television stations. About the only time an outdoor story gets any exposure is when there is some controversy—such as protectionists opposing a special hunting season—or when an unusual creature appears. A great white shark in the sewer system will get play, as will a moose wandering down Main Street, but these are considered news features and are not a part of regular programming.

I think one reason the fishing field, for example, has not been given the proper coverage in network television sports is that so few sportscasters (Curt Gowdy being a notable exception) know anything about the subject. Another reason is the difficulty of photographing the sport. While it is relatively easy to set up cameras all around a football field, baseball diamond, or basketball court, it is a far different matter to photograph freshwater and saltwater fishing where so much of the action is underwater. Not only can you not "cue" a fish when you want it, but a boat deck or stream bank is usually rough walking. Most saltwater fishing boats don't stay still in the water, and chances are that TV cameramen (at least the dozen or so I have met) are either not familiar with boats or get seasick. It is probably no wonder there has not been too much enthusiasm to photograph outdoor sports. However, the few good, hardy, and imaginative photographers, producers, and directors I know—people the caliber of Glen Lau—may change all this.

Hunting shows too have had a discouraging history. ABC's excellent "American Sportsman" had an auspicious beginning showing not only fishing but big-game and bird hunting. An unfortunate batch of tastelessly done big-game hunts (elephants being shot and collapsing to the ground in a cloud of dust) did not appeal to a large segment of the public—especially with all the human death we saw each night on the TV in reports from Viet Nam. Regardless, the program won a number of Emmy Awards, and some excellent shows were done in the upland-game-bird and waterfowl-hunting fields (with stars such as Bing Crosby and Phil Harris). I think the show's failure to remain in a fixed prime-time spot (it appeared sporadically on Sunday afternoons—when most outdoor sportsmen were out doing their thing) caused it to lose ratings.

One of the developments in the television field which will make it easier to film outdoor shows in the future is ENG equipment: battery-powered recorders that permit instant replay of outdoor events without the time-consuming chores of processing and editing film. Cameras are lighter and portable—as is sound equipment. Huge strides have been made in the development of telephoto and zoom lenses, necessities for photographing wildlife. These technological advances will do much to increase opportunities for the outdoor writer in broadcasting.

In talking about the practical aspects of writing for radio and television, I will assume that you have already learned the basic techniques of how to write news and feature stories for the print media. I shall therefore discuss here only the differences in writing for electronic journalism. The techniques of good feature and news writing apply equally to both print and electronic journalism. It is only the immediacy and tense of the writing that differ, and this is really not that difficult to learn.

As I said at the beginning of this chapter, writing for radio and television is writing for the ear, not the eye. The story is read and heard only once. I cannot tell you how many times I have been annoyed with a radio writer—obviously new at the job or simply unskilled—who has handed a newscaster a piece of radio copy that begins something like this:

> A TWA plane crashed into a mountain today, killing one hundred fifty people. Police and firemen who arrived on the scene said bodies were strewn over a half-mile area. Flames and smoke could be seen rising into the sky for several miles. We will be back as soon as possible with further details.

The chances are ten to one that either I was talking or someone else was talking to me when that radio bulletin came on. In either case, the result would be the same: I would have missed the first sentence.

While this would be "getting the news into the lead" for a newspaper story, it just doesn't work for radio or TV. When you are writing a story for these media, you have to assume that the listener is going to be at least a sentence behind you. *Ease* into the story. You can get the *same news* in. Just give the listener time to focus his attention on the subject. This is how it should have been done:

> Latest reports reaching our newsroom indicate that a large number of people were killed moments ago when a giant airliner crashed into a mountain in the vicinity of Butte, Montana. A spokesman for the Civil Aeronautics Board said the plane was believed to be a Trans World Airlines DC-9 carrying an estimated one hundred and fifty persons. Reports from police and firemen in the area....

This technique applies to every radio and TV story, not just to fast-breaking news. Write radio and TV news as if you were conversing with the listener. Use the informal style in which a person ordinarily speaks. Sentences should be kept short and straight to the point. Avoid complex sentence structure and little-known words. While the following example might do for a newspaper, it will not work for radio or TV:

> Climbing to the aid of an injured companion high on a wind-swept mountain, Bill Brown, a ski instructor for the Alpine Ski Resort at Aspen, Colorado, was himself seriously hurt when he collided with a downhill skier, Jane Grove, 27, of Santa Fe, New Mexico, who the rescuers said later, was suffering from a fractured leg after the accident.

By the time you get through listening to this report, you are going to be wondering who did what to whom. Start out with a short sentence, as if you were talking to somebody; then work into what happened in detail.

> Three skiers were injured in a series of bizarre accidents on the slopes of White Mountain today.

Then tell what happened.

The same is true when it comes to getting ages and titles into a story for radio or TV. While newspapers might use:

> Henry H. Steeles, 46, Director of the State Department of Environmental Protection, said today that his agency was recommending that off-road vehicles be prohibited from the Mendez Wilderness Area.

Radio and TV should use:

> The director of the State Department of Environmental Protection, 46-year-old Henry H. Steeles, said his agency was recommending that off-road vehicles be prohibited from the Mendez Wilderness Area.

Print media is a captive of the time element. In a magazine or newspaper story, something has already happened and the story usually tells when. Most newspaper stories carry a "dateline"—the date on which the action occurred or the story was written. Example:

> Boston, Mass., Feb. 2 (AP)—The United States Coast Guard, during a press conference held here today, expressed support for the licensing of all small boats carrying motors of more than 4 h.p.

An outdoor writer working for radio or television is able to update this story and make it sound more *immediate*. For example:

> The United States Coast Guard has given its support to a measure asking for the licensing of small boats. The federal agency is calling for passage of a law requiring licensing of all boats with motors of more than 4 h.p.

Verb tenses are all-important in broadcast journalism. Print media utilize the past tense:

> The Secretary of the Interior *said today* he would announce to Congress. . . .

Radio and TV can bring the story up to date with the use of the present tense:

> The Secretary of the Interior *is preparing* an announcement. . . .

Or a mixture of tenses:

> The Secretary of the Interior *is preparing* an anouncement which he *will deliver* to Congress tomorrow. Secretary Cecil Andrus *said today* he would tell Congress. . . .

In titles, always use the title before the name of the person. It gives the listener time to get ready for the "meat" of the statement. Many times the listener may not catch the name involved if if comes at the beginning of the sentence.

> James Smith, Curator of the Museum of Mammalogy, is calling for. . . .

It is far better to write:

> The curator of the Museum of Mammalogy, James Smith, is calling for....

The same rule applies to military, political, and religious titles.

Naming the news source is just as important in radio and TV writing as it is in print media. Statements like, "Sources close to the Department of Game and Fish" or "Informed sources close to the director of the National Wildlife Federation" are a cop-out (unless it is vital that the source be protected). It is important that the listener be absolutely certain whether the newscaster is speaking personally or for a news source. Otherwise it is opinion and not news.

> The alligator will soon be taken off the Endangered Species List in Florida and put on the Threatened Species List, it was intimated by game biologist Roy Needles today at a meeting of the Florida Game Commission.

Hell. If he said it, *say so.*

> A game biologist for the State Game and Fish Commission, Roy Needles, says the alligator will soon be taken off the Endangered Species List in Florida. It will be moved to the Threatened Species List instead, he said.

Another good way to handle a statement on radio or TV is by the use of the word "quote," like this:

> A biologist for the State Game and Fish Commission, Roy Needles, said today, and we quote, "It's about time we took the alligator off the Endangered Species List. It should be put on the Threatened Species List instead."

Of course, there are cases where the attribution is not necessary in outdoor writing, anymore than it would be in straight news writing. It depends upon where the story came from. A radio or TV writer should postpone or omit attribution in a story only where there is absolutely no question of the credibility of the source. Hence it is safe to say:

> The President will propose to Congress that six million acres of Alaska wilderness area be turned over to the Eskimos.

In other words, it is not necessary to say:

> The President, Jimmy Carter, said today he will propose to Congress that six million acres of Alaska wilderness area be turned over to the Eskimos.

It is not necessary to use the word "unquote" at the end of a quote in radio or TV writing. Rather than say:

> The head of the Department of Archeology, Dr. Percy Boneholder, said, quote, "The skeleton was more than a million years old," unquote.

Say this instead:

> The head of the Department of Archeology, Dr. Percy Boneholder, said of the find, and these are his own words, "The skeleton is more than a million years old."

For heaven's sake, don't say so-and-so "pointed out" anything. "Pointed out" indicates it is so. How do you know it is? It may be a matter of opinion.

Since we use conversational language on radio and TV, it is permissible to use contractions. You can say "don't" instead of "do not"; "they'll" instead of "they will"; "doesn't" instead of "does not"; "he's" instead of "he is"; "they're" instead of "they are"; and "isn't" in place of "is not."

Don't start sentences with long, modifying clauses such as:

> After weeks of bickering with other agencies within the state government, and despite constant threats from the governor's office that an injunction will be filed unless action is taken soon, the head of the State Highway Department said today he will not propose a new highway through Vermejo Canyon.

This is better:

> The head of the State Highway Department says he will not propose a new highway through Vermejo Canyon. This came in spite of threats from the governor's office and....

Read your story aloud before it goes on the air or on the tube. If it sounds concise, correct and comfortable to you, fine.

As for style in radio and TV writing, get a style guide. Just as in magazines (we at *Field & Stream* use the *United States Government Printing Office Style Manual* and newspapers in wire-service work use

The Associated Press Style Book) there is a style guide for broadcast journalism. I suggest using the one in Mark W. Hall's *Broadcast Journalism* (pages 115-130), Hastings House Publishers, New York. It is excellent.

Writing for radio and television, rather than print media, simply calls for a few special writing techniques, as I said earlier. But there are other factors that set one apart from the print media writer. The electronic journalism writer is working for a medium regulated by the government—in this case, the Federal Communications Commission. This may not seem like a great problem or difference to the novice writer, but it causes some basic rules of the game to change. While good taste, honesty, and devotion to facts are as important to the radio and TV writer as to the print media outdoor writer, owners of radio and TV stations are, understandably, more "under the gun" from the federal government than the publisher of a newspaper or a magazine is. While the owners of newspapers and magazines may, say in the case of a libel suit, get off with a stiff fine, the radio or TV station could conceivably have its broadcast license revoked. Since this represents millions of dollars in investments, it is also understandable that general managers of stations, network executives, and station owners are a bit more reluctant than the print media people, on the whole, to tackle highly controversial, expose writing. Speaking from my own experience I found stations to be much more cautious than newspapers and wire services about running expose or investigative material. I am not making a judgment—just an observation.

There was a time when the outdoor writer was rarely confronted with the issue of libel or slander. You were pretty safe even when you disclosed the real weight and size of somebody's fish in your column, because who ever believed a fisherman? But in this day of environmental controversy, court decisions, charges and countercharges, the chances of libel are far greater than they used to be, and it is good to know the dangers.

It is worth remembering that the First Amendment of the Constitution states plainly enough there shall be no law abridging the freedom of the press. Courts over the years have clouded certain areas in the work of journalists. My suggestion to a beginning writer in the electronic journalism field is to brush up on the latest rulings concerning libel, slander, and a journalist's rights and responsibilities. Laws pertaining to communications are constantly being changed by court rulings, so it is difficult to give you a constant set of rules here. It is important to understand libel and slander so you know what you *can* and *cannot* do.

The American and English Encyclopedia of Law defines libel as: "a malicious defamation expressed either by writing, printing, or pictures which tends to blacken the memory of one who is dead, or to impeach the honesty, integrity, virtue, or reputation, or to publish the nature or alleged defects of one who is alive and thereby expose him to public hatred, contempt or ridicule; or to cause him to be shunned or avoided, or injure him in his office, business, or occupation." Slander is simply the spoken form of libel—which brings up an interesting point: is malicious defamation by radio or TV libel or slander?

There has been no definitive ruling by the courts on this, but they seem to be leaning toward libel—as the spoken words usually come from written copy. There are no federal guidelines for libel. Each state has its own libel laws.

A good defense against libel or slander is that the statement written was the truth. But even then there are extenuating circumstances. A man may have served a prison term and paid his debt to society. A reporter may mention the fact that the man has a prison record and served a sentence for a crime. This is a matter of public record. But if the writer keeps referring to it, it can be a form of libel or slander. It is unnecessary to keep referring to it, since it could be injurious.

Privilege is a defense against libel. Privilege is a statement extracted from public records, hearings, testimony, or documents. Fair comment is a defense against libel since it assumes it is fair to comment on matters of public interest. The absence of malice is considered a defense against libel—and in many cases, the prompt public retraction of the written statement or spoken word—if libel is claimed—may serve as a defense.

Another rule of thumb in investigative reporting is that it is difficult to be sued by a politician. When somebody runs for office he is sticking his neck out. If the statement concerns the person's ability or action while in public office, you are generally on safe ground. It is always best to use common sense as a yardstick. Every American is protected against invasion of privacy—the violation of a person's right to be safe from public display and criticism of private matters. Privacy is a hazy concept. If you have any doubt, hold off and consult a libel expert.

On the other side of the coin, all writers (including outdoor writers) are protected by "shield laws." Protecting one's news sources has been a highly controversial issue. Shield laws vary from state to state, so check your local laws. As the result of many court cases, a number of states and the federal government have passed so-called "sunshine laws." These laws are to ensure freedom of information. They give an investigative outdoor writer a lever he or she did not have before. As an example, assume you are dealing with the United States Army Corps of Engineers and you find out they have been holding secret meetings regarding the construction of a highly controversial watershed project. You may not be able to get the minutes of the meeting right away, but if you write long enough about the secret meetings being held, the public can force the Corps to produce the minutes.

The one really bright spot in being a writer for TV is that the medium is expanding every year. Only a fool would deny that over the next few decades, most of our entertainment—and a great deal of our information—will come from the tube.

The future for outdoor writing may well be in the area of video cassettes. There are indications that film-production companies are starting to get into this field and that they are backed by large sponsors who have done some research and have discovered the vast audience available for their product. After all, sixty million fishermen comprise a considerable audience. Sixty million *anything* is a vast audience! A few years from now, one may simply go to his nearest film library and buy or rent a video cassette. It can be slipped into the TV set at home where a special channel will be set aside for this purpose. These shows can be in color and sound and can run anywhere from thirty-minute segments to ones lasting several hours. As we close in on the year 2000, we will learn how to catch a big game fish, or how to fly cast for trout, or how to properly backpack, cross-country ski, or operate a small powerboat—all while resting comfortably in that big chair in front of the TV.

Writing Outdoor Books

10.

I have written eight books on outdoor subjects, counting this one. That experience (and the lessons learned from it) is the basis of this chapter. Book writing may seem too advanced a topic for a beginner's how-to book, but it does have a certain application for the novice. Books, whether they sell well or not, are a more permanent and prestigious form of publication than articles or columns. They add authority to a person's list of credits and can serve as excellent door-openers to opportunities that may otherwise be inaccessible.

Even if you don't plan to write a book, you should be alert to the possibilities. For instance, if you are taking a long or unusual trip, keep a log or journal. And don't forget your camera. To already have those slides of your Iceland trek is a big selling point. If and when the time comes to write a book, you will have a written and photographic record of details and impressions otherwise impossible to recall.

The outdoor book market is more limited than the outdoor magazine market in the number of readers reached. Consider how many people would be willing to pay seven to ten dollars and up for a book on fishing, as opposed to those who would plunk down a dollar for *Field & Stream,* or perhaps $2.50 for a fishing annual. Yet, there are fishermen, hunters, boaters, etc., out there who will gladly pay any price for books on their favorite subjects.

A typical printing of a nonfiction or how-to book, a category which includes most outdoor books, will run from five to ten thousand copies. The publisher will be happy to sell this many in a year. The highly illustrated (and expensive to print and publish) color outdoor books will often have a larger printing, say fifteen thousand. This is because of the high printing costs and the need to keep the list price within reason. In this case, the publisher might not expect to sell all the copies, and some books might eventually wind up as remainders.

Then there are the labor-of-love books on such subjects as fishing for Atlantic salmon, or hunting woodcock, or wild turkey. Or conservation/nature books such as *American Sportsmen and the Origins of Conservation* by John F. Reiger, Winchester Press. These books may never get beyond a printing of three thousand, and yet be excellent. Usually these are done by a writer who does nothing but his specialty, has plenty of time on his hands (and perhaps an independent income), and does not really care how many books he sells, as long as he has the approval of his associates and peers. What really matters to him is that he has converted his love for the subject into lasting physical form.

I am assuming that, like me, when you write an outdoor book, you want it to sell as many copies as possible. Not only that, but you would also like it to become a best-seller, be translated into at least a dozen foreign languages, and be the basis for a movie. The chances of any outdoor book's doing this are very slim, but we can always dream!

As a realistic example of how outdoor books do, I can tell you how my various books are doing. Two of the best-selling are: *The Best of Corey Ford,* a collection of Corey Ford's best writings, from his books as well as his *Field & Stream* columns. *A Fine and Pleasant Misery,* a collection of the humor writings of Patrick McManus, associate editor of *Field & Stream,* is about hunting, fishing, camping, canoeing, and all the strange people Pat McManus knows and writes about. Both these books (*The Best of Corey Ford* was published in 1974 and *A Fine and Pleasant Misery* in 1978) have sold well and steadily. These men are fine writers and (probably very significant in the success of their books) have a wide and faithful following.

The third book that has sold the best for me as of this writing is *Falconry Today*—a book I wrote for youngsters in 1976. It is a thin treatise on the history and art of falconry, the ancient sport of kings. Because falconry excites young teens (as it did me, and later my own sons), the book continues to sell well year in and year out.

I wrote a large, relatively expensive ($25) book, called *The Worlds of Ernest Thompson Seton*, in 1976. It was part biography and part art book, was printed in Italy in magnificent color, and is a very impressive book. It took two years to write and has sold more than eight thousand copies. It is one of those books that may sell steadily for years.

I did not have such good luck with a clean, well-designed book called *The Sportsman's World*, published by Holt, Rinehart and Winston, Inc., in 1976. It was a collection of my hunting and fishing stories from around the world, with four-color photos and special sections, following each chapter, discussing accommodations, travel arrangements, rates, etc. It did not sell well. It may have been overpriced ($16.95). As I said earlier, color printing is expensive.

One of my favorites was one I wrote in 1973, called *Line Down! The Special World of Big Game Fishing*. It was a collection of my experiences catching big game fish the world over. It was beautifully illustrated with pencil sketches by my wife, a professional artist. It did not sell too well, possibly because big game fishing is a very expensive sport and the number of people actively involved in it is relatively small.

I have a nature book called *The Pond* published in the spring of 1979 by Knopf; another called *The Bear Book*, a limited edition by Amwell Press, N.J.; and this book you are reading. We will see what happens with these.

Outdoor books, again, are a limited market, and you would be well advised to pick a topic that has a large or a growing following. Be particularly careful when writing about a specialized branch of this already specialized field. On the other hand, writing about a very faddish topic will put you in competition with instant books and unknown numbers of books still in the works. By the time your book comes out (fifteenth or sixteenth in an endless stream), the publisher may have lost his initial enthusiasm. So, unless you are lucky enough to be in the advance guard, a steadily warm topic is better than a hot one.

The time you spend in thought and research before you write a book will save you time and disappointment in the end. Be sure that your topic has enough scope for book-length treatment. Many half-baked outdoor books are based on what is really only a magazine-article-sized subject. On the other hand, there are some nice ideas for books that really don't answer any clear need of the reading public. Nice books, but they don't sell well (probably because they are nice to read only if somebody *else* buys them).

Each year, many outdoor writers have books published that are collections of their stories which have appeared in outdoor magazines. This is a relatively painless way to write a book. We frequently give permission to writers who work for us to do this—providing they credit the magazine. Do not be surprised, as your articles begin to appear regularly in newspapers and magazines, if an editor calls *you* for a book. Book editors are always sifting through publications for up-and-coming authors who might have a book in them, or skilled writers who could be matched up with a book idea the editor already has in mind.

Other outdoor books fall into the how-to category (as in the case of my *Falconry Today*) and are just plain work to write. They are extensions of how-to magazine stories, and I have never met an outdoor writer yet who did not admit that instructional books are difficult to write. No matter how well you know your subject, analyzing it and expressing it well enough to convey it to others is a formidable task.

Before you begin to write a book on the outdoors, be sure you know enough about the subject to do it properly. You are going to have to convince a publisher you *do* know enough to do it, so you had better be prepared. Publishers are businessmen, and they have a keen sense about what will and what won't make money for them.

Regardless of whether you present your book idea to an agent or to a publisher, you should first outline your plans for the book. A letter describing the book you have in mind, and an outline of chapters and their contents, should suffice. Especially if you are a new or unestablished writer, you may want to include a sample chapter or two to show the style and execution you're capable of. Include a brief biography establishing your expertise (in outdoor books, too, knowledge and experience may be more important than writing style). A publisher or agent can tell from this whether you are capable of handling the book. If you have a personal platform for the promotion of the book—a column, radio or TV show, etc.—mention it. A run-down of the competition and why your book is different, or better, will help. I would include statistics on the breadth of the market for the book. Editors may not always be as familiar with your subject as they would like to be, and hard facts from you will help them convince the marketing department. Having the enthusiasm of the editor will also give your book a boost that will help it through the whole production and marketing process.

Picking a publisher deserves some careful thought and research. You should find a publisher that is familiar with outdoor books and is equipped to handle and market them. For an overview of publishers, find the current *Literary Market Place* in your library, or review the book publishing entries in *Writer's Market*. Compile a list of publishers that deal with your specialty. Then, back in the library, go to the multivolume *Publisher's Trade List Annual*. This mammoth compilation consists of the bound-together actual catalogues of most publishers. This book will show you what each publisher on your list is actually doing in your field, and whether or not your book fits in.

In my experience, some publishers do very little promotion on outdoor books and seem to depend upon word of mouth to sell. Elaborate plans for special-market penetration somehow go unrealized. They simply put the book on their fall or spring lists and hope the hunting, fishing, or nature public will flock to the book stores to order the book. 'Taint so.

Take for example a pleasant little book called *My Moby Dick*, written by William Humphrey. It was about a monster brown trout that he tried to catch, finally hooked, and lost. It was a well-written short story which was made into a thin book (ninety-six pages) and published by Doubleday. *Sports Illustrated* ran it in condensed form; considering the three million circulation of *SI*, the book got considerable publicity. On the other hand, one of the best books I have ever read on trout fishing, *A River Runs Through It, and Other Stories*, by Norman Maclean, University of Chicago Press, was published a few years ago, and the only review I ever saw of it was in the *New York Times* Book Review. It was nominated for a Pulitzer Prize, but I'll wager *My Moby Dick* outsold it by a bunch. Promotion and advertising mean a great deal to a book. Even a lightweight and terribly written book can make millions when promoted well. If there was ever a worse novel than *Valley of the Dolls* (I am a writer, not a prude), I never read it. Yet millions were poured into the promotion of that book, assuring its success no matter what.

As a final note to locating a publisher, don't give up if you can't find one that will take your book. If you are convinced that you have a book that will sell, you can publish it yourself, using one of the good books on self-publishing that are available. Publishing is not an Act of God, and in certain instances you may have surer access to the market for your book than a large national publisher would.

Selling your book to a publisher sometimes takes considerable convincing. That is why I got an agent years ago. He negotiates book contracts for me and does a fine job. Unless you have considerable business talent, I suggest you try to find a reputable literary agent.

In a nutshell, an agent's job is to be responsible for any business dealings involving the literary works of the author. He has to stay on top of the field (although a good writer can do so too by reading such periodicals as *Publisher's Weekly*) and know who needs what and when, plus the highest—and the average—prices they are willing to pay for it.

There are several ways you can get an agent. You may ask successful writers if they will recommend one, perhaps their own. I have seen this done several times, particularly if the writer thinks you are good. You can send for a list of literary agents from the Society of Authors' Representatives, 101 Park Avenue, New York, NY 10017. Write to some of them telling what you do and what you would like to do in the future. Another suggestion is to get the current *Writer's Market* and look under the Opportunities and Services section. There you will find listings of agencies, with information as to what kind of materials the agency is willing to handle, what percentage the agent receives as his commission (usually 10-20 percent), and so forth.

Don't sign up with an agent until you know a little about him. Be sure you know what rights he is handling for your material, and make sure there are no charges for services (such as editing or marketing) other than those you have contracted for. Some agencies charge the writer a reading fee, which usually ranges from around $25, for a short story or magazine article, to $100 or more, for novels and plays. The listing in *Writer's Market* indicates what fees for reading, evaluating, or criticizing, if any, are charged. Most reputable agencies refund these fees, or credit the author's account from the first sale they make. Be careful, as there are a number of them who will read your book outline or manuscript, charge you a fee, and do nothing with it. On the other hand, there are a great many fine literary agents, most of whom are members of the Society of Authors' Representatives.

An agent can be a valuable asset to you, but I would not worry about obtaining one until you have established a name for yourself in the writing field—in magazines or newspapers at least. Most good agents are reluctant to take on a new writer without a track record. When you are consistently making $10,000 to $15,000 per year as an outdoor freelance writer, you should consider an agent, and an agent should be happy to consider you.

The amount of advance is between you and the publisher, or between you, your agent, and the publisher. There is no rule of thumb on this. Some writers like to get as much cash in advance as possible. Others take small advances and hope the royalties will pile up. The ideal royalty arrangement is for the writer to get 10 percent royalty on the cover price of the book on the first five thousand copies, 12½ percent on the next five thousand copies, and 15 percent thereafter. There are publishers who will offer a flat fee for certain types of books, mostly how-to's. Before entering into such an arrangement, give it a close look. It is not always the best way to go.

I am satisfied if I am able to get an advance in the $10,000 area and have the book sell about that many copies. If you are a beginner, don't try to shoot that high for the advance; somewhere in the area of $3,000-7,500 is about average. In judging the size of an advance, you must realize that it does not reflect upon the merit of your book. It is usually based on a very sober analysis of first-year sales potential, which is another reason why you should choose your subject very carefully.

The amount of time necessary to complete a book, obviously, is determined by the size of the book and the complexity of the work involved. Especially if it calls for a great deal of travel, research, or photography, it will be important to set a realistic deadline for turning in the finished manuscript. Half the advance is typically given to the writer on signing the publishing contract, and the other half is given to him when the book is submitted in satisfactory shape; or it may go one-third on signing, one-third on delivery of half the manuscript, and one-third on delivery of complete and final ms. Because I am a deadline writer—brought on by years with wire services—I usually allow about six months for the deadline when my finished book is due. Usually it takes approximately nine months, from the time the copyedited manuscript is turned over to the printer, for a book to come out.

Another important consideration when writing your outdoor book is that the majority of them are illustrated, especially the how-to books. In most cases, the author is required to supply the illustrations, photographs, or drawings. Unless you are a competent photographer, you will have to go elsewhere for these. Using professional sources for the pictures, or buying them one by one, can be very expensive. An alternative to this is to form a partnership with a photographer, either for a flat fee or a percentage. This same approach applies to illustrators.

The other option is to make use of the numerous free sources of photographs, such as public relations departments of manufacturers and the state fish and game departments. The drawback of this is that some of their photos are dated or posed, which can give your book a low-budget look. This can be avoided by thoroughly researching a number of sources and choosing carefully. There is also a tendency (simply because they are free) to go overboard and include unnecessary pictures. Going in this direction will give your book a padded look. The last thing to remember is that because of the cost of color printing, most books (outside the very expensive coffee-table types) will use black and white. So, if you take your own photos, use black-and-white film or be prepared to pay for the cost of conversions.

Writing is work, as I have said before, and writing a book is harder than writing a magazine story—just as building a house is more work than building a porch. I have found that if I think of each chapter of a book as a separate magazine story—from the standpoint of length and content—writing a book comes easier. However, it is still a matter of sitting down and doing it.

Inevitably writing a book has some major differences from writing a string of magazine articles. A book is an interrelated whole which will pose more organizational and developmental problems than a magazine story, and will have many more details to be checked and snags to be untangled. A book is a huge commitment of time and effort—a very different thing from writing an article a week. No matter how limited or familiar your topic is, researching and writing a book is a long and strung-out process, one that appears to have no end.

When you (at last) turn in the perfectly typed, illustrated, captioned, all-permissions-gotten manuscript, which the publisher wanted last month, it still isn't over. After that come the endless and aggravating processes of editing, copyediting, expert reviewing, proofing, indexing, and promoting—more problems and deadlines.

The galleys will arrive as soon as your reservation is confirmed to Kodiak Island, and you will be scheduled to speak at the Des Moines Authors Club on opening day of deer season. To make it through all this happily and intact takes a special kind of purpose and application—and, I am tempted to say, a special kind of temperament.

Book writing is a highly specialized area of the outdoor writing field, not something the average freelance beginning writer will be concerned with. However, it is something to consider in later years as one gains experience and perhaps has a number of magazine stories which he or she would like to incorporate into book form. Meanwhile, I suggest you concentrate on writing your outdoor material for newspapers, magazines, radio, or TV, and think of books as a long-range goal.

The Fishing Writer

11.

One of the attributes of a good fishing writer is that he will admit to not knowing everything. It is frightening to look back over the years and see how much I did not know about fishing. It is even more sobering to realize that what I have learned in half a century of fishing is no more than a scratch on the surface of the subject. But this is the confidence (and ignorance) of youth and the gradual enlightenment of age.

As a trout and bass fisherman in my mid-twenties, there was little I did not know about the subject—according to me. I had done some saltwater fishing as a youngster, so I was also an authority on that—although my triumphs in the saltwater area were somewhat more modest. Having been born in Providence, Rhode Island, and having fished as a boy on Narragansett Bay, I had managed to catch flounder, tautog (blackfish), skipjacks, eels, weakfish, and some small sand sharks. Such was the awesome basis of my expertise. Upon moving to New Mexico at the age of nine, I discovered the joys of trout fishing and pursued that with a vengeance (with everything from worms and salmon eggs to spinners, spoons, and flies) for years.

When I began to write outdoor columns in the late 1940s—after returning from World War II—I was convinced I knew a great deal about both hunting and fishing. This is a common failing of outdoor sportsmen. If you are a beginner, don't take me too seriously. We all have to start somewhere, and if you have been fishing as far back as you can remember, at least you know more than the person who is just starting to fish.

On the other hand, you will be writing a column for fellow anglers, and many of them will be experts. There is no field I know of in which there are so many "experts." *Everybody* knows more than the next person. Admitting that *you* don't know everything will immediately put you in the proper perspective for those many expert readers you have. They will forgive you your errors if you are humble enough to admit to not knowing everything.

Let us assume that you are living in a fairly small town or city, and that you are an avid fisherman. You are the young man or woman who regularly reads the outdoor magazines and spends a lot of time fishing. You are not an accomplished photographer yet but, as I recommend in Chapter Eight, you are going to try to become at least a competent one. You would like to write a fishing column for a local newspaper, or magazine, or a regular feature spot for a radio or TV station, and to start trying to sell freelance stories on fishing to regional and national magazines. How do you begin and what should you know?

You are going to have to spend a little money in order to build up your reference library. First I would write to the *Sporting Goods Directory*, published by the Sporting Goods Dealer, St. Louis, MO 63166. It lists the manufacturers of every conceivable type of sporting goods from golf and baseball through hunting, fishing, and camping gear. The directory sells for a nominal charge—somewhere around five dollars. Say you are looking for fishing tackle manufacturers. Write to each one listed, saying you are an outdoor writer specializing in fishing and would like their current catalogue.

Next write for the current year's *NSGA* (National Sporting Goods Association) *Buying Guide,* 717 North Michigan Avenue, Chicago, IL 60611. This guide carries an alphabetical listing of suppliers in the sporting goods industry, with names, addresses, and phone numbers. You never know when you are going to need to ask a technical question on fishing tackle. The guide also lists manufacturers' representatives who are NSGA members; associations and industries serving (in your case) the fishing tackle industry; and suppliers listed by category of sporting goods produced and sporting goods brand names. This book costs five dollars for nonmembers of NSGA.

The next book I would order is *McClane's New Standard Fishing Encyclopedia and International Angling Guide*, by A. J. McClane, longtime fishing editor of *Field & Stream* before he retired after thirty years with the magazine. The encyclopedia is published by Holt, Rinehart & Winston, 385 Madison Avenue, New York, New York. This sells for a whopping forty dollars, but it is worth every penny. It contains just about everything the fishing writer will need to know about fish, fish food, geographical location, tackle, techniques, and Lord knows what else. It should serve as the backbone of your fishing library. As time goes on, you can pick up specialized books on different types of fish and fishing, but for now this giant volume will suffice.

Because it is important for you to know what is going on in the fishing world outside your home state or county, I would write to the National Wildlife Federation, 1412 Sixteenth Street N. W., Washington DC 20036 and ask them for the current *Conservation Directory*. This will be invaluable in your correspondence. It lists every agency from all the federal ones concerned with conservation through international, national, and interstate organizations. In addition, it lists commissions, colleges, and universities; state fish and game commissions and departments in all fifty states; wildlife refuges; national forests; national parks; national seashores; private and independent conservation organizations; periodical and other directories of interest; and even the conservation agencies of foreign governments. It also contains audiovisual source information.

I would look up every organization I thought would have any connection with fish and fishing (from Trout Unlimited and the Izaak Walton League to the American Institute of Fisheries Research and the American Littoral Society) and ask to be put on their mailing lists as a fishing writer. You may be ignored occasionally, but most times these organizations are happy for more exposure in the media. Since the *Conservation Directory* lists the public information director of each of the state departments of game and fish, I would write to them asking that you be put on their mailing lists for both news releases and their monthly state magazines. There again, you may not receive copies from all of them, but most state agencies are happy for more coverage of their work—especially in the outdoor press. If you have not already been doing so for years, start collecting all possible back issues of fishing magazines—national, regional, and local. Start a clipping file on all material you run across pertaining to fishing.

I would write to the OWAA, the Outdoor Writers Association of America, as soon as you have sold a few columns or stories (or photographs) and ask to join. The dues are only $25 per year. Its many members do more to aid the outdoor profession than any other organization in America, and you will make several valuable friends. Also, the OWAA, which is located at 4141 West Bradley Road, Milwaukee, WI 53209, puts out an annual outdoor writers directory. It lists all outdoor writers in alphabetical order. Look up members close to you and begin a correspondence with them. I have never met a member of OWAA who was not happy to help a beginning writer, broadcaster, or photographer in the outdoor field. In addition, the Association holds an annual convention which focuses on the problems that beset all outdoor writers, broadcasters, filmmakers, and photographers. You will get far more out of OWAA than you can ever put into it. I have been a member for many years and am proud to be one.

You are now at the stage where you should try convincing your local newspaper editor that he should run an outdoor column on fishing. The first thing you should do is call your local game department and find out how many fishing licenses are sold each year in your state. With that figure as a starter, bear in mind that youngsters under fourteen years (in most states) do not require one, nor do "senior citizens" over sixty-five. Remember too that saltwater fishermen are not required to purchase a fishing license. You can come up with a round figure based on total state population. The state tourist bureau can give you figures on the number of people who visit the state each year, as tourists, to fish. They can probably also give you a good ballpark figure on the amount of money spent for gasoline, food, lodging, tackle, etc., in one season. Usually the figures are astronomical. These make a good selling presentation to a newspaper or magazine editor, sports editor, or director of a radio or TV station.

If you do not succeed in selling a regular column or spot to any newspaper, radio station, TV station or regional magazine, you might as well consider freelancing fishing stories for national publications. The subject matter is up to you. I would try to think of an unusual twist to a story. Perhaps there is a local fishing guide who has been around for a very long time. A profile of him might make a good feature. A new dam or impoundment may be under construction. How will this affect the fishing? Did anyone recently catch a very large fish in your area, and does he or she have a photograph of it for a story?

There may be companies in your area manufacturing lures or fishing tackle. If so, there might be a story on what the company is doing in the way of new developments. Many times a local game warden or fisheries biologist makes a good profile. You are going to have to use your imagination.

The first freelance outdoor story I ever sold was to *Field & Stream* while I was still a journalism student at the University of New Mexico in 1948. A friend of mine and I had been hunting ducks in our spare time along the irrigation ditches south of Albuquerque. Since the ditches were straight and the banks heavily overgrown with willows and tamarisk, it was difficult to surprise the mallards, pintails, gadwalls, teal, and other ducks when we parted the growth and stepped into the ditch. They would leap skyward, far out of shotgun range.

It occurred to me that if I obtained a large truck inner tube, inflated it, sat in it with my shotgun, and floated silently down the half-mile or so of ditch, I would surprise some of these ducks. Dressed in battered Army fatigue shirt and trousers, and clutching my trusty Ithaca side-by-side 12-gauge shotgun, I made the float. It worked like a charm. By the time the ducks discovered me, I was only a few yards away, and I tumbled them out of the sky as they climbed frantically for altitude. I came out at the end of the float cold and wet but with a limit of ducks. My friend took a black-and-white photograph of me holding the ducks and standing in the inner tube.

I wrote the story in about twenty-five hundred words, called it "Tire Tube Ducks," enclosed the photograph, and sent them off to *Field & Stream*. I nearly fainted when I got a check for seventy-five dollars in the return mail. I later asked Hugh Grey, the editor who bought it, why he did so.

"It was a neat gimmick," he said, "a new twist."

It's as simple as that. Think of something new, interesting, and different concerning fishing in your area, and send off queries or a manuscript. It is the only way I know to start. Don't be discouraged if you get a rejection slip the first, second, or third time; we all did (and still do, for that matter). Keep trying. This is the ultimate answer.

Now start collecting books on fishing in earnest. My library contains several thousand volumes on the subject, and I know many outdoor writers and editors whose libraries are far larger than mine. There is such a vast world of information on fishing that one could never find all the books on it. From Dame Juliana and Izaak Walton on, fishermen have been writing about their favorite sport. With the possible exception of love and war, I doubt if there is another subject which has more written about it than fishing.

I don't have a recommended list of books, as there are too many to name. I have my own favorites. They are ones which cover specific types of fishing, such as Peter Goadby's *Big Fish and Blue Water*, the definitive book on fishing Pacific waters for big-game fish, and Ernie Schweibert's *Trout*, a two-volume monumental work on everything and anything anyone would ever want to know about trout and trout fishing.

Perhaps your long-range goal is to be the fishing editor of a national magazine or a large metropolitan newspaper. If so, there is an incredible amount of knowledge you will have to acquire. Many years ago, fishing tackle was simple. It was not complicated even for saltwater big-game fishing. About the only big-game reel around was one manufactured by the Von Hoffe brothers of Brooklyn, New York. Lines were woven thread, and there were but few rods. When I was a youngster, you used a switch pole and string for such fish as sunfish or yellow perch. If you were really sophisticated, you fished with a fly rod or level-winding reel and rod. I grew up with a True Temper steel casting rod and a Pfleuger Supreme level-winding reel with which to cast plugs and spoons for bass, pike, pickerel, and walleyes. I owned one split-cane bamboo fly rod and a Pfleuger Medalist fly reel until I was almost thirty years old. I used that for trout and bass—casting flies and bass bugs.

Today just open a catalogue of fishing tackle, and the variety of rods, reels, lines, leaders, and lures is dazzling. Now the saltwater tackle field is so varied and so highly developed that it takes a specialist to write about it. Space-age materials have resulted in a vast array of new rods, reels, monofilament lines, and lures of all sorts in the freshwater field. And new equipment means new fishing techniques. Nowadays a fishing editor must know how to write about fly casting, bait casting, spin casting, and spin fishing. In addition, he should know saltwater and big-game fishing—and all the gear that goes with it. He should be familiar with every species of both freshwater and saltwater fish in a particular region, and if he wants to be a national fishing editor, as many as possible in the world.

A good fishing writer must be part ichthyologist and part naturalist. He must know environmental problems that beset rivers, lakes, streams, and oceans. He must be an expert on pollution, industrial development, mining practices, timber techniques, and tidelands. He must be part meteorologist, part entomologist, part botanist, and part marine biologist. On a first-name basis, he must know not only all the heads of tackle companies, but also most of their employees. He must be as at home in an AFTMA (American Fishing Tackle Manufacturers' Association) convention as he is on his favorite bass pond. To be able to write about fish, fishing, tackle, and boats, he must be *proficient* with all this tackle and gear.

Ultimately he will be able to discuss the parabolic curves of rods as casually as he might the time of day. He will know how to read the water of a trout stream in the Rockies or a salmon river in Labrador as easily as he can tell a tarpon fin on a Florida Keys flat or the dorsal fin of a striped marlin off Ecuador. He will know the best baits for catfish in Louisiana and the most productive methods of taking coho salmon on the Great Lakes. He will be expected to know how to flycast one hundred feet or more for steelhead in the Pacific Northwest and how to properly filet a dolphin in the Bahamas. He will or should know the name and action of every spinner, spoon, crankbait, and plug on the market. He will be expected to know the best times to catch stripers off Montauk, New York, or sea trout off Padre Island, Texas. The "Good Ole Boys" will respect him because he will know how to handle a spinnerbait in a "honeyhole" in Alabama for bass, and a guide on the Moise River in Quebec will admire his handling of a forty-pound Atlantic salmon on an eight-pound tippet.

He will know the local names of every fish in the United States—as well as what a Mahseer is in India and a Peacock Bass is in South America. He will be expected to take sharp color photographs under any and all light conditions and of things traveling at incredible speeds.

He will have to know the attributes of shooting head lines, weight-forward floating and sinking lines, and double-tapered lines for the fly fisherman who fishes in both fresh and salt water. He will know the relative good and bad points of fiberglass, split bamboo, graphite, and boron in rods. He will be expected to remain in a fighting chair for hours in the hot sun as giant marlin and tuna try to tear his arms from the sockets. And he will have to learn to laugh when the fish get away—all of them.

Most of all he must be able to write about this wonderful sport. Doing it is one thing, as all of us who love it know. Making it come alive on paper is something else. And that is where the real work comes in.

The Shooting Writer

12.

The field for a shooting or hunting writer has narrowed since I began writing outdoor columns.

There are still twenty million persons each year who buy a hunting license in this country. That does not count youngsters under the age of fourteen who may hunt if accompanied by an adult but need no license, but who must pass a hunter safety course first.

Even so, the field has narrowed, and for a number of reasons. More and more people live in large metropolitan and suburban areas. There is not the hunting I had as a youngster. All of my boyhood chums had BB guns, if not .22-caliber rifles, and we were always stalking something, whether an English sparrow or a ground squirrel. Since those days cities and towns have passed laws forbidding not only .22 rifles but air rifles. As a result, only the youngster fortunate enough to be raised in a rural area has a chance to grow up hunting.

Another factor contributing to the decline in the number of hunting and shooting writers is that our hunting lands keep shrinking as our population keeps growing. Lands I roamed at will as a youngster, with a rifle or shotgun under an arm, have long since been paved over or

developed into housing areas or industrial sites. Even in the West many areas I once hunted have been developed or posted.

Well-financed and highly vocal anti-hunting groups have sprung up—such as The Defenders of Wildlife, The Friends of Animals, The Fund For Animals and The Committee to Abolish Sport Hunting. They object to hunting on moral grounds; they do not think it right to kill wild creatures. In this free country they are entitled to think and say anything they wish. However, their attacks upon the hunting community are more often based on emotion than on scientific fact. They reach into the school systems and get their message out through the media—newspapers, magazines and television. They influence a number of youngsters who have never had the opportunity to hunt, shoot, or learn the facts about wildlife and scientific game management. The National Wildlife Federation (with a membership of six million), The National Audubon Society, The Wildlife Management Institute and other groups have taken the public stand that hunting is a valuable wildlife management tool, which it is.

Each year our colleges turn out graduates with degrees in wildlife management, and it is here that hope remains for the hunting public. The sound, scientific management of game as a renewable resource, carried on by trained personnel of the state and federal wildlife agencies, will ensure the continuation of this sport.

Those of us who hunt and who write about hunting find ourselves bewildered at times by the almost theological zeal of the persons who object to hunting on principle. These objections may have more to do with the old Puritan Ethic than a desire to protect wild creatures. I suspect the anti-hunters dislike the hunter because they believe he *enjoys* hunting and killing, which really bothers them. They would prefer their killing be done for them by an anonymous person at a slaughterhouse, so they will never witness death and can pretend the steak or chop eaten was never a living creature.

The Viet Nam War did much to turn a generation of young people off to killing. Many of these people do not hunt, but they do shoot.

There is still a great audience out there for the shooting writer or editor. The current *Writer's Market* lists at least forty consumer magazines that buy hunting and shooting stories. A look at the OWAA membership directory will show several thousand newspaper columnists across the country who make a living writing outdoor columns on hunting and fishing. Books on hunting and shooting are published constantly by almost all the major publishing firms.

The competitive areas have no dearth of enthusiasts. In addition, there are gun collectors and those who have become interested in antique guns and black-powder shooting, a growing and exciting field. The devotee can build his own replica from a kit or buy one already assembled. There is something nostalgic about loading and shooting these old-fashioned guns. Making one's own balls of lead in molds and loading the old-style guns from the muzzle is fascinating. Many people have begun hunting for birds as well as big game with the black-powder muzzle-loaders.

For the young writer today who is fond of shooting or hunting I would give the same advice I gave to fishing writers in the previous chapter. First, obtain the *Sporting Goods Directory* and write to the gun and ammunition companies listed. Then, purchase the *NSGA Buying Guide* for the same reason the fishing writer should. I would also buy some specialized catalogues and books unless, as a hunter and shooter, you already have them in your library. I would subscribe to the annual *Gun Digest,* published by John Amber, Digest Books, Inc., Northfield, IL 60693 which will keep you up to date on the latest guns, related equipment and prices. It is a fine book on what is new in the guns and shooting field. Digest Books also publishes *The Handloader's Digest;* a shooting writer must know handloading of ammunition.

And, just like the fishing writer, the shooting writer should ask The National Wildlife Federation for its current *Conservation Directory.* I would—if you are not already a member—join The National Rifle Association. A shooting writer should certainly support the only large national organization looking out for the rights of gun owners.

Write to the organizations listed in the *Conservation Directory* that you think might have some connection with guns or shooting and ask to be on their mailing list. Then, write to the public information directors of the fifty state game and fish departments and to federal agencies, also listed in the directory, and do the same. I would establish correspondence with the Amateur Trapshooting Association at Vandalia, OH 45377, and the National Skeet Shooting Association at Box 28188, San Antonio, TX 78228.

If you don't already have it in your library I would recommend that you purchase *The Experts' Book on the Shooting Sports,* edited by David E. Petzal. It covers everything from target shooting, bench-rest shooting, small-game hunting, varmint hunting and big-game hunting (close and long range) in the rifle field. It also covers handgun target shooting and handgun hunting. In addition, it serves as an excellent reference book on trap and skeet shooting and the hunting of all sorts of game with a shotgun. It is a book written by experts and is the best of its kind in the field. It is available at your local book stores or from Simon and Schuster, Rockefeller Center, New York, NY 10020.

A list of all the books I could recommend for your library would take up pages. I will name a few I think of as classics, indispensable to a beginning shooting writer. A good library will have them. *Hunting Big Game in North America,* by Jack O'Connor; *The Rifle Book,* also by Jack O'Connor, longtime shooting editor of *Outdoor Life* Magazine; *One Man's Wilderness,* by the late Warren Page, for many years shooting editor of *Field & Stream; Keith,* the autobiography of the great Elmer Keith, one of the deans of American shooting; *Ed McGivern's Book of Fast and Fancy Revolver Shooting,* a fascinating treatise on handguns; *Shotgunning,* by Bob Brister; *The Modern Shotgun,* a two-volume work by Maj. Sir Gerald Burrand; *The Bolt Action,* by Stuart Otteson; *The Hunting Rifle,* by Townsend Whelen; *The Shooter's Workbench,* by John Mosher; *The American Shotgun,* by Charles Askins; *How to Measure and Score Big Game Trophies,* by the late Grancel Fitz; and *Bow Hunting for Big Game,* by Keith C. Schuyler. That should give you a solid foundation of reference books.

Then, like the fishing editor or writer, I would start a clipping file of all matters pertaining to guns and hunting from periodicals. Try to locate some other shooting writer who belongs to OWAA and correspond with him—and with other experts in the field. As soon as you have sold a story or two or some photographs, become a member of OWAA, for reasons I discussed in the previous chapter.

The gun or shooting editor—like the fishing editor—must acquire an incredible amount of knowledge to be successful. I have been actively hunting for almost fifty years in North America, Asia and Africa—and I still consider myself a rank amateur compared to the professional gun writers. I started hunting at age eleven in New Mexico, both with a .22-caliber rifle and a 20-gauge shotgun. I hunted big game there as late as 1950 with a lever-action .32 Special Winchester Model '94. The Winchester had iron sights, and with it I killed deer, elk and antelope. I did not own a rifle with a scope until I was in my late thirties. After that I began hunting on a worldwide scale. I have hunted most species of North American big game and a good many of Africa and Asia. I consider myself a good wing shot on birds with a shotgun, an adequate rifle shot and a passable pistol shot. I have written hunting columns and stories for years, but I would no more put myself in the category of a *gun writer* or *shooting editor* than I would claim to be a Nobel Prize calibre poet!

Decades of study and experience go into the making of a professional gun writer. A man the stature of John Amber, former editor and publisher of *Gun Digest*, for example, makes most hunters feel as if they are using slingshots instead of guns.

A shooting writer or gun editor must be part ballistician, part gunsmith, part historian, part engineer, and must be a *good shot* with every type of gun. What those with the reputations of Charles Askins and Elmer Keith know about a subject so seemingly simple as the chokes of shotgun barrels is astronomical. It could (and did) fill books. Warren Page and Jack O'Connor learned about ballistics and such subjects as muzzle velocity through decades of testing and research. Open up a copy of *Modern Guns*, published by Collector Books of Paducah, Kentucky, for example, and you will find a catalogue of more than two thousand guns, with identifying information, operation and prices. A gun editor probably knows *each one* of these guns by heart!

A shooting writer must not only be able to converse intelligently with gunsmiths, he must be able to hold his own in discussions with zoologists, ornithologists, and game management experts. He has to have a vast knowledge of the world's wildlife. A good professional gun writer must be as at ease discussing the proper shotgun loads for grouse at the Holland & Holland Shooting School in England as he is explaining the mistake of resting a rifle barrel on a rock while aiming to a Texas rancher. He must be able to tell the best time for hunting Greater Kudu in South Africa as easily as he reels off the prime pheasant hunting areas in his home state.

There is no shortcut to being a successful gun writer. You are going to have to read everything on guns you can get your hands on; you are going to have to learn from the professionals before they pass on. You are going to have to learn gunsmithing and Lord knows how many aspects of ballistics. In addition, you are going to have to become proficient in the use of every conceivable type of sporting gun, because you are going to be judged by your peers.

And, the toughest part of all is you are going to have to learn to write well about a subject so complex it boggles the mind. You *will*, that is, if you want to become a professional and successful gun writer.

That word *write* is the key one. The fact is that the most successful gun writers in the business were writers first and foremost. Jack O'Connor, who is generally acknowledged to be the greatest of them all, was a professor of journalism at Arizona State University and a successful novelist and screenwriter long before he signed on with *Outdoor Life* as its gun editor. Warren Page, who was O'Connor's contemporary at *Field & Stream*, was a Harvard graduate, an English teacher at Lawrenceville (one of the nation's most prestigious prep schools), and a highly cultured and literate man. Bob Brister, Page's successor, brought long years of highly eclectic newspaper experience to his post. He won numerous prizes for general news reporting and was a Pulitzer nominee.

What these men never lost—or lose—sight of is that the object of the sport is not the kill itself; it is the countries to which you travel, the people and the cultures you encounter, the animals, their habitat, and the lessons you learn about yourself. This ancient pursuit is a kind of crucible. You put yourself in, simmer, and see what comes out. That process is the core of the experience. If you can recreate that process successfully, you'll succeed.

The Conservation/ Nature Writer

13.

The young person today who is beginning a career as an outdoor writer in the conservation field is carrying on a great tradition. The outdoor sportsmen of years gone by—whether they were hunters, fishermen, novelists or poets—were all interested in the same thing: preserving nature and its wild creatures for generations to come.

You can put any tag you wish on this type of outdoor writer—environmental writer, ecology writer or nature writer—but I grew up in the outdoor field to think of them as conservation writers. In the 1960s the public discovered the word *ecology* and began to use it rather than *conservation*—although the two words have different meanings. Ecology is described in Herbert C. Hanson's *Dictionary of Ecology* (1962) as "the study of the interrelationships of organisms to one another and to the environment."

The word *conservationist* is a far more correct term to describe those who were and are interested in conserving America's natural resources. The principles early conservationists understood a long time ago are just as true today: Renewable resources such as wildlife and forests can be successfully exploited indefinitely as long as a certain amount of "capital" is maintained. Even nonrenewable resources such as coal and oil can be made to last infinitely longer if managed on an efficient basis. As John Reiger wrote in his book *American Sportsmen and the Origins of Conservation,* "Historically, conservation has not been a science like ecology, but a reform movement using political and legal methods to obtain what Theodore Roosevelt called the 'wise use' of resources." The sportsman has always been among the most concerned and active in the fight to save wildlife and wild lands in this country.

Theodore Roosevelt was a conservation activist and writer; he was also a big-game hunter. John James Audubon, the famous bird artist, was a hunter. So was Ernest Thompson Seton, the great artist-naturalist and cofounder of the Boy Scouts of America. Most of the well-known naturalists and conservationists around the turn of the century were hunters and fishermen who were vitally concerned about the future of wildlife. Roosevelt teamed up with other famous sportsmen of his day—Seton; William Hornaday, founder of the New York Zoological Society; ornithologist Frank Chapman of the American Museum of Natural History; and Roosevelt's chief forester, Gifford Pinchot—to make *conservation* a household word in America in the first decade of the twentieth century.

The great naturalist John Burroughs, in commenting on his trip in 1903 with Roosevelt through Yellowstone Park, wrote:

> Some of our newspapers reported that the President intended to hunt in the Park. A woman in Vermont wrote me, to protest against the hunting, and hoped I would teach the President to love the animals as much as I did—as if he did not love them more, because his love is founded upon knowledge, and because they had been a part of his life.

What greater tribute could be paid the outdoor sportsman who truly loves nature and its wild things?

Fishermen, too, become an integral part of nature when they fish. Henry David Thoreau once wrote of a fisherman he had observed from his *Week on the Concord and Merrimack Rivers* (1849):

> He was always to be seen in serene afternoons haunting the river, and almost rustling with the sedge.... his fishing was not a sport, nor solely a means of subsistence, but a sort of solemn sacrament and withdrawal from the world, just as the aged read their Bibles.

And yet so many of today's young "ecological writers" look down on the outdoor sportsman as a lout who kills wildlife simply for the fun of it.

Even the Sierra Club, a well-respected conservation organization, founded in 1892 by the great naturalist John Muir and with chapters in all fifty states, has taken swipes at the sportsman. Such attacks strike many conservationists as more divisive than helpful to the movement as a whole.

It matters little today whether it is fashionable to dislike hunting or for outdoor sportsmen to rant and rave at what they term the "lunatic fringe" of animal protectionist organizations. What really matters is that we all—in our own way—attempt to save our forests, streams, rivers, oceans and all wild creatures from the kind of exploitation or neglect that could lead to extinction. A sportsman/conservationist should be as concerned with the status of the California condor as would be a student of ornithology.

There are hundreds of conservation organizations in this country today that raise funds and work hard to save wildlife and the habitat necessary for its survival. Leaf through the *Conservation Directory,* published each year by the National Wildlife Federation, a conservation education association organized in 1936 and with a membership of three and a half million. The Federation alone has regional directors covering all fifty states, and many of the state game departments are now federated with the headquarters of the organization in Washington. It is doing a fine job of increasing public awareness of the need for the wise use, proper management and conservation of the natural resources upon which all life depends: air, water, soils, minerals, forests, plant life, and wildlife. It distributes numerous periodicals and educational materials, sponsors outdoor education programs in conservation, and even litigates environmental disputes.

Under the federal government listing of the *Conservation Directory* you'll find the Department of Agriculture, which includes the Forest Service and the Soil Conservation Service. You will also find the Department of Commerce, with agencies such as the National Oceanic and Atmospheric Administration, the Office of Coastal Zone Management, the Office of Sea Grant, and the National Marine Fisheries Service; and most important the Department of the Interior with such conservation agencies as the Bureau of Land Management, the Bureau of Outdoor Recreation, the Bureau of Reclamation, the United States

Fish and Wildlife Service, the Geological Survey, and the National Park Service.

There are dozens more fine conservation organizations listed under independent agencies of the federal government, from the Environmental Protection Agency to the U.S. Water Resources Council. Dozens more organizations devoted to the protection of our natural resources are listed, in alphabetical order, under the heading of International, National, and Interstate Commissions. There are groups ranging from the excellent Audubon Society under A to the equally prestigious Zero Population Growth at the end of the list. All the organizations listed—and there are hundreds—are working toward the same goal: making sure we all manage to survive on a well-preserved Earth. I cannot think of a directory more important for the library of a budding environmental/conservation/nature writer.

All across this land there are conservation groups steadily going about their business. Each of them represents a potential story for the conservation writer.

One such private organization, which puts out its own magazine, is Ducks Unlimited, a loosely knit group of outdoor sportsmen and waterfowl lovers who first banded together during the dust bowl days of the 1930s when the great wetlands of the Canadian provinces—nesting ground for most of the waterfowl that migrate south to the United States each year—began to dry up. Without fanfare and without government or other outside financial aid, DU began to obtain long-term leases on existing or potential Canadian wetlands. Water control structures were then created to maintain water at constant and proper levels. More than a thousand of these marsh projects were built and today encompass more than *two million acres* of prime waterfowl habitat, where more than 80 percent of the North American waterfowl population is raised.

More than $32 *million* in tax-exempt donations has been raised by individuals to finance this incredible program. It is even more inspiring when one realizes that it was begun during the Great Depression—when few people had the funds for the necessities of life, let alone conservation projects! DU today has organized similar projects in Mexico, where much of the North American waterfowl go in the winter months. DU is also affiliated with its sister organization in Canada and has pledged millions of U.S. dollars to help support Canadian DU.

There are stories on all sides for the writer who is truly concerned about our environment and wildlife. George Reiger, conservation editor of *Field & Stream* and one of the most knowledgeable men in the environmental field today, each month in the magazine reveals the very real dangers that exist for our wildlife, its habitat and the environment as a whole. He is as concerned about ocean oil spills as he is about strip mining and is as worried about Northwest Coast Indians netting and selling spawning salmon as he is about the devastation being wrought by the U.S. Army Corps of Engineers.

There is *never* a shortage of material in the investigative reporting field of the conservation writer.

I wrote an expose in *Field & Stream* in 1977 on the disgraceful practice of illegally poaching and selling ivory by the late Jomo Kenyatta of Kenya, a story covered also by the *New York Times* and the British Broadcasting Company. The impact of the three stories resulted in the law—passed six months later by the Kenya government—prohibiting trade in wildlife products of any kind, including ivory. It succeeded in closing down the curio trade in that country which was the primary cause of poaching. Outdoor writing is a satisfying career when it results in the passage of laws that prohibit destruction of the environment or harm to wildlife.

One of the advantages of the conservation writer is that he or she is not restricted to the outdoor magazines. Conservation stories are constantly being picked up and run by the large general circulation publications. For example, the January, 1979, issue of *Reader's Digest* reprinted five pages of art and captions from my book, *The Worlds of Ernest Thompson Seton*. And books on conservation and the environment are in constant demand—particularly by publishing firms which deal in the young-adult field.

Nature writing, though somewhat different in approach, is not really a separate field from conservation writing. What we want to conserve, after all, is nature, so anything that makes people better understand and appreciate the value of some creature or natural phenomenon is bound to help the cause. Les Line, editor of *Audubon* magazine, writes a monthly nature column for *Field & Stream* because most outdoorsmen are amateur naturalists. Les devotes his columns to such subjects as dragonflies, whip-poor-wills, toadstools, and the birds, plants and mammals that the outdoor person is likely to see in the wild. George Harrison, another fine nature writer, writes a similar monthly column for *Sports Afield*. Nature articles can convey important messages in an easy-to-understand, even entertaining way, and sometimes this approach can accomplish more than a scientific treatise could. This is also a field with many possibilities, since almost anything connected with the land or its inhabitants—including people living on easy terms with nature—is a potential subject.

One fine example of the great range that nature and outdoor writing allows is the *Foxfire* book series, first published by Doubleday in 1972. These books began as a school project by a group of young students, under the guidance of Eliot Wiggington, who hoped the project would, among other things, preserve the skills the mountain people of the Great Smokies had handed down for so many years.

In a series of excellent stories, the young writers of *Foxfire* show how for centuries the descendants of early settlers made things with their own hands. They write of building log cabins, making chairs and soap, preserving fruit, churning butter, butchering hogs, planting by the signs, creating home remedies, moonshining, faith healing, and snake lore. It is outdoor writing at its best. If one were to be allowed a single book following a nuclear holocaust (in addition to the Bible, perhaps), I would certainly suggest *Foxfire*.

Although conservation writing is serious business, in many ways central to all other aspects of the outdoor writing field, it is far from limited. It can range from people-related material like that in *Foxfire*, to natural history, to profiles on groups or individuals working on conservation projects to hard facts-and-figures reporting on problem situations.

Outdoor magazines may be most interested in articles dealing with threats to fish and game, such as water pollutants, destruction of habitat, or loss of open space to development. Family magazines may be interested in hazards that threaten health, such as chemical wastes in municipal water supplies. General magazines may be interested in land-use scandals, energy questions, resource waste, or any situation of magnitude affecting the lives or pocketbooks of many.

In short, the conservation writing field is limited only by the writer's interest and nose for a good and important story. Don't overlook the fact that though much conservation writing seems to deal with bad news, there are also lots of positive things to report. Rivers have come back from the dead; parks have been saved; eyesores have been cleaned up and made beautiful. These too make good stories. And sometimes a bright side exists because some conservation writer earlier alerted the public that something was wrong.

The Camping Writer

14.

    The many facets of camping, such as cooking, hiking, wilderness living and the like, make it a good, general area of the outdoor field. A camping writer can be a sort of jack-of-all-trades and write for a number of publications, both in and out of the outdoor magazine category.

    The camping editor of a magazine such as *Field & Stream* traditionally has been concerned with the camping that is done by hunters and fishermen. Our camping editor, Steve Netherby, sticks to the main thrust of *Field & Stream,* and that still leaves him a tremendous field about which to write.

    However, there is a world of camping that is completely outside of the hunting and fishing field. There is the scenic and wildlife photography area of backpacking; there is canoe camping, kayak camping, and boat camping; there is trail ride camping, when a group may camp for weeks; there is camping while rock climbing and mountain climbing; there is camping while cross-country skiing and snowshoeing. Add to that bicycle camping, motorcycle camping, RV camping, and even survival camping. All make good subjects for magazine stories, columns or books.

The camping scene in the past two decades has had a complete overhaul. When we camped before and shortly after World War II, we lugged a lot of heavy bulky equipment into mountain areas by mule or horseback, or drove to a cabin that we made our center of operation. Even in a cabin we toted around heavy-duty sleeping bags, canned goods, large saws and axes and the old-fashioned massive camp cooking gear—sturdy cast-iron frying pans and Dutch ovens. Our cooking fires were either campfires in the woods or pot-bellied stoves in cabins.

The development of space-age metals and fabrics, plus the introduction of dehydrated foods, has changed the entire concept of camping. One of my sons, who likes to backpack and fish the high country, carries a pack on his back that would have weighed seventy or more pounds in my youth. In it he carries all the gear and food necessary to keep him warm, dry and well-fed—including such items as ultra-light fishing gear, a saw, knife, ax, stove, camera and flashlight, first-aid kit and binoculars—a total weight of less than thirty pounds!

I am constantly amazed and interested—as an editor as well as an outdoorsman—at the versatility of each year's new developments. The field has become a gold mine for the outdoor writer who knows his subject.

The development of modern-day recreational vehicles has made it possible for individuals or entire families to camp in luxury. National parks each year are filled with trailers and motor homes of all makes and models. Some are luxurious enough to make one wonder why the family ever left home. I have seen families in Yellowstone Park with huge motor homes parked side-by-side with TV antennas sticking up like deer antlers, and I've heard the sound of radios carrying for miles on the night air. I don't call that camping, but a lot of people do! This type of camping may well fall more into the realm of the recreational vehicle writer than the camping writer, but the dividing line is somewhat nebulous. In fact, there is really no such thing as *a* camping market. For a writer, camping is whatever various publishers and readers believe it is, which is what makes this such an open, diversified field.

Two good examples of approaching camping from opposite directions are Colin Fletcher's *The New Complete Hiker* (published by

Alfred A. Knopf), a sort of bible for spartan backpackers, and Norman Strung's book, *Camping in Comfort* (published by Lippincott), which is concerned with recreational vehicle camping, tent camping, boat camping (such as houseboats) and recipes, all for camping in comfort. Both are excellent books by well-known outdoor writers, but their contents couldn't be more different.

Even what might appear at first to be specialized areas within the field of camping usually have, upon closer inspection, infinite possibilities. For example, take a look at the book *Winter Camping*, by Bob Gary, an Environmental Sports Book. Gary covers everything from making a home in the snow (brrr) and winter sleeping gear to freeze-dried food that simply needs boiling water added. How many people today know how to make a snowshoe? A lot of hikers and backpackers have a notion that it is a simple thing to slog miles through heavy snow in your Vibram soles. Making snowshoes is almost a lost art, but it's an art that can be easily learned. Snowshoes or skis may save your life in snow. Winter camping is an excellent subject for articles, and far too few people who do it write about it. It is one of the only sports I know—that and cross-country skiing—that offers opportunities to photograph wildlife in winter. Big-game animals act far differently in the winter than in summer, and pictures of them under snow conditions are rare.

There are subjects commonly associated with boating that could just as easily fall into the province of the camping writer/editor. Take for example an excellent book called *The Complete Wilderness Paddler*, written by James Davidson and John Rugge and published by Alfred Knopf. It covers portaging, navigation, scouting for campsites along rivers and lakes, as well as more typical camp topics as insect protection, building fires, and food.

A camping writer can find almost no end to his subject. While it certainly does not fall into my personal definition, to some people camping is spending the night on the sheer face of a rock wall while mountain climbing!

The outdoor camping, hiking and backpacking area is a natural one for women outdoor writers. Maggie Nichols, assistant managing editor and seventeen-year veteran of *Field & Stream*, wrote an excellent book in 1978 entitled *Wild, Wild Women*, published by Berkley Publishing Corporation. In it, Maggie covers the gamut of the outdoors from the woman's view. Starting with the theme that it is about time to dispel the idea that the outdoors is a "man's world," Maggie goes on to extol the joys of everything from fishing and shooting to looking and feeling well in the outdoors. She also lists some good reference guides to camping and associated fields that may come in handy for the novice camping writer, such as:

Getting Into Wilderness Camping, by Sheila Link, who also writes on almost any outdoor subject; *How to Enjoy Backpacking, How to Camp and Leave No Trace* and *How to Keep Warm*, available from Gerry, 5450 N. Valley Highway, Denver, CO 80216; "Outdoor Living: Problems, solutions, guidelines," Tacoma Mountain Rescue Unit, Box 696, Tacoma, WA 98401; and "Search for Solitude," Department of Agriculture, U.S. Forest Service, 14th and Independence S.W., Room 3238 South Building, Washington, DC 20540 (includes a list of wilderness areas).

A traditional subject for women outdoor writers is camp cooking. Although no longer thought of as a woman's specialty, it is still a good and fruitful field. Sylvia Bashline, a long-time professional OWAA member, for example, does a monthly food column for *Field & Stream*. She and her husband Jim Bashline, *Philadelphia Inquirer* outdoor editor, have teamed up on a number of books, including one on game and fish cookery. Another woman who has made a successful outdoor writing career based on her knowledge of cooking is Karen Green, author of two books and many magazine articles. And cooking is certainly not the exclusive province of women; there are all sorts of excellent books by men on cooking game and fish and preparing camp meals.

Another popular subject for women and men is wild food gathering. There are several books in this field; one by a woman named Alyson Knap called *Wild Harvest: An Outdoorsman's Guide to Edible Wild Plants in North America* is particularly useful for campers. Published by Pagurian Press, Knap's book is a fine guide not only on how to survive in the wild but on how to enjoy eating plants that grow in the wilderness. Of course, this is a rather specialized area and not one to be entered into by the novice. Both eating and writing about eating wild food are too risky to be done without considerable expert knowledge of the subject.

A subject very pertinent to a feminine slant is camping with children—not only the special problems of children in the outdoors, but the opportunities and importance of guiding a child's early experiences in the natural world.

Another subject that is far from exhausted is the physical problems faced by women in the wilderness. For example, in the book previously mentioned, OWAA member and professional writer Maggie Nichols talks of the problems that may be of particular concern to women such as sunburn, dry skin, and how to keep your hair in good shape in the wilds. Going to the bathroom may not seem like much of a problem if you are a guy, but, as Maggie explains, it can be a problem if you are a lady and there are lots of men on the trip. It can be a special problem in a fishing boat or when there is not a shrub in sight.

But a woman outdoor writer need not feel confined to such obvious areas. There is plenty of room for women in the whole range of outdoor writing. The extracts from Maggie Nichols' book in Appendix Nine will give you some idea of just how broad a subject range can be tackled by the woman outdoor writer. In many cases a woman's views and experiences of the outdoors will be subtly different from a man's. Men and women perceive and approach things in different ways. These differences, however subtle, are assets to the woman outdoor writer, not liabilities.

The camping writer, as much as the hunting and fishing writer, should write away for *The Sporting Goods Directory,* and then obtain a copy of the *NSGA Buying Guide* for the same reasons given in Chapters Eleven and Twelve. There is so much new equipment associated with the backpacking and camping field that it will fill volumes. If you are going to be a backpacking or camping writer you will need to be familiar not only with existing equipment but with the new products that come out all the time.

It is the vital responsibility of the camping writer today to inform, and inform properly; especially when the vastly swollen ranks of camping, hiking, backpacking, etc. aficionados include many people new to the outdoors, from city or urban backgrounds. Many young people simply assume that buying a backpack and filling it with food is all they need to enjoy a trip into the wilderness. Levis and jeans are comfortable—at home. At an altitude of eight thousand feet in the mountains, with a brisk wind blowing during a summer rainstorm, one might as well be naked. Sneakers, running shoes or new hiking shoes, without the proper socks, can cause blisters and infection. Not many neophyte hikers or backpackers, especially from nonrural areas, know the first thing about heat exhaustion, heat stroke or hypothermia. Many have died for that same reason.

A few years ago I was in Taos, New Mexico, when a group of

youngsters left Taos—all dressed in lightweight jeans and carrying backpacks—headed for a jolly week in the high country. Why worry? It was August and the weather was warm and pleasant in Taos at a little more than a seven-thousand-foot elevation. Four days later, the Forest Service had to rescue the group by helicopter. They had run into cold rain at high elevations, gotten cold, and one youngster caught pneumonia. Several others had infected feet from blisters, and all were suffering from exposure. A little judicious reading of a good book on wilderness camping and survival could have prevented a near-disaster.

Although all this may seem obvious to the experienced camper, it is wrong to assume that everyone will know to check on the availability of water before leaving on a camping, hiking or backpacking trip or that learning how to read a chart or map may save a life. Some will not understand the importance of climate and weather, and the writer addressing a beginner audience should stress the danger signs. If on a hot, sunny day, a hiker or camper starts to feel faint and look pale, this may be a sign of heat exhaustion. The cure is to rest in the shade, drink fluids and get salt into the body, for which purpose salt tablets should be carried while hiking or camping. Heat exhaustion is not too serious and should pass quickly if treated properly.

Heat stroke, on the other hand, is serious and can cause death if the victim is not cooled off right away, which makes it doubly important for writers to warn of this danger. Symptoms of heat stroke are dizziness or outright collapse; the skin is hot, red and dry. The best immediate treatment is to wrap the victim in wet clothing or immerse him or her in water as soon as possible.

The dangers of hypothermia should be conveyed also in articles on backpacking and hiking. Many people hiking today do not know that the cooling of the body can be a real problem in mountain areas or during cold weather. The two most common causes of chilling, when a cold wind comes up, are not enough clothing or insufficient food. If the body core becomes chilled, the victim can die from exposure. It is important that a camping writer tell readers to watch their companions carefully under cold conditions. They must be especially alert with anyone who has suffered an accident, such as a fall. If the companion starts to shiver violently or becomes short-tempered or irrational, they should look for signs that he or she is getting cold, such as bluish lips and nails. The person should be warmed immediately with either heavier clothing or a fire. Sugary foods are also needed for energy.

If the body temperature continues to drop, the victim will become listless, will act in a clumsy manner and may become incoherent. Before this happens it is important to get him or her into a sleeping bag, supply plenty of sugary liquids and build a fire. Hypothermia can cause death, especially if combined with shock. It, along with heat-caused problems, is a very real danger faced by campers, and responsible outdoor writers will do their best to inform readers of what to look for and how to respond to emergencies.

In addition to life-threatening situations, the writer can alert a beginning camper/backpacker/hiker to other areas. Among these are wilderness ethics (to build or not to build a fire, how to keep a clean camp, proper toilet making, respect for nature, and the like). As with helping people stay alive, it is the writer's responsibility to teach proper wilderness behavior, so that the values campers and hikers seek in the outdoors will not be spoiled by careless visitors.

If you are a camping enthusiast and like to hunt or fish, there are many angles you might choose for your stories. For instance, there is camping in remote spots such as Baja California where the surf fishing is excellent. Not everyone knows how to camp and be comfortable under those conditions. If you do, you have an excellent chance of selling such a story to a national outdoor magazine or such magazines as *Camping Journal*. Lightweight backpacking in conjunction with trout fishing in high mountain areas makes interesting reading; so does winter camping and ice fishing in high mountain lakes.

Most stories that combine hunting and camping tend to be concerned with the utilization of heavy equipment. Any big-game hunt in which one travels into mountain ranges or the tundra requires horses or mules to carry the bulky supplies. Tents pitched for an elk hunt in Wyoming, for example, resemble the old canvas military tents and generally sleep at least two people. Since most elk outfitters take as many as a half dozen hunters at once, plus a cook, horse wranglers and guides, a lot of tents need to be set up for sleeping. Usually a large cook tent is also erected. All food, cooking utensils and tools must be packed in saddle boxes and saddlebags. This is camping by logistics, and it requires experienced outfitters. A writer who learns to do it on his own could write an interesting story. "How to Build an Elk Camp" by Doyle Kline, which ran in *Field & Stream* in 1978, is an example of one such story. The magazine received a number of letters thanking us for printing Kline's many useful tips and shortcuts. Other similar topics might be how to properly cut firewood for camp, including information on what kinds of trees are best and which wood creates smoke; or ideas for planning the meals for a week or two in a hunting camp, including shopping and packing tips, cooking shortcuts, storage suggestions, and ways to calculate needed quantities.

The subject of pack weight is ever popular. Some of the tips a good backpacking camper can come up with are truly astonishing. For example, in *America's Backpacking Book,* by Raymond Bridge, published by Scribners, the author has this advice about cutting weight to a minimum:

> Having assembled all that stuff, put on the clothes you would expect to wear on the trail, pack the rest of it up, then pick up that pack. Heavy? You haven't finished chopping yet; dump it on the floor again and get to work. A whole cake of soap? How long is this trip going to be anyway? Break off a little weekend-size piece. A complete roll of toilet paper? Come now, leave the remains of the roll in the bathroom instead. Put that family-sized tube of toothpaste back in the cabinet and take a little plastic bag with some tooth powder. The stub of a candle is probably quite adequate for a supplemental fire-starter, and it weighs less than the full-sized candle you have. You will be amazed at how much weight you can eliminate with this kind of examination, at least until you have gotten down to your basic pack. When you find yourself sitting up one night boring holes in the handle of your tooth brush to make it lighter, go into the bathroom and look in the mirror. Do you see the gleam of the fanatic in your eyes? Congratulations, you're now a confirmed weight-watcher!

There are all sorts of gimmicks about camping that make excellent, short how-it's-dones for national outdoor magazines. The pay may not seem stratospheric but, for example, *Field & Stream* pays $250 each for short two hundred fifty-word how-to items. Here is an example:

> If you are a backpacking fan and would like to reduce the weight of that pack, there is a simple method of taking off pounds in a hurry.
> The days are long-gone when a backpacker or camper needed to lug heavy cooking pots or frying pans.
> Today's lightweight metals are featherweight compared to the old gear, but they do weigh *something.*
> The next time you spend a few days on the trail take along a slim roll of aluminum foil.

The foil may be torn off the roll in squares and, folded properly, may be used to cook almost anything. Flat on the coals and with low sides, foil makes a great frying pan. One can fry bacon, broil trout or scramble eggs and the foil will not melt.

Folded and with higher sides, foil can be used to cook dehydrated soup or vegetables. It is easy to shape foil for hot coffee or tea containers.

And what is perhaps the best part, there is no need to wash dishes after a meal. Simply fold up the used foil, carry it home and dispose of it in the garbage can.

Now that does not seem like a very ingenious bit of advice, but you would be surprised at how many backpackers and campers never thought of it. The story of how you foiled the pack weight problem could make you good money.

Editors like to get queries on such seemingly small and inconsequential ideas. Short pieces fill space where the editor needs small spaces filled. You'd be surprised how often editors need to fill one page and have nothing "in house" that can be used in that limited a space. Cartoons help, but with the premium on space today (due to increased paper and postage costs) no editor is going to run full-page cartoons as they did years ago. If something is going to fill a page, it had better be good, solid, nuts-and-bolts informative writing.

It can just as easily be camping copy as anything else.

The Boating Writer

15.

For our purposes, we will concern ourselves only with the writer whose audience is the boater who uses his craft primarily for fishing or hunting, or for "outdoor" water sports such as whitewater rafting, canoeing or kayaking. The type of boating writer/editor who writes about powerboating or sailing for their own sake does not really fall into our outdoor writer category, even though he certainly gets outdoors a great deal.

Boating writing per se is an elaborate specialty all its own, with a tradition, a technology, and an array of subspecialties and publications which could well take a whole book just to outline. Bill Robinson, former editor of *Yachting,* has written several dozen books and hundreds of magazine stories on such subjects as the great classic yachts, sailing around the world, and the various national and international sailing races like the America's Cup. If I asked Bill if he knew what OWAA was, he would look blank.

This reminds me of the time several years ago when I was taken to the New York Yacht Club for lunch by Larry Nelson, former advertising director of *Yachting*. Larry and his wife Claudia are ardent big-game fishermen, and we had fished together in the Bahamas and off Florida a number of times.

When we walked into the dining room, there was a group of men at a corner table—dressed in the typical blue blazers of yachtsmen. Larry took me over and introduced me to them. One was Critchell Rimmington, then publisher of *Yachting;* Bob Bavier, also of *Yachting;* two members of the crew of the United States America's Cup team, Buzz Mossbacher and Bill Robinson, editor of *Yachting;* and several others, all yachtsmen. Upon being introduced and shaking hands, I was asked by Bob Bavier if I were a sailor.

"No," I said. "I am not. The only kind of boat I like is one that will get me out where the fish are."

There was a stunned silence and a few polite coughs as I smiled and Larry and I walked to our table.

"Cripes!" he whispered to me as we sat down, "did you have to say *that* in the *New York Yacht Club!*"

The kind of boating writer I am talking to in this book is the one like me—the outdoor writer whose camping, hunting, or outdoor travel stories may often have a boating slant, or whose fishing stories may occasionally be more boating than fishing. I have owned a number of boats during my life, from canoes and rowboats to oceangoing powerboats, and I have learned a great deal by owning them. I am convinced that the *only* way to learn about boats it to own one or spend a whole lot of time on one owned by a friend. You can read about boating for years and not learn what you can in a week aboard a boat.

I have done about as much fishing from a center-console boat in salt water as anybody I know. When my three sons were small, I went through a series of saltwater boats until I finally settled upon a seventeen-foot fiberglass-hulled Menemsha Boston Whaler. It was specially designed by Dick Fisher, then president of the Boston Whaler firm. Unlike most Whalers, which are open, it had a molded fiberglass cuddy cabin as part of the hull. It completely sheltered the forward half of the boat. In the cabin was a small galley, two bunks, and a head. Exit forward from the bow could be made by opening two ingeniously designed "clamshell" doors. I could cast from the bow platform with the doors either open or closed. When closed, the cabin was absolutely watertight, and the boat shed seas over the bow beautifully. There was room enough aft of the center console and seat for a fairly roomy cockpit in which I rigged a small fighting chair. I installed fifteen-foot collapsible outriggers. Beneath the console seat, there was room to store two twelve-gallon gas tanks and, if necessary, I could also stow two more six-gallon tanks. It gave me quite a cruising range. I used an 85 h.p. Johnson outboard as a power plant for years—later switching to a four-cycle Bearcat engine.

My sons and I fished for years out of Cape May, New Jersey, with that boat—running it in all sorts of weather, from dead calm summer days to the leaden, gray, storm-tossed seas of late fall and winter. We ran her fifty miles offshore to the Baltimore Canyon and back with no more concern than a skipper running a forty-five-foot Hatteras Sportfisherman. Later we trailered the boat to Ft. Lauderdale, Florida, and ran her out of there for years.

During the time I owned the Whaler, and afterwards, I fished from big sportfishing boats around the world—from Ecuador and Cuba to Hawaii and New Zealand. In addition, I spent years in saltwater boats designed for the flats. I am an addicted tarpon, bonefish, and permit fisherman. Hewes Bonefishers, Makos, Aquasports, and half a dozen other shallow-draft, center-console boats have carried me fishing from the flats of the Florida Keys and the Bahamas to Costa Rica. I have handled canoes in the north woods and spent many a marvelous day in big work canoes with Eskimos. I have gone through all this to indicate the experience that stands behind even the relatively minor boating writing that I do. No matter what field of boating writing you intend to pursue, you will never be able to be an armchair writer.

Two of the basic functions of a boating writer are to prevent beginners from making mistakes—dangerous and even fatal ones—and to keep the experienced boatman abreast of new developments in equipment and regulations. The outdoors boating writer has the additional task of focusing on fishing (and hunting) modifications and applications.

There are a number of good publications around for the beginning boating writer. As far as boating equipment is concerned, I would recommend, again, the *NSGA* (National Sporting Goods Association) *Buyers Guide*. There is a boating guide which comes out annually that is relatively unknown to the novice boating enthusiast and that is *Boat Owner's and Buyer's Guide,* which appears on newsstands in September. It is published by *Yachting* magazine and can be ordered from them at 50 West 44th Street, New York, NY 10036.

Another good source of information for a beginning boating writer is a small paperback written each year by Jim Hardie, fishing editor of the *Miami Herald;* Jim Martenhoff, boating editor of the same paper; and Bill Ward, editor of *Outdoor Guide.* It is called *The Miami Herald Fishing, Boating, Camping Outdoor Guide* and it contains all sorts of valuable tips. It can be ordered through the *Miami Herald,* 1 Herald Plaza, Miami, FL 33101.

Jim Martenhoff, incidentally, is a good example of a successful boating writer. He writes a regular boating column for the *Miami Herald* (a huge metropolitan daily newspaper), writes frequently for national outdoor magazines, and has written a number of excellent books on boating. Most large daily newspapers close to the sea employ regular boating editors, and even a number of large dailies inland—particularly in the Great Lakes area—have boating editors. All the national outdoor magazines have boating editors, and so do a number of smaller regional outdoor magazines. Writing boating stories can be a lucrative field, and boating books sell well.

Anyone who plans to become a boating writer, mainstream or otherwise, should do one thing as soon as it is practical. In almost every major city in America, even those not too close to water, there is a branch of the United States Power Squadrons. It offers a basic safety and operating course (among other courses), and one is certified upon completing it. A boating writer should urge all his readers to do the same. Our waters today are teeming with craft, and, unfortunately, a great many people handling these boats are not only inexperienced and uninformed but downright dangerous. Many of them do not even know on what side of buoys to run when leaving or entering a harbor! They also have *no* idea what safety gear to stow aboard a boat or what is required by law.

At the end of this chapter I've included a list of other organizations you may want to consider becoming a member of, depending upon your field of interest.

Another "must" for the aspiring boat writer is boat shows. Chicago, Detroit, Los Angeles, New York, Philadelphia, and Miami are among the big ones. Exhibitors at these shows have brochures on their products which should be useful for your files. If you have never confronted the complexity and diversity of modern boating, you are in for a surprise upon attending a major boat show. In addition to every manner of boats, there are booths devoted to radio and radar equipment for communication and navigation; compasses; cleats; ropes; depth finders; paddles; oars; oarlocks; anchors; lights; clamps; swivels; deck, hull, and bottom antifouling paints; trailers; trailer hitches; winches; federally required safety gear, such as flotation seats, cushions, life preservers, and flotation jackets; inboard, stern-drive, and outboard motors; manual and automatic pumps; and every conceivable gadget known to freshwater and saltwater boaters.

The outdoor boating writer will find no shortage of items in his specialty: elaborate displays of small craft such as canoes, kayaks, bass boats, inflatables; fishing tackle, electronic fish finders, fishing charts, outriggers and downriggers, fighting chairs, live wells, gaffs, towers, and gunwale rod holders—just to skim the surface.

A successful outdoor boating writer must be as familiar with this incredible collection of paraphernalia as the average man or woman is with the dashboard of the family car. This knowledge (and your typewriter and camera) are the tools of your trade as a boating writer.

By the time you have earned a title equal to boating editors such as Bud Paulson of *Field & Stream,* Zack Taylor of *Sports Afield,* or Bob Stearns of *Outdoor Life,* you will not only *know* more than most boat owners will ever know about boats and boating in their lives, but you will also be proficient in *handling* boats and equipment. The same is true of the writers and editors on such magazines as *Sea, Motorboat, American Boating Illustrated, Yachting, Powerboat Magazine, Outdoors,* and numerous other magazines published for the powerboat owner and fisherman.

A boating writer need not be concerned about powerboats at all in order to sell boating stories. There are excellent outdoor writers who have never used a motor on a boat and who specialize in rowboats, canoes, kayaks, inflatable boats, and rafts. They use them for fishing and, in many cases, simply for float trips, nature photography, or whitewater runs down swift rivers. The fraternity of kayakers has grown enormously in the past decade, and the back-to-the-earth movement of the late 1960s and early 1970s saw a tremendous awakening of interest in canoeing. This is a fertile field for the outdoor writer who wants to combine outdoor and wildlife photography with boating. A silently gliding canoe can take the photographer along those countless small waterways that even in developed areas are a refuge for wildlife.

There are all sorts of interesting angles that can be used by an imaginative outdoor writer in this area. Recently I read a well-written and very humorous account of a group of young people who wanted to trace the early Indian canoe watercourse of the Bronx River in suburban Westchester County near New York City. They wanted to canoe down this river, as the Indians did more than two hundred years ago bringing trading goods to the city of New Amsterdam. The trip was made and—outside of having to portage the canoes every half mile or so because of either refuse or small dams—the canoeists finally reached the Hudson River. They paddled around the island of Manhattan, catching the attention of most residents of the big city, as well as the media. I have always wondered what it would be like to attempt to duplicate some of the great canoe and raft trips of some of our early explorers—such as Lewis and Clark. That would make a fine boating story for *any* magazine.

In 1907, the late, great naturalist Ernest Thompson Seton, one of the first true outdoor writers, made a historic canoe trip lasting six months and covering two thousand miles in the northwest territories of Canada to the region north of Aylmer Lake. What a story it would make to take *that* trip again! It would not be difficult either, since the entire trip was written up in a book called *The Arctic Prairies*, published by the International University Press, New York City, in 1911. The book is scarce and out of print, but it could be found, perhaps, in a library.

There is an inexhaustible supply of material for the would-be boating writer no matter where he travels or lives.

With the invention of the fiberglass hull several decades ago, the boating public saw an almost miraculous growth in the number of boats that would not sink when filled with water. Flotation could be built into the hulls—as in the case of my Boston Whaler. While they were by no means guaranteed against capsizing or being swamped, they would stay afloat until help arrived. Since the first primitive man hollowed out a log and made a dugout canoe, man had been plagued by boats' breaking up and sinking at sea. The strong, double-hull fiberglass boat changed all that.

Following World War II, there was a sudden increase in small, powerful and lightweight outboard motors which allowed the saltwater as well as the freshwater angler and boatman to venture far out and return in the same day. Small- to medium-sized boats capable of planing (skimming across the surface of the water) at considerable speeds suddenly began to show up far offshore in both the ocean and the Great Lakes. Only the very expensive large boats had been able to reach these fishing areas previously.

Big-game fishing had always been (and still is) a very expensive sport. It is not at all unusual to spend from a quarter- to a half-million dollars on a well-equipped sportfishing boat from twenty-four to forty-five feet long. One can spend far more than that today for boats upwards of thirty-eight feet—particularly when it comes to tuna towers, ship-to-shore radio equipment, loran navigational equipment, and radar. Charter fees for big-game fishing are not cheap. In the better boats and popular areas, three hundred dollars per day is not unusual.

And so it is not surprising that a number of imaginative and ardent fishermen began to see the sense in buying boats in the eighteen- to twenty-one-foot class, equipped with one or two powerful outboard motors and with outriggers (or downriggers), depth finders, and CB radios. With these boats, they would challenge the big boats in the Hatteras, Bertram, ChrisCraft, Merritt, Rybovitch or Egg Harbor class on both the sea and the Great Lakes. The investment was not that high. A decade ago, one could purchase a strong and safe fiberglass hull for three thousand dollars, pay another eight hundred to one thousand dollars for a new outboard motor, and be ready to go. For a total investment of about five thousand dollars (as opposed to a quarter-million), the small boat angler could travel to the same fishing grounds. Granted, the small boatman had to stay home when the seas came up, but even the larger boats have a bad time in "sloppy" seas. The small boatman, able to travel at twenty-five to thirty knots, if he heard of bad weather approaching, could reach home port (or shelter) far faster than could the bigger boats.

So the legions of fishermen and small boaters grew rapidly in the 1950s, 1960s, and 1970s, until now the sea is literally dotted with boaters during much of the year. In areas such as Los Angeles and Florida, the boaters operate happily year-round, while in the north, the boats go into the boatyard or are trailered home for the winter. Most of the fishermen in the north—particularly in the Mid-Atlantic and New England areas—keep their boats in the water right up through November, for it is then that the striped bass and other migrating fish head south, and the fishing is excellent.

I can remember fishing the full moon in November with a great boating and fishing writer, Al Ristori, in Al's twenty-one-foot Mako. There were three- to four-foot seas running, a twenty-knot wind was blowing, and we were dressed in long underwear, down jackets, hip boots, and foul-weather gear. It was so cold we needed gloves, and it is difficult to cast wearing gloves, but the stripers were running over

Shagwan Reef off Montauk Point and we did not return to the marina until after dark—wet and half frozen, but with a boat half full of striped bass. You don't have to be crazy to be a saltwater fisherman (though it does help!). It is this fanatical dedication to the sport that marks the best writers.

Years ago when I lived in New Mexico, my friends and I used to travel to such bodies of water as Elephant Butte Lake, Conchas Lake, or Bluewater Lake where they had small, aluminum boats for rent. We rented these beat-up boats with their not-very-dependable motors by the day and fished for trout, bass, crappie, and walleye. Today, driving through the Southwest, it is common to see boats and trailers parked in driveways and beside houses. Boat and trailer companies have done a land-office business there and in other "desert" states in the past ten years—all because boats, motors, and trailers have become so strong, fast, and light.

The same is true of the houseboat—a marvelous invention if one does not foolishly consider it an oceangoing craft. It has revolutionized boating on the large lakes of America. One has only to travel to Lake Powell or Lake Mead in the Southwest to see what the houseboat has done there. Whole families may now spend a vacation on a houseboat—fishing, swimming, sunbathing (even waterskiing, if one tows a small speedboat behind). Houseboats are also seen in increasing numbers on the larger rivers and canals where they serve the same purpose as mobile homes, allowing those aboard the opportunity to meander along the waterways at their own pace. An astonishingly large number of people live year-round aboard houseboats.

All this is grist for the mill of the budding boating writer. Go get 'em!

Boating Organizations You Should Know
by Joanne Fishman

(Courtesy of Sea **Magazine, February 1979, CBS Publications Division, 1515 Broadway, New York, NY 10076.)**

National Boating Federation

The need for a federation of national boating organizations was recognized years ago, but nationwide liaison was lacking. In 1958, passage of the Federal Boat Safety Act renewed interest. Under the act, states began developing their own boating programs with Coast Guard assistance.

NBF objectives include autonomy for state boating agencies, more and better aids to navigation, higher safety standards built into boats and equipment, and more accurate marine weather reporting.

For a membership application for your club or organization, or if you wish information on joining groups already affiliated with NBF, write the delegate in your area.

Chesapeake Bay Yacht Clubs Association, Al Simon, 9211 Sligo Creek Parkway, Silver Spring, MD 20910.

Chespeake Bay Yacht Racing Association, C. Edward Hartmann II, Box 3323, Annapolis, MD 21403.

Federated Boatmen of New Jersey, William J. Garry, 106 Lakedale Dr., Trenton, NJ 08648.

Federated Boatmen of New York, Inc., Barry Golomb, 275 Madison Ave., New York, NY 10016.

Massachusetts Bay Yacht Clubs Association Inc., Henry F. O'Connell, Jr., 20 Belcher St., Winthrop, MA 02152.

Outboard Boating Club of America, Jeffrey W. Napier, 401 N. Michigan Ave., Chicago, IL 60611.

Pennsylvania Boating Association, Carl F. Sheppard, 30 E. Springfield Ave., Philadelphia, PA 19118.

Coast Guard Auxiliary

"None of those early auxiliarists, absorbed in such duties as patrolling a beach in anticipation of Nazi spies debarking from U-boats, could have foreseen that they were but the vanguards of civilian volunteers whose newly formed organization would within three decades both outnumber and assume increasingly important assignments of the parent U.S. Coast Guard," explains Lt. Cmdr. James D. Prout, director of the Ninth Coast Guard Auxiliary district.

By the late 1930s, boating safety had become a growing problem, and when Coast Guard Commandant Adm. Russell Waesche convinced Congress to authorize a nonmilitary reserve, its purposes were delegated as the following: To promote safety and to effect rescues on and over the high seas and on navigable waters; To promote efficiency in the operation of motorboats and yachts; To foster a wider knowledge of and better compliance with the laws, rules and regulations governing the operation of motorboats and yachts; To facilitate certain operations of the Coast Guard.

The backbone of the educational effort now is the thirteen-lesson course in boating skills and seamanship. Optional lessons also are available in the following areas: charts and compass, marine engines, marlinspike seamanship, sailing, weather, marine radiotelephone and locks and dams.

Auxiliary membership is open to men and women who are U.S. citizens and own at least a 25 percent interest in a motorboat, yacht, aircraft or amateur radio station, or have other qualifications which would prove valuable to auxiliary programs. For more information, contact the auxiliary director in your district.

United States Power Squadrons

Since 1917, the United States Power Squadrons has been a mainstay of boating education in America. In all, some two million people have completed the squadrons' free basic boating course.

The idea of the power squadrons was conceived by Roger Upton of Boston, one of the original advocates of the marine gasoline engine.

Slowly, interest in powerboating spread out from Boston in widening circles. A seamanship course was added to the advanced instruction; then engine maintenance and weather courses were added. Next followed a sail course, and a marine electronics course. Currently, the more than sixty thousand members are operating in 425 squadrons across the country.

In New Jersey, a modified and expanded piloting course, based on the public boating course, is now required for all new members. The next four levels of instruction are available throughout all the squadrons. The seamanship course covers the various types of boats, additional marlinspike and boat handling. The advanced piloting course prepares one for cruising in coastal waters, covering coastal navigation, the tides, currents and radio-direction-finder work.

Membership in the USPS is at the invitation of a member and dues usually are $25 but may vary slightly with individual squadrons. Dues include a subscription to the squadrons' monthly magazine, the *Ensign*.

Outboard Boating Club

The Outboard Boating Club was established in 1945 to provide boating clubs with a means of sharing ideas and promoting greater interest in the recreational use of the waterways.

Today the primary purpose of the club remains the same, but the membership roles have been expanded to include manufacturers and dealers of outboard motors, boats, trailers, and suppliers of marine equipment and services as well as outboarding enthusiasts.

The OBC staff tracks the progress of various bills affecting boating in the state and federal legislatures. And a subscription to its newsletter, *Legislative Ledger,* is sent to each member. Members also receive copies of the club newspaper, *Outboard Boating,* which contains club news and boating safety tips.

OBC has helped more than 2000 clubs to organize and establish a year-around program of activities. Membership is $10 for each club, regardless of the number of members. For further information, contact: OBC, 333 N. Michigan Ave., Chicago, IL 60601.

American Power Boat Association

Someone once said of Americans: give two of them anything with a motor and the first thing they'll do is race them. By 1902, boat owners were racing on Long Island Sound, seeing which boat could travel fastest over a given distance with a given handicap.

Since the early boats were of varied styles and capabilities, there were nearly as many differing opinions as to what constituted a fair method of handicapping as there were owners.

Accordingly, the Columbia Yacht Club in New York issued a call to all interested clubs to meet and arrange racing rules. And, in 1903, twenty representatives of clubs organized and adopted the name American Power Boat Association.

The association established the first racing commission in 1913, and the powers delegated to this commission remain the backbone of the present function of the APBA.

Today, though, the APBA sanctions all types of powerboat racing—from the exciting thunderboats and offshore powerboats to jet skis and predicted log contests. More than six hundred regattas are sanctioned annually in the United States and Canada. More than five thousand racing boats are registered by racing members while officials and other members bring the total enrollment to some seven thousand.

Membership in the APBA is open to individuals as well as clubs.

For racing members, dues, including insurance premiums, vary from $5 to $70 a year depending on the type of racing class to which one belongs. Associate membership is $15. Contact: American Power Boat Association, 22811 Greater Mac, St. Clair Shores, MI 48080; telephone (313)773-9700.

The Recreational Vehicle Writer

16.

If you don't think the recreational vehicle market is booming, just take a trip across your country.

Highways, especially during the vacation months, are jammed with motor homes, towed trailer homes, campers, pickup trucks, vans, and all sorts of four-wheel drive and off-road vehicles—many of them carrying motorcycles, trail bikes and bicycles. In the winter, many of the vehicles in the northern and western states will be towing snowmobiles.

One needs only to drive to an area like Yellowstone or Yosemite National Park to see the astonishing assortment of recreational vehicles available to the outdoor-minded individual or family today. Drive to the surfing beaches of southern California, the dunes of North Carolina or the woods of northern Michigan, and you'll see recreational vehicles you never knew existed.

Americans are always on the go. It is to me a characteristic that distinguishes us from the inhabitants of Asia and Europe. We are a nation on the move—constantly—and have been since the first pioneers began the move westward in search of new lands. And because we are such a mobile society, we have developed a world of specialized equipment to make our mobility easier and more comfortable.

Since the end of World War II the development of light and strong trailers and mobile homes—plus hundreds of new lightweight, durable materials—has made getting around and living in comfort far easier than before. I can recall the days when a "trailer" meant a two-wheeled, small square metal hut that would sleep four at the most (in bunk beds) and contained a sink and a fold-out table. We towed these into the mountains for hunting and fishing trips. If one wanted to go to the bathroom, there was just the great outdoors or a Park Service latrine.

Living in a trailer in those days had a sort of social stigma attached to it—as though one lived on the wrong side of the tracks. I drive in wonder today past the thousands of luxurious mobile home parks and trailer parks in such areas as Florida and the Southwest. Some of them are more attractive and better-planned than housing developments a few miles away. But the outdoorsman or woman—whether a fisherman, hunter, backpacker, nature lover, hiker, cyclist, trail bike enthusiast or snowmobiler—is more concerned with the vehicle that enhances recreation, whether it's a car, pickup, four-wheel drive, van, or larger home-on-the-road type of rig. And the multitude of accessories associated with recreational vehicles—winches, trailers, pumps, racks, sanitation facilities and tanks, fuel savers, air-conditioning, heating, Citizens' Band Radio (CB), and all sorts of gadgets that have grown to be part of the vocabulary of the outdoor vehicle enthusiast—are also a rich field for the writer to mine.

There is a great deal of activity going on in the outdoor recreational vehicle field, and the people who are involved in it like to read about what is new. For example, the 1979 issue of *Writer's Market* lists thirty-three separate magazines under the heading of "Travel, Camping, and Trailer" publications. All of them buy stories on rec vehicles from freelance writers. In addition, many daily newspapers have travel and automotive editors. Books on recreational vehicles sell like hotcakes in areas where a great number of them are in use. National general-circulation magazines take stories on trips to unusual places by trailers and rec vehicles. *Sports Illustrated* has run stories on rec vehicle safaris to Baja, and *Sunset* magazine, with a million-plus circulation on the West Coast, not only takes stories on rec vehicles but has an outdoor living editor on its staff.

THE RECREATIONAL VEHICLE WRITER

Okay, you love cars, trucks, motors, and cycles, and you have since you were barely able to sit on a parent's lap and turn the wheel. You can write a clear, concise story. You want to make a living out of your talent and your interest. You can do it by becoming a rec vehicle writer. Lots of people have, from the columnists on the major outdoor magazines—Bill Kilpatrick, recreation vehicles editor of *Field & Stream*; Jack Seville of *Sports Afield*; and Bob Behme of *Outdoor Life*—to the many writers who cover the subject for a myriad of small regional magazines. In addition, there are staff writers on magazines devoted full time to the subject, such as *P4V* (power, four-wheeled vehicles), *Mobile Living*, *National Motorist*, and *Van World*.

How do you get started as a rec vehicle writer? There are several steps I would suggest that will help. Like the would-be hunting, fishing, camping, etc., writer, you should contact one organization first—the National Sporting Goods Association, 717 North Michigan Avenue, Chicago, IL 60611—and ask for their *NSGA Buying Guide*. It will put you in contact with not only automobile manufacturers but manufacturers of accessories in every area of the automotive field. I would then contact the Recreation Vehicle Industry Association (RVIA), Box 204, 14650 Lee Road, Chantilly, VA 22021. RVIA is the national trade association representing recreation vehicle manufacturers (motor homes, travel trailers, truck campers, camping trailers, and pickup covers) and related companies. It can tell you what publications you should subscribe to and will put you on their mailing list. This will keep you up to date on the latest developments in the rec vehicle field and also will put you in contact with fellow rec vehicle writers. RVIA is a fine organization and has done much in the way of aiding rec vehicle writers and editors. It has worked hard also for safety standards and effective regulations in the industry.

Writer's Market lists the many publications that take stories on the rec vehicle field. Most important of all, the rec vehicle writer should subscribe to the weekly newspaper *Automotive News*, the bible of the industry.

Rec vehicle enthusiasts come in all sizes, shapes, colors, and ages. They range from wild-eyed kids who compete in dune buggy and desert cycle races to senior citizens who travel from Florida to Alaska slowly and carefully driving their motor home or truck camper. They represent a cross section of every economic, age, color, and religious segment of this nation, united in their love of travel and comfort. Most of them are incurable "mister-fix-its" and would rather discuss new developments in safety tow bars than politics, religion, or the weather. Most of them are nature lovers and photographers, or hunters and fishermen who appreciate four-wheel-drive rec vehicles because they enable the outdoorsman to reach places inaccessible except by foot or horseback years ago.

I am a recreational vehicle lover, and I live right in the middle of New York City. While most of the people in my neighborhood park their small foreign-made sports cars or their Mercedes sedans in under-apartment garages, I keep a 1969 Jeep Waggoneer in my garage. I am recognized and well known by neighbors and garage attendants alike. Not many people negotiate the east side of Manhattan in a bulky, high station wagon equipped with a top roof rack, CB radio, adapters for a snowplow, four monstrous mud and snow tires (year-round) and a bulky, electric winch jutting out in front of the radiator. That winch has uses other than pulling myself, or other cars, out of snow or sand. Except for bus drivers and the drivers of the local garbage trucks, I am about the only driver in the city who never gets out-bluffed by a cab driver. At the last minute he sees those snowplow attachments and that huge winch, and he can imagine what his cab is going to look like if he doesn't stop trying to cut me off!

I love the big monster and so does my wife. We can travel in all kinds of weather when most vehicles in Manhattan are slipping and sliding all over the streets in a mere two inches of snow. We have no fear of visiting friends in the country in the worst weather. The 1969 Jeep Waggoneer has the big eight-cylinder Buick engine in it (it was built before the company was bought by American Motors), and it pulls a heavy boat and trailer very well. We have a small cabin in the woods not too far from New York, built on the side of a steep hill. I can back the old Jeep down that hill in the worst weather—rain or snow—load or unload it, and get out with those big snow tires churning in four-wheel drive.

Like many other coast dwellers, one of my favorite sports is surf casting for stripers or bluefish. And like many other surf casters, I have found my four-wheel-drive invaluable. It has traveled the soft beaches from Cape Hatteras through Long Island and on Martha's Vineyard, moving smooth as silk through sand that would bog down a Mack truck. Nothing can stop that old Jeep. I keep the snowplow near the cabin and, although it must weigh five hundred pounds at least, it is easy to attach and use. You would be amazed at the offers I received for the Jeep and plow in New York City during the blizzards of '78.

No way, I have repeatedly said. I wouldn't trade my old rec vehicle for a new Cadillac, and I mean that. What good would a luxury car be in the places an outdoorsman would want to go?

I mention this to show how widespread the rec vehicle interest is—from city to country to suburb to small town—and how varied the possibilities in this field can be for an imaginative writer. The machines have many uses, and each use is worth a thousand words, give or take a few. This is true not only of the rec vehicles' obvious and not-so-obvious benefits, but of its drawbacks as well.

Let's face it, a rec vehicle is not the most economical vehicle when it comes to gas mileage, and it is possible that this will cause changes in the field—and in the writing on this subject, too. Some of the larger motor homes get frightful gas mileage (many drivers tow a small car behind to use when the big motor home gets where the owner wants to go) and, depending on how severe the fuel problem becomes or continues to be, there may be a lot of upheaval in this market.

On the other hand, manufacturers are getting better gas mileage out of almost all cars today, in spite of anti-pollution controls required by law. The average four-wheel-drive rec vehicle gets gas mileage comparable to the conventional or standard car. Pickups and station wagons, which can be converted into four-wheel drive by clutch, get good gas mileage when in conventional two-wheel drive. Motorcycles (a form of rec vehicle being used increasingly by campers, especially in the West) get excellent mileage. Obviously, there will be much interest in stories on how to save energy in the recreation field—and the alert author will undoubtedly find a ready market for his or her ideas on making the best of the situation, whatever it turns out to be.

Where do you gain all the knowledge necessary for you to qualify as a professional rec vehicle writer? From the same place the hunting, fishing, camping or boating writer does: a combination of *experience* in doing your thing and *reading* what others say about it. And there is a tremendous amount to be learned about the subject. RVIA can help you with a recommended list of research material, and the various manufacturers also can assist by sending you operation manuals and catalogues. But it is going to be up to you not only to learn the field well but to find different slants—which could range from energy-saving information to trip-planning ideas to human-interest stories to whatever you can find that would not only be enjoyable to read but would make an editor take notice, too.

Recreational vehicle writers have much to do with maintaining the good image of rec vehicle users, and this is an important part of their writing job. Some recreational vehicles have caused considerable concern in environmental circles. And in many cases the environmentalists, as well as private land owners, have been justified in protesting the abuses of certain recreational vehicles. The hundreds of motorcycles and trail bikes that tear across the flats of California and much of the Southwest *do* damage the fragile and delicate ecology of a desert. Such motorcycle, trail bike and dune buggy races should be restricted to designated racing areas approved by official racing associations. The indiscriminate use of cycles and trail bikes in wilderness areas not only causes harm to the environment and arouses the animosity of those concerned with nature but hurts the public image of the recreational vehicle user. Fortunately, the trade associations for such products as motorcycles and trail bikes have policed their own ranks and, along with publications in their field such as *Cycle World,* have called for restraint and common sense in the use of such machines.

A few years back snowmobilers got into a number of hassles with private land owners and environmentalists because the snowmobilers went wherever they wished. It was not until organizations such as the International Snowmobile Industry Association, the trade association of snowmobile manufacturers, stepped in that the furor died down. The association and its members, for the most part, now observe sensible and safe rules in the use of snowmobiles, sticking to designated trails and areas and carefully observing the rights of both private land owners and wildlife.

Rec vehicle associations have served the industry well, and there is every reason to believe they will continue to do so. It is a good fraternity for you to join.

The Dog Writer

17.

When outdoor writers talk about dogs, they mean gundogs—the pointing, flushing, and retrieving breeds—plus the hounds. The general or "pet market" writers are just as interested in poodles and Yorkshire terriers as in any other breed. They cover dog shows for newspapers and magazines, and write pet columns and books about dogs in general.

But the gundog writer is a specialist. He or she is concerned only with the dogs that, down through the centuries, have been taught to help man find and retrieve game. Since the dawn of man, the dog has been with him as companion in the search for small game, game birds, waterfowl and big game all over the earth. The hunting dog was far more important to man in centuries past than it is today since we no longer *have* to hunt for our food as we did in the past. Yet in those centuries of association people and hunting dogs have developed a relationship which is very close.

There is no more beautiful or more satisfying sight to the outdoorsman who likes to hunt than a finely trained dog doing his job well. Whether watching a pointer freeze on point over a covey of bobwhite quail, or seeing a Labrador retriever swim back through ice-filled water carrying a Canada goose, the thrill of the experience is rooted deep in man's memory.

I am one of those people who love bird dogs. I have raised Labradors and was lucky enough to be owned by an excellent German shorthaired pointer for a number of years. My Labs were good dogs, and especially fine retrievers. Also, as many a dog writer will confirm, they sometimes make excellent upland-game bird dogs. They have good noses, and though they don't point, they will flush birds such as woodcock, grouse, pheasant, and quail—and they will retrieve them well.

I have hunted over just about every strain of bird dog there is. I have seen marvelous springer spaniels trained by the dog handlers at Nilo Farms in East Alton, Illinois. I have hunted over fine Brittany spaniels at Remington Farms in Maryland, particularly with one named Jigs, owned by *Field & Stream* shooting editor Bob Brister who lives in Houston. George Reiger, conservation editor of *Field & Stream*, has the best golden retriever I have ever hunted over. His name is Rocky, and he is so good he will hunt with strangers as well as with his owner.

George Bird Evans lives in West Virginia, and it is doubtful if anyone has better setters than his. Larry Mueller of Jacob, Illinois, is about the best hound expert I know, and he eats, sleeps, and talks hounds—from beagles on up. I have hunted lions and bears behind some of the best hounds ever bred, owned by Cass Gooder in New Mexico. Also I have hunted with Chesapeakes on the Eastern Shore and weimaraners in Texas. I am familiar with most sporting-dog breeds. I have hunted with dogs that were not worth a damn—and dogs that were poorly trained or had some defect.

Each man or woman has his or her favorite individual bird dog, and mine was a big eighty-five-pound German shorthair who would rather hunt than do anything else in the world. He would slide to a point while running in full stride when he got a whiff of scaled quail. He could trail and point running birds like no other dog I have ever hunted over, and he would plunge into ice-filled rivers to retrieve waterfowl without a thought to the below-zero temperature. When that dog was killed, I never bought another. Perhaps I will some day.

There is no easy way to become a good gundog writer. You have to know the animals first and then try writing about them. You have to own and work with dogs to know them. You don't have to be a hunter or a shooter to become a good gundog writer, but it would certainly be an advantage.

Training a hunting dog is a long, difficult, and frustrating process. Yet when one succeeds, the rewards are worth every bit of time, expense, and agony. You have to live gundogs and experience the realities of dog training before you can think of writing about them.

To be a good dog writer, like Bill Tarrant of *Field & Stream*, or Dave Duffey of *Outdoor Life*, you will have to know almost as much about dogs as a veterinarian. Tarrant, and not because he is gundog editor of *Field & Stream*, is the best dog writer I have ever read. He knows more about gundogs than most vets and bows to only one man in his knowledge of training—Delmar Smith, his friend—and about the best dog trainer alive. Smith is five-time winner of both the National Open and the U.S. Open Brittany championships.

Regarding specific career prospects, most outdoor magazines have dog editors on the staff. There is a market for freelancers, though not a large one. The best possibilities probably lie in the book field. Dog books sell steadily to a specialized audience. Bill Tarrant's fine book, *Best Way to Train Your Gun Dog*, David McKay, New York, is the one I would recommend to the beginning gundog writer.

For those who are interested in specialized fields, I would suggest:

Spaniel Training for Modern Shooters, David & Charles, North Pomfret, VT, 1974;

The Practical Dog Hunter's Book, John R. Falk, Winchester Press, NY, 1971;

Labrador Retriever, S. Kip Farrington, Jr., Hastings House, NY, 1976;

Training the Versatile Gun Dog, Jerome and Alyson Knap, Scribner, NY, 1974;

Dave Duffey Trains Gun Dogs, Dreenan Press Ltd., Croton-on-Hudson, NY, 1974;

The New German Shorthaired Pointer, C. Bede Maxwell, Howell Book House, NY, 1963;

Troubles with Bird Dogs, George Bird Evans, Winchester Press, NY, 1975;

New Bird Dogs, Larry Mueller, Stoeger Publishing Co., NJ, 1973.

The next step I would suggest is to get yourself on the mailing lists of the following organizations:

Amateur Field Trial Club of America (AFTCA), Hernando, MS 38632. Comprised of more than three hundred member clubs, this organization sponsors regional and national competitions for the pointing breeds.

American Brittany Club, Rt. 3, Box 14, Sherwood, OR 97140. AKC parent club for the Brittany spaniel. Publishes *The American Brittany* monthly.

American Chesapeake Club, Rt. 2, Box 762, Flagstaff, AZ 86001. AKC parent club for the Chesapeake Bay retriever. Publishes a club bulletin quarterly.

American Field, The, 222 W. Adams St., Chicago, IL 60606. Weekly publications primarily about the pointing breeds. Contains listing of Field Dog Stud Book.

American Kennel Club, 51 Madison Ave., New York, NY 10010. Largest registry of dog breeds. Licenses competitions. Publishes *Purebred Dogs—American Kennel Gazette* and will send, upon request, "Orange Book" of Field Trial rules.

German Shorthaired Pointer Club of America, 125 Arlene Dr., Walnut Creek, CA 94595. AKC parent club of the German shorthaired.

German Wirehaired Pointer Club of America, 4645 W. 97th Place, Oak Lawn, IL 60453. AKC parent club of the German wirehaired (Drahthaar).

German Shorthaired Pointer News, Box 850, St. Paris, OH 43072. Monthly.

Golden Retriever Club of America, The, Route 1, Constantine, MI 49042. AKC parent club for the golden retriever. Publishes *Golden Retriever News* bimonthly.

Gordon Setter Club of America, 938 Millwood Rd., Great Falls, VA 22066. AKC parent club for the Gordon setter. Publishes *Gordon Setter News* monthly.

Irish Water Spaniel Club of America, Center Road, RFD, Bradford, NH 03221.

Morris Animal Foundation, 531 Guaranty Bank Bldg., Denver, CO 80202. Sponsors and coordinates research in animal health.

National German Shorthaired Pointer Association (American Field affiliate), Rt. No. 2, Box 169, Cambridge, WI 53523.

National Red Setter Field Trial Club, R.R. No. 1, Newton, IL 62448. Publishes *Flushing Whip* monthly, same address as above.

North American Versatile Hunting Dog Association (NAVHDA) R.R. No. 1, Puslinch, Ont., Canada. Sponsors trials that emphasize the versatility of certain hunting breeds. Dog tests on land and water. Open to any dog registered in National Stud Book.

Orthopedic Foundation for Animals (OFA), University of Missouri—Columbia, School of Veterinary Medicine, 817 Virginia Ave., Columbia, MO 65201. Founded to help eliminate hip displasia in dogs through effective X-ray program.

Pet Food Institute, 111 E. Wacker Dr., Chicago, IL 60601. Will provide material to help celebrate National Dog Week which is observed in September.

Retriever Field Trial News, 1836 E. St. Francis Ave., Milwaukee, WI 53207. Primarily reports Field Trial results of retrievers; ten issues annually.

Springer Bark, The, Box 2115, San Leandro, CA 94577. Quarterly. Covers Field and Show activity for springer spaniels.

Vizsla Club of America, The, Box 2461, Carmel, CA 93921. AKC parent club of the Vizsla breed. Publishes *Vizsla News* monthly.

Weimaraner Club of America, Greenway Road, Sun Prairie, WI 53590. AKC parent club of the weimaraner. Publishes *Weimaraner News* monthly, same address as above.

Wirehaired Pointing Griffon Club of America, R.R. No. 1, Puslinch, Ont., Canada. Publishes *Gun Dog Supreme* bimonthly, same address as above.

For Beagles: *Hounds & Hunting*, Dept. FS-10, Bradford, PA 16701.

Coon, Lion, Bobcat and Tree Hounds: *Full Cry*, Box 190-FS, Sedalia, MO 65305.

Coon Hounds: *American Cooner*, Box 211-C, Sesser, IL 62884.

There are no hard-and-fast rules in dog writing. Each person will eventually fall into his own style. Many might be called "nuts-and-bolts" dog writers, experts in their field who write straight, simple, factual stories about dogs and dog care. But every so often will come along a dog man who lifts dog writing to the level of literature. The late Corey Ford was one such writer. Ford wrote a number of books and contributed regularly to *The New Yorker* and *Saturday Evening Post*. Former *Field & Stream* editor Hugh Grey read his stories and, knowing Corey was an outdoorsman and a dog lover, convinced him to write a monthly column called "The Lower Forty" for *Field & Stream*. It was one of the most widely read columns that ever ran in the magazine, and it was published for sixteen years until Ford's death of cancer in 1969.

Corey Ford's first story for *Field & Stream* was written for the late editor Ray Holland in 1952, and it was about a dog, but it was not his first appearance in the magazine. Twelve years earlier, he had written to Holland about a man's accidentally shooting his bird dog to death; his letter appeared as an editorial, "Just A Dog," in 1941.

Ray P. Holland
Editor of *Field & Stream*
New York, N.Y.

Dear Ray:

I know this is a kind of unusual request; but I'd like to borrow some space in your columns to write an open letter to a man I do not know. He may read it if it is in your columns; or some of his friends may notice his name and ask him to read it. You see, it has to do with sport—a certain kind of sport.

The man's name is Sherwood G. Coggins. That was the name on his hunting license. He lives at 1096 Lawrence Street, in Lowell. He says he is in the real estate and insurance business in Lowell.

This weekend, Mr. Coggins, you drove up into New Hampshire with some friends to go deer hunting. You went hunting on my property here in Freedom. You didn't ask my permission; but that was all right. I let people hunt on my land. Only, while you were hunting, you shot and killed my bird dog.

Oh, it was an accident, of course. You said so yourself. You said that you saw a flick of something in the bushes, and you shot it. All you saw was the flash of something moving, and you brought up your rifle and fired. It might have been another hunter. It might have been a child running through the woods. As it turned out, it was just a dog.

Just a dog, Mr. Coggins. Just a little English setter I have hunted with for quite a few years. Just a little female setter who was very proud and stanch on point, and who always held her head high, and whose eyes had the brown of October in them. We had hunted a lot of alder thickets and apple orchards together, the little setter and I. She knew me, and I knew her, and we liked to hunt together. We had hunted woodcock together this fall, and grouse, and in another week we were planning to go down to Carolina together and look for quail. But yesterday morning she ran down in the fields in front of my house, and you saw a flick in the bushes, and you shot her.

You shot her through the back, you said, and broke her spine. She crawled out of the bushes and across the field toward you, dragging her hind legs. She was coming to you to help her. She was a gentle pup, and nobody had ever hurt her, and she could not understand. She began hauling herself toward you, and looking at you with her brown eyes, and you put a second bullet through her head. You were sportsman enough for that.

I know you didn't mean it, Mr. Coggins. You felt very sorry afterward. You told me that it really spoiled your deer hunting the rest of the day. It spoiled my bird hunting the rest of a life-time.

At least, I hope one thing, Mr. Coggins. That is why I am writing you. I hope that you will remember how she looked. I hope that the next time you raise a rifle to your shoulder you will see her over the sights, dragging herself toward you across the field, with blood running from her mouth and down her white chest. I hope you will see her eyes.

I hope you will always see her eyes, Mr. Coggins, whenever there is a flick in the bushes and you bring your rifle to your shoulder before you know what is there.

Corey Ford

Gene Hill, associate editor of *Field & Stream,* writer of books and many magazine stories on all phases of the outdoors, is also a dog writer when the spirit moves him. He raises Labrador retrievers on his New Jersey farm. The spirit moved him in 1978 to write about a dog in one of his "Hill Country" columns in *Field & Stream.* I would like to include it here because I think if I run what I consider the best of dog writing, it will teach far better than I can.

Brown Dog
By Gene Hill

Lately there's been an upsurge in the popularity of what's called the "versatile gun dog." The term covers several breeds, all European in origin. Now, while I'm not knocking any claims about them as such, I'd like to point out that this country has had such a dog for longer than I can remember. It's not really a breed; it's more of a type. I had one when I was a kid and nearly everyone else I knew had one at some time or another. You might call it a "brown dog."

Brown dogs are not really all brown. Some run a little orange in the coat and others have a pronounced greyish, but lackluster cast. Still, common brown is the predominant shade. The hair is sort of long, though not necessarily, and can be either smooth or rough or in between. They have a peculiar three-quarter sidewise gait as if the front wheels were out of alignment, and they tend to use only one back leg at a time, resting one or the other alternately unless an emergency occurs requiring full power.

No farm can be said to be properly run unless there's a brown dog in some position of authority. They will herd cows and pigs, keep the chickens out of the house garden, and keep the area free from skunks—

which accounts, in large measure, for their rather distinct odor. No small boy can be properly raised without one.

I think it was Robert Benchley who once remarked, "Every boy should have a dog; it teaches him to turn around three times before lying down." Brown dogs do a great deal more than that. They provide excuses for adventures, teach him how to whistle loud and clear, improve his throwing arm, and, most important, instill in him the incredible responsibility that comes with being loved unquestioningly, totally, and irrevocably.

Brown dogs are famous for their nonchalant, sophisticated attitude. They have an air of having seen it all before—an attitude of preoccupation. Mine would stop now and then and stare into middle distance, as if pondering some crucial question for a minute or so; then, having resolved it to his satisfaction, he'd shake his head as though wishing he could impart this gem of knowledge to me, but somehow feeling it would be wasted or more likely that I simply would not understand its value.

The narrow achievements of ordinary gun dogs—pointers, setters, or retrievers—seem to amuse the all-capable brown dog. Anyone who has owned one knows that they will bring back anything they can carry or drag. They will turn a brush pile inside out for the rabbit hunter, or circle a squirrel tree at precisely the right pace and distance to put the squirrel just where you want him. Pointing birds seems to bore them, but get one working pheasants and he'll herd and flush them your way as easily as he'd run a pasture full of Holsteins back to the barn. For a farm boy who wants results, fried rabbit, or squirrel stew, the brown dog is guaranteed to get the job done.

A brown dog will tolerate a boy's family, but will not get too involved. If the boy is absent, say during school days, he will mope around or curl up close to where the master will first appear on coming home, and wait. If there are things he has to attend to, rounds to make or whatever, never doubt that the sound of the school bus will fall on his ears first and farthest away.

When the owner of a brown dog I know went off to college, the dog would move out to the end of the lane about a day and a half before his pal was due home. How did he know? I haven't the foggiest idea. Since the boy's father didn't know when to expect him home either, it's even more mysterious—except that, if you're a brown dog, you're expected to know such things and it's your job to act on them.

Brown dogs are never trained in the common usages of words. They just sort of figure out what has to be done and they do it. If you need someone to sit and listen to your problems, they'll lend a most sympathetic ear. If you're bursting with spring, they'll race up and down the brook with you and even walk a little taller when you bring Mom the first sprigs of myrtle or watercress. I suspect they like summer best of all because everyone's home. Brown dogs are very fond of parties: swimming hole picnics, hayrides, summer softball games, fireworks, bicycling, fishing trips, and camping out. They make good outfielders and lifeguards, and I wouldn't have dreamed of sleeping on the lawn without my brown dog to watch over me; nor would he have allowed it in the first place.

Most problems with brown dogs stem from their intelligence and unswerving desire to please. Mine went along with me and my first .22 to watch me get rid of a few groundhogs in one of the pastures. I suppose I shot two or three; I forget. But he got the idea that we wanted groundhogs, and nearly every day, all that summer, he brought one home. The problem was that he didn't bring them home immediately, but waited a day or so until they were more impressive—in both size and smell. That little lesson wasn't lost on me either. I learned that there were certain outings I went on alone after that, especially when I was going to shoot snakes in the ice pond or around the place in the brook where we liked to swim. What would have happened if he had decided we wanted water snakes strung out on the porch still fills me with pangs of desperation.

One neighbor had to keep a chain around the kitchen icebox door after his brown dog learned to open and close it. It was a mystery where the food was going for a while, since he was smart enough not to take a lot or too big a piece . . . just a small snack now and then to tide him over in the evening hours. Another had to tie the dog in the cellar or the barn if he felt he had to spank his son—and even then the dog would snarl a little at him for two or three days, as if to say he knew and didn't like the idea at all.

It's a shame that not everyone has a brown dog to help him over the rough spots, or to share that time of incredible wonder and discovery. A brown dog is a kind of special gift we should each have at a certain time of our life to round it out. A brown dog belongs to that time of life which was filled with dreams of what we see today as small things indeed: a hammer .22, slingshots, a first knife of your very own, and hip boots; the little keys that opened the first doors to the outdoor treasures we now prize above price. Somehow brown dogs understand these things and know how to share them.

I used to think, with pride overflowing, that my brown dog was mine. Now I know better. We never really own a dog as much as he owns us. Where he led I would follow without fear, and even now, remembering how he would curl up with his back against my bedroom door, I know again how it was to feel safe and protected from anything and anyone.

Once when I was very small and very sick my mother put him in bed with me against everyone's advice. "They need each other," she said, and that was that; she understood brown dogs and their peculiar magic.

It's getting about that time for another brown dog to come and live around the place. Sometimes I feel a strange cold draft at night and a brown dog would know just how to curl his back up against the door to keep it from troubling me.

Want to know how to get a job as a gundog writer on a national outdoor magazine?

One day in 1973, a manuscript arrived on my desk from a writer in Kansas. It was about dogs, and the writer's name was Bill Tarrant. Our gundog editor had died a few years earlier, and we had not found a man we thought could fill his job. After reading Bill Tarrant's story, I put down the manuscript, called him in Kansas, and offered him the job of gundog editor. He accepted and has been with us ever since. Neither he, I, nor any of our readers have ever been sorry.

This is the story he submitted:

And I Do Not Walk Alone
By Bill Tarrant

W. C. Fields said, "I never met a drink I didn't like." Will Rogers said the same thing about men. I say the same thing about dogs. The way I feel, God proved His love of man when He gave him the dog.

I've been spun around by my fellow man, forsaken by loved ones, used and discarded by friends. Man has a way of playing a game called "You play ball with me and I'll ram the bat up your left nostril." I've never met a dog similarly disposed.

I've walked cross-country in deep snow—late at night—and had the companionship of a dog that I didn't need to ask to come along.

I've sat alone in a sad house and cursed my fortune while the dog curled at my feet had a faith in tomorrow I could not find.

I've been hours late getting out a dog's feed pan and never heard a complaint.

I've yelled in rage to clear a room of man and beast only to see a few minutes later one black nose and two bright eyes poke around the doorjamb to scent the spell of the room. I but shifted in my chair and the rascal was in my lap. The men who cleared the room? They may never come back.

I've picked up dogs with broken bones and taken them to a vet. No pain could make the dog cry out to his benefactor.

I've seen children calmed at night with a dog on their pillow. There could be no better pacifier, no finer protector. I might sleep through whatever befell the child, or shy from an intruder. The dog would do neither.

I've seen dogs break ice to retrieve a duck, stand on point with a thorn in a pad, go down a 70 percent grade to corral a sheep, chase a car crosstown to be part of a family outing, sniff out a warehouse while a policeman crouched outside with drawn pistol, lick a sick man's feet, kiss a crying child's cheek, stare beseechingly at a mother's worried face, raise an arm of a dead-tired man who'd worked too hard to make ends meet.

I've seen men bury their dogs and not be able to stand up to leave the grave. And I've seldom known a man to mention a dog's parting.

Last year most of us read in the newspaper about a woman who died and left $14 million to her 150 dogs.

I can hear 'em now. "That's stupid," the disgruntled said. "Lots of people could have put that money to good use." And likely, among that group of worthy recipients would be—themselves.

But I ask the critics of this woman's will to consider this:

Remember that time you came by a pup? All the doubts? Puddles on the carpet. Gnawed shoelaces. Milk-drips on the kitchen floor. But for reasons of your own the pup moved in anyway.

And how did he come through the door?

Did he say, "Hi" so you could understand? I mean, was he fluent in the American language? Did he come bearing gifts? It's always good to see those types. Did he represent a social coup? Had he done things? Been places? No?

Well, if he didn't have any of these human attributes, then surely he was pedigreed; they're worth money, you know. Oh, you say you gave $2 for him at the dog pound. Well, was he pretty to look at, then? "No, kind of rangy," you say, "and wobble-kneed and pinched-nosed." Well then was he strong or fearless? Could he do some work, help protect the place? What's that? "How strong and fearless can a pup be at ten weeks?" I see your point.

Then let's face it. That dog came into your home absolutely worthless and a total foreigner. I ask you, how many of those have you taken in lately?

And then when this improbable guest got through the door, what did he do? I see. He puddled on the carpet, gnawed shoestrings, dripped milk.

So you threw him out, right?

Nope, wrong.

Why was this?

Well, when that dog came through the door he had three things going for him: a wagging tail; a rough, wet tongue; and an eagerness to say hello to everyone he met.

It was like just meeting you made his day. He quivered with excitement. Rolled over in submission. Nuzzled up so's the warmth of his body came soothing to your heart through the skin of your ankle. So you picked him up. That's the way with love. It's contagious.

And you stood there holding this pup close to your cheek, smelling that last-night's-ice-cream-carton-smell of him, your fingers sunken into his soft belly, woven through his silken fur, when across your face goes that rough, wet tongue.

What you had in your hands was absolute, non-diluted, ever-growing, non-demanding, can't-live-without-you, take-me-wherever-you-go, hurry-back-if-you've-got-to-leave love.

PR Careers for the Outdoor Writer

18.

There is probably no area of outdoor writing that has been more neglected than public relations work. As Tom Kimball, executive director of the National Wildlife Federation said in the introduction to *Natural Resources and Public Relations* by Douglas L. Gilbert:

> Countless young people contemplating a professional career in conservation reached such an important decision because of their love for outdoor life and their interest in wild birds, fish and mammals. Both are certainly prerequisite to satisfaction in this type of life's work.
>
> They will soon find, however, that most of their time will be spent working with people, rather than with the natural resources. Most of their days and nights will be spent in offices or indoor meeting places rather than tramping the fields, waterways and forests.
>
> Thousands of others who have already started their conservation careers can attest to this fact. They have completed their formal training and have been successful at finding jobs as wildlife biologists, game managers, law enforcement officers, range managers, foresters, agronomists or administrators. Most of these professionals long since have realized their technical knowledge is of little avail if their publics

do not understand their conclusions nor accept their recommendations.

No suitable management program for our nation's natural resources—soils, waters, forests, range lands and wildlife—can succeed without public support. Technical knowledge in recent years has constantly been far ahead of public acceptance. This characteristic of American conservation efforts is epitomized by the imaginary (but typical) character who reputedly said, "Don't confuse me with the facts, my mind is already made up."

Natural Resources and Public Relations was published in 1971 by the Wildlife Society, Washington D.C. It's a good book and I would suggest that anyone planning to go into outdoors public relations get a copy. The author is a professor of wildlife biology and head of the Department of Fishery and Wildlife Biology, College of Forestry and Natural Resources, Colorado State University.

One thing that sets the outdoor PR person apart from the freelance outdoor writer is a steady income. Having been a freelance writer myself for a number of years, I grew to appreciate the regular salary associated with public relations for the public or private sector.

There are a number of opportunities in the public relations field for outdoor writers in the state and federal departments of game and fish. My outdoor PR career started as public relations director for the New Mexico Department of Game and Fish. I learned a lot about the PR field as well as about game and fish management, the administrative problems of game departments, visual aids, public speaking and how to work with the public. Fortunately my great interest in the outdoors meant that I did not have to learn as much as the non-hunter or non-fisherman might have had to learn in order to do my job. Also, I had been trained in journalism so that news releases and a monthly magazine were not unsurmountable problems to me. I did not know much about radio or TV in those days, but I developed a good, solid background in using those two media to disseminate news about the state's game and fish programs.

A knowledge of the mechanical techniques and requirements of the various forms of media—newspapers (daily and weekly), wire services, radio and television, and film—is of outmost importance to the PR writer. A basic education in journalism is probably the best foundation for a PR career.

In those days—early 1950s—I was about the only member of my state's game department with any formal training in the news media. Today, colleges that give degrees in wildlife management and related careers have begun to include courses on public relations. Tom Kimball was right—the biggest problem in conservation today is lack of communication. The natural sciences and their many highly specialized branches are filled with experts whose findings are critical to all of those concerned with our environment. But many of these experts have no desire or are unable to communicate their findings to fellow workers or to the general public, and conversely the general public has trouble understanding them. Explaining complex and critical environmental issues requires not only skilled and informed writing, but expert public relations.

Take for example the concept of multiple use of public lands. There are factions that would insist that wilderness areas, for example, be established and maintained strictly for the use of wild creatures and the few backpackers hardy enough to climb into them. They would not permit use by hunters, fishermen, recreational vehicles of any kind, or even allow small planes to fly over them. There are others, such as myself, who agree with them on some points (such as keeping trail bikes and four-wheeled vehicles out of wilderness areas) but feel that the restriction of such huge areas to single-use recreation is selfish and impractical, given the size of our population and the broad need and desire for outdoor recreation.

I was on a panel a few years ago with a group of young environmentalists, and we were discussing the wilderness area question. The group had decided that the wilderness areas should be left "just as God created them," untouched by man.

"What about forest fires?" I asked a young lady.

"Oh that's different," she said. "We have to put those out, naturally. They destroy so many trees."

I asked her if she thought God put out each fire that sprung up, and she became confused. I asked her if she thought early Indian tribes put out forest fires, and she did not know—and yet she sanctioned every action taken by early Indians. I told her the Indians knew that burned-over areas in forests provided food for game and that rain would—in most years—put out fires. We finally reached a level of mutual understanding, but this was public relations in action.

The outdoor writer who works for a state or federal conservation agency will spend most of his time selling ideas and concepts or convincing the public of the advisability and benefits of programs.

He or she probably will have much to do with publishing a monthly state magazine as well as writing newsletters and news releases. An education and information program is only as good as its staff. Many of the states do a creditable job of reaching the public and young people in particular with scientific information on wildlife and wildlife management. Some states—bowing either to political pressure or protectionists in the educational systems and elsewhere—put out monthly magazines that would be better suited to the Walt Disney Studios than game and fish departments.

Unfortunately, employees of state and federal wildlife agencies and conservation agencies, like those in many civil service programs, may ultimately find that retaining one's job becomes the prime motivation. Longtime employees of many state and federal conservation agencies tend to avoid rocking the boat over controversial issues. Some conservation departments (or departments of natural resources, as they are sometimes called today) are struggling internally, with Young Turks challenging wildlife management programs that have been in effect for decades. The PR person in this situation may find more politics than Great Outdoors in his or her daily job.

Nevertheless, there is important work to be done in informing the public about state and federal fish and game programs and about the true nature of wildlife management. With all the adverse and frequently ill-informed publicity being generated by a wide range of special-interest groups, the PR person speaking for the state may have to fight hard to be heard, but it is a job that needs doing.

In the private sector of the outdoor field there are all sorts of good public relations jobs for PR agencies, resorts, or industries that manufacture outdoor equipment. Many of these jobs pay well and do allow the public relations man or woman to spend a good deal of time outdoors where the product is used. The public relations director for a major sport firearms company, a fishing tackle company, a boat company or the manufacturer of camping equipment has a satisfying and rewarding job. He or she associates with people in the outdoor field constantly, attending conventions and trade shows and sharing ideas with other members of the outdoor press.

One of the first things I would do—and I realize it does cost money—is to join the Public Relations Society of America, Inc. (PRSA), headquartered at 845 Third Avenue, New York, NY 10022. The national dues are $96 per year and the local chapter dues are $45 per year, but even so it is a bargain investment for the public relations man or woman. You are kept abreast of all the developments in the public relations field and receive a directory of other PR people. The organization helps greatly with all the questions that arise for a young PR person.

PRSA was a big help to me when I worked as an account executive in the New York offices of Ketchum, MacLeod & Grove—a large Pittsburgh-based advertising and public relations agency which, in the years I was with them, handled accounts on the scale of the U.S. Army, Alcoa, Pittsburgh Plate and Glass, and Rockwell International. Because I was known as an outdoor writer (and also because I am a pilot), I was hired to handle the public relations for the Aero Commander division of aircraft owned by Rockwell International. During that time I became what is known as "accredited" to PRSA. I took a comprehensive study course on the history of public relations, early concepts, transitions in PR thinking, current trends, principles of PR, and the various tools of the trade. When I passed the examination I was then able to use the "accredited to" PRSA line on my stationery and the masthead insignia of the organization. This accreditation means a lot in professional public relations circles—especially in industry and large agencies. The study provides a better understanding of the history and practice of public relations as a profession. Your local chapter of the PRSA will be listed in the directory sent you by the national headquarters.

My job at Ketchum, MacLeod & Grove, just to give you an example of public relations in an agency handling outdoor products, was to get as much exposure as possible for the Aero Commander Division of North American Rockwell (as it was called before it became Rockwell International). I worked with people who bought the industrial jet—the Jet Commander—such as golfer Arnold Palmer. Arnold is a bird shooter, and we did several stories for outdoor magazines on his use of his jet, between tournaments, to travel to good spots for quick hunts such as quail plantations in Georgia. I did a number of stories on twin-engine Commanders for outdoor magazines such as *Sportfishing* and managed to place stories in many outdoor magazines on the small and light single-engine Aero Commander 100 series. These planes are ideal for the hunter and fisherman who wants to get away quickly to remote areas and avoid highway congestion. Then-outdoor editor of the *New York Times*, Oscar Godbout, ran a number of columns on the use of light planes on hunting and fishing trips.

Photography skills are less important in this type of job, since the agency usually will supply you with a professional photographer. Being a good photographer yourself can only help you, however.

Work for a public relations agency can be lots of fun. When I opened my own public relations firm, John Samson Associates, on Park Avenue, New York, some years later, I took on the type of assignment most outdoor writers dream about. My client, again, was North American Rockwell, and my job was to develop a Bahama island into a first-class big-game fishing resort. In addition, I was to explore and develop the potential for bonefishing and reef fishing. The island was Cat Cay—fifty miles across the Gulf Stream from Miami—and I spent eight months on that assignment. Today it is one of the best fishing resort islands in the Bahamas. Unfortunately, such clients do not come along often enough!

Other types of clients an outdoor-oriented PR person might work for (or try to get) include makers of camping equipment, clothing, compasses, and anti-sunburn lotion—just to name a few of the wide variety of products in this field. And getting away from outdoor products, the PR person who really knows the outdoors might find good opportunities as a consultant to manufacturers of such general merchandise as cereal or shampoo who want to show their product in a "natural" setting, but—as all too many commercials show—have no idea what a campground is.

Obviously, a PR person for a company making anything connected with the outdoor field should make himself known to the outdoor writers who work for magazines and newspapers. OWAA has memberships open for writers other than those who work as full-time freelance writers in newspaper, magazine, radio or TV work. The organization says in its bylaws:

> Supporting and Sustaining Memberships shall be open to individuals, organizations and firms with an interest in the outdoor field and desirous of supporting the Association's programs for expanded public information on outdoor recreation and conservation, professional craft improvement and increased recognition of outdoor writing as a specialized field among media and educational institutions.

That way you or your firm may join OWAA; you may attend their conventions and receive the monthly publication, *Outdoors Unlimited*, and the OWAA membership directory. When that arrives, write to all the OWAA writers listed, telling them of your firm, your product and what you have to offer.

There is an area about which you have to beware if you work for a company that manufactures outdoor products: Naturally, everybody is going to want your product or your service free. You cannot, obviously, supply this to everyone. The best rule of thumb I know is to honor requests only from editors or writers who work for a magazine or newspaper that might reasonably be expected to run a story on your product, or from members of OWAA. The organization has a code-of-ethics committee that works hard to keep the outdoor writing business honest, so that equipment sent on consignment will be returned unless the manufacturer or public relations director tells the writer to keep it; and reasonable efforts to get articles on the tests printed will be made. Years ago, the larger boat, gun, fishing tackle and RV companies frequently gave outdoor writers equipment to test. But so many unscrupulous "outdoor writers" took advantage of these fine offers, never writing about the product, that these companies have stopped the practice. Now the larger companies will only consign equipment to well-known outdoor writers, and I can't say I blame them.

Airlines and resorts have taken the worst beating from these people. At *Field & Stream* we receive mail constantly complaining that some outdoor writer, claiming to represent this magazine, came to a hunting or fishing resort and indicated he or she was doing a story for us. Naturally the story never appeared, and the resort people were angry at us. Our answer is that all resorts, transportation companies or manufacturers who are approached by any outdoor writer claiming to be with *Field & Stream* should call us first before dealing with them. That should be a good rule of thumb for you if you take a job as a public relations representative for a resort or company.

OWAA has done a lot to change this, maintaining excellent relations with airlines and companies in the outdoor industries. As a matter of fact, many firms that manufacture outdoor items are supporting members of OWAA.

I personally believe honesty is the most important attribute of a public relations writer. I think—within reason—one has to believe in the product one is being hired to sell. An honest enthusiasm will shine through your copy, give an edge to your creativity and ensure your success. On the other hand, if you are being employed to write of the benefits of a hunting/fishing/camping/boating/golfing/tennis resort and the place stinks, you are going to have a personal problem in deciding whether to continue to work for the owner.

I once worked for a trade association of the liquor industry. It was my task to write of the joys of liquor, the beneficial effects of same, the dangers of moonshine and other tenets of the trade. I quit, after a year, and not because I do not like to drink—I enjoy a drink very much, especially after a long day in the field. But I was finding myself writing stories saying that liquor was not the prime cause of alcoholism. I was being asked to write press releases and feature stories trying to prove that alcoholism was the end result of psychological problems—that the alcoholic was destined to be addicted to something because of his inherent problems and it might just as easily be marijuana, heroin, morphine, or cocaine as alcohol. I quit because I personally believe alcohol causes alcoholism. It was that simple. I don't profess to know all there is about the subject, but this was my personal opinion and I could not continue to write something I did not believe. But this was a very personal decision and it is up to each individual outdoor PR person to determine his own cut-off point. Being a good public relations person in the outdoor field entails common sense, honesty and integrity.

Outdoor public relations is good way to earn a living. The pay is generally good. Outdoors is healthier than indoors, and where would you meet a better class of people?

Appendixes

The following is a sampling of successful outdoor writing. All of these articles and extracts had accompanying visuals of which only the merest hint could be included. "Arctic Spring," for example, had truly stunning photographs which surely contributed to its acceptance by an editor.

My intention was not to seek out the classic—transcendent—examples of outdoor writing, which are well illustrated and preserved in anthologies and other books. What I was looking for were workmanlike, recent examples of various categories of outdoor writing.

Each of the following has been successfully proposed, and published. Each illustrates a different facet of everyday outdoor writing and is successful in its own way for different reasons. What is clear in all of the examples (given their varying degrees of "literary" merit) is authenticity of experience and depth and accuracy of information. This leads back to what I have stressed so many times in this book: you do not have to be a great writer to be a successful outdoor writer. If you can do as well as these, you should succeed, and then, if you insist, go on to write the Great American Wilderness Epic.

1. Some Useful Feature Techniques

There are several changes I have made in my feature writing style over the years. One is to make a conscientious effort to get away from the first person as much as possible. It is very difficult at times in outdoor writing since so much of it is concerned with trips you have taken yourself. But, I have attempted to substitute other words for "I" when I can. For example: "I cast the fly in the direction of the cruising tarpon. It made a swift turn and swallowed the fly. I struck instinctively and looked at my feet to make sure the coils of fly line were not under my feet . . ."—can be done this way:

"The fly landed about five feet ahead of the cruising tarpon. It turned and took the fly in a swirl of water. There was that frantic second when the most important thing in the world was to make sure the coils of fly line were free to leave the deck as the huge fish made its first towering leap."

Also, the use of "we" sometimes gets away from the present first person—as in the ending of this story called "Tarpon Madness" which appeared in the May, 1978 issue of Field & Stream:

The fight lasted about 45 minutes and wound up a quarter of a mile from where the fish had struck. The tarpon was whipped in shallow water, not more than 3 feet deep. It finally turned on its side close to the boat. Knowles took a couple of pictures for me as it lay gasping on the surface. Then he reached out and flipped the fly from the side of the jaw. The fish sank to the bottom, rolled on its side once, righted itself, and began moving slowly away.

"Nice fight," Knowles said. "He should go maybe 95 to 90 pounds. Not quite 100, but a real nice fish" He reached over and we shook hands.

"Thanks," I said and grinned. "That was nice boat handling, Knowles."

"Name's Billy," he grinned back. "Let's go catch some more of these rascals."

And catch some more we did. We fought tarpon that got off after half a jump; one that took us halfway across the flats before getting off; missed two more on the strike; caught another of about 75 pounds, and lost a monster—one Knowles thought might have gone 125 pounds—on the second jump because I was too immobilized by shock at his first jump to properly set the hook the second or third time.

The sun had sunk toward the western horizon, and the heat and humidity rose as the breeze fell to a near calm. Thunderheads began to build up in the west and northeast as they usually do in June, and lightning flickered under them on the distant, dark horizon.

We finished the sandwiches and cola, and drank up the cold beer from the ice chest.

And we jumped and fought fish and talked the talk of fly rod fishermen—flies, rods, reels, battles recent and long-past. We spoke of other fishermen and other guides, who had said what about whom, who had lost what fish because of stupid mistakes or bad luck, and who caught what for the opposite reasons. We breathed the odors of the steaming flats and were happy.

When the clouds grew too close and the wind began to pick up, we headed in to Bud 'n Mary's Marina to call it a day—for a good day it had been. That night there would be sitting around with the guides and tarpon fishermen and hearing the tales—some lies and some truth just stretched a bit. And there would be the taste of conch chowder and baked dolphin, fresh from the Gulf Stream and seasoned with just a little garlic sauce and butter. I would go to bed later that night with face and forearms burned a mahogany color in spite of having used half a bottle of suntan lotion. Sleep would come as quickly as to a child, and there would be that sweet knowledge that the withdrawal symptoms from tarpon fishing didn't have to start for two more days—when the jet was scheduled to carry me north again.

Digression is another method I have come to use as a means of breaking up what could be a monotonous chronology of a story. An example of that appears in a story I wrote in 1977, for Field & Stream called "Day of The Elk" and which appeared in the Best Sports Stories of 1978, E. P. Dutton, New York. The digression begins with paragraph seven on page 200 and ends with paragraph two on page 201. I think it changes the pace of a story and gives it more life.

We had been walking for almost three hours and the wind was gusting intermittently at about 40 knots, carrying with it the fine powder snow that tugged at an exposed cheek with all the delicacy of a wood rasp.

The air, which had seemed to congeal at 22 below zero at 4 a.m., had soared up to somewhere near 5 below by midmorning as the sun climbed into the incredible blue of the New Mexico sky. But the northwest wind, whipped down from the arcticlike air at the top of Costilla Peak and Ash Mountain, added a wind-chill factor that was bone-penetrating. With me was Bob Dougherty, my red-haired, red-moustached, red-bearded guide. He was lean and as rugged as the twisted, wind-wrenched cedars that studded the rocky ridge below where we had been breaking trail in the knee-deep snow. More than 20 years younger than I, Bob did not notice the lack of oxygen at almost 9,000 feet. Like most of the hands who worked year-round on the half-million-acre Vermejo Park ranch, his lungs had adjusted to the altitude. Mine, used to the sea level of New York (and probably still tinged with carbon monoxide from the deafening Madison Avenue buses, plus half a dozen other toxic chemicals spread over Manhattan by Con Edison, taxis, and the Jersey oil refineries), were struggling to keep me alive, let alone moving.

We had hoped to find the elk in a big meadow just to the east of a saddle between two small hills. Bob said they had been there four days ago when he had ridden by, herding a recalcitrant Hereford bull that had evaded the other ranch hands who had driven the cattle down to winter range a month earlier.

We had reached the meadow an hour before—just at sunup. There had been no elk and no tracks. The weather had changed all the rules, and with several mountain ranges on the 750 square miles of ranch, it was anybody's guess where the elk were. After failing to locate them near the meadow, we had tried scouting ridges, hoping to cut sign of traveling elk moving down to the lower canyons and mesas that were spread out below us like an undulating sea of dark-green trees and gray rocks poking up through the glare of sunstruck snow. Still, there had been no tracks of elk. We had come across the pugmarks of one lion—fairly small by the prints—a couple of coyote trails, and some mule deer sign. Our glasses failed to pick out elk at the base of the peaks or any fresh tracks in or near heavy spruce timber.

"Hard to tell," Bob said, lowering his glasses. "The storm could have them all down in the heavy spruce at the bottom of the slopes, or then"—he rubbed a mitten across his moustache, white with frozen moisture from his breathing—"they could be all the way down to the scrub oak if they had really been hurried by the big freeze."

I doubted it and I knew Bob did too. Elk move down to winter range when the big storms hit the high country, but they usually feed down—not rushing all at once. They might come off the peaks in a hurry if a huge blizzard struck, stumbling and poking their way down the steep trails almost head-to-tail in the swirling snow (as I had seen them do once in Wyoming), but only down to the heavy blowdown spruce timber for shelter. Once the storm abated they would emerge and paw through the new fall for grass in the high peaks and meadows, continuing their slow descent to the flats and foothills.

"Tell you what," I said, shifting a numb foot in the deep snow, "let's try behind the Wall. They might have come down behind it."

Bob thought a moment then nodded slowly. He stuffed his glasses inside his fur-lined parka.

"Might just work," he said. "It's going to be some walk in this snow." He stopped and grinned. "You up to it?"

"I'm up to it," I said. "Yesterday didn't kill me and I guess today won't. Besides, you're breaking trail."

It made a difference walking behind the one who had to plow through the wind-packed drifts. In most places it was about knee-deep, but there were areas where it was thigh-deep and it was necessary to thrash through these low spots. We could have hunted on horseback, but I don't like wearing a horse down in deep snow. A good mountain horse will go until it can barely walk in soft snow, but it can't speak to tell you how damn rough it really is. I *know* when I reach the edge of exhaustion and I can always stop, rest, and eat some raisins or sip hot, sweetened tea while resting in the lee of a big tree or boulder. Besides, I like to hunt afoot. I like to hunt any way I can, or for that matter, anywhere.

It does cause problems. Having one's body stationed in Manhattan, overlooking Madison Avenue—and one's heart in the Rockies, or Kenya, or on a caribou tundra near Ungava Bay or a Virginia marsh, can cause the mind to bend some.

"Why must you hunt?" asks another of the very bright ladies at yet another of the endless New York cocktail parties. "We have come a long way from having to hunt for food. You can buy anything you need to eat at this time in history. Is it a need to hunt for trophies? Do you kill for sport? Tell me, I have an open mind. Why must you hunt?"

That is the time of the mind bending.

No, dear lady, I do not *have* to hunt for food in 1977, nor did I in 1937 nor will I in 1987 or 1997, if I am granted life long enough to hunt then, but I *will* still hunt. I will not go into all the reasons why hunting is a legitimate wildlife management tool—as I have done for decades—because you will not accept my logic. In spite of what you say, you have already made up your mind. I am a hunter because I grew up one and I must be one until I am too old to hunt anymore. And few men love nature or its wild creatures more than I do.

Each year my freezer is filled with the delicious meat of white-tailed deer, elk, mule deer, antelope, caribou, upland game birds, waterfowl, and all the freshwater and saltwater fish I am able to catch.

You may keep your USDA-inspected beef, your butterball turkeys, your kosher corned beef, your plastic hamburgers and hot dogs; your Colonel whosit's chicken, and your Mrs. what's-her-name's breaded fish. You can have somebody else do your killing for you if you wish, and you may absorb all the chemicals for quick fattening and artificial coloring they pump into growing, living things today as long as you wish. I will get my antelope steaks after a long, careful stalk under the endless blue sky; my venison backstrap after a successful shot at a whitetailed buck; and my caribou roasts from the plump young bull climbing the slope above the river. I savor magnificent roast Canada goose I dropped from a flock climbing out of a cornfield; succulent quail from coveys that burst from a palmetto patch; pheasant from the magnificent cock bird that almost outflew a pattern of No. 6 shot last year; and roast ducks from the myriad of mallards, blacks, teal, widgeons, pintail, and other waterfowl that have brought me so much joy.

And if I am able to keep up with this strong young man breaking snow ahead of me, and if we are lucky enough to run across the elk moving down from the frozen peaks in the wake of the big blizzard, I am going to dine on elk steaks—the best-tasting meat I know of—all next year.

The blizzard, lashing and savage, roared across the Southwest in early December, piling snow spruce-tip high in the mountain passes, bringing cross-country driving to a halt on the drift-choked highways, and sending temperatures plummeting far below zero....

You can also introduce atmosphere into an outdoor story through historical background. It sets a mood and, I think, moves an outdoor story up a notch in the literary sense. An example from my work may serve well. One is a story called "The One-Shot Antelope Hunt" which I wrote and which appeared in January, 1973 issue of Field & Stream. *You will notice the historical perspective makes a very effective introduction to a localized outdoor story.*

Winter comes early to the rolling tan prairies of Wyoming, and the winds are chilly after the sun sinks behind the Wind River Range to the west. The aspens and alders have already turned a flaming gold and red by mid-September along the twisting bed of the Sweetwater River, Beaver Creek, and Wind River near the small town of Lander in the west-central part of the state.

The same cutting winds shake telephone wires running along highways leading to places with historic Oregon Trail names such as South Pass, Bridger, Gros Ventre, Sheridan, Clark, Powder River, North Platte, Big Horn, Crazy Woman Creek, Saddlestring, and Dead Indian Peak.

And as they have done since before man first hunted the great country southeast of the Grand Tetons, the chief, medicine men, braves, women, and children of the Shoshone Indian nation gather around campfires for the ceremony of the hunt, praying that there will be no hunger in the lodges of people in the approaching winter. But it is no longer just the Shoshone who hunt the swift pronghorn antelope in this starkly beautiful land. They are joined by the white men who came to Wyoming an instant ago in Shoshone time—a mere century and a half—hardly enough moons to make one a part of the land.

But these men come for the same reason the Indians once gathered around the campfires: to be blessed, for they will leave the next morning before dawn to stalk America's swiftest big-game animal.

Lander, Wyoming, has become the annual site of a unique hunt that is peculiarly American and yet known to sportsmen around the world—the One-Shot Antelope Hunt. The hunt, from a modest start twenty-nine years ago, has grown in reputation until today expert riflemen from every state in the United States and every foreign nation vie for an invitation to be a member of one of the six three-man teams competing. To win the coveted one-shot trophy the hunter must kill his pronghorn with one bullet blessed by the Shoshone chief and his medicine men. If he misses, he can never try again—

although he automatically qualifies as a "past shooter," allowing him to return annually to target shoot and mix with the hunters. But he can never again enter the one-shot event.

I was fortunate enough to be chosen as a member of an outdoor editors' team last season....

2. Making Fishing Come Alive

The following four examples are from stories of mine. They represent one writer's way of making fishing come alive on paper. There are as many ways to do this as there are writers.

The first piece is the ending from "The Black Marlin of Hawaii." One thing you might notice about it, besides how good I felt (mentally at least) after battling that fish is that I made my inexperience in big-game fishing (at that time) clear to the reader.

The second extract is the end of "The Rockies: Timberline Trout." The whole mood at the end of a day's fishing is evoked in the passage. Every sentence brings in several distinct physical images and impressions.

The next example includes the beginning and ending of a story called "Iceland: Land of the Salmon." In this case, leading in with the exotic names of the rivers, the sensory details of the wind, the water, and the salmon themselves, sets the scene and brings the reader along in anticipation.

The final example is "Montauk: Day of the Striper." Here again I have included both beginning and ending. You can see how the ending restates what was introduced in the lead, tying things together. The interweaving of knowledge and experience is much of what makes this work, knowing the feeding grounds, the tackle used, the sequence of events at the end of the day. But most important, in all these examples is knowledge of the emotions of every stage of the fishing experience. This—no matter what style you employ—is what really makes fishing come alive on paper.

"The Black Marlin of Hawaii"

I dimly remember—through the pain of my arms and back—seeing the double line and big brass swivel come up several times and catching a glimpse of the wire leader. But each time the fighting fish would thrash across surface, and the mate would have to let go of the line.

Finally there was the blur of a gaff, the sound of the skipper landing on the deck to help, and the shower of water over me as the marlin was gaffed again and held against the side of the hull. I didn't know enough to help tail-rope the fish and just sat in the chair, exhausted, as the two hauled the fish over the starboard gunwale. It landed with a slithering thump on the deck, and the mate whacked it several times on the forehead with a wooden club.

And after that everything was a melee of slaps on the back, handshakes, whoops, grins, shouts, and the headiest feeling I had ever felt, up to that day, in my entire life.

And there was suddenly a need to lean over the side—my stomach wrenching and the bitter taste of bile and beer in my mouth. When I stopped and slid back to the deck, the skipper slapped me on the back and poured a cold can of beer over my head.

"Don't worry about it son," he shouted. "Nothing to be ashamed of. You whipped hell out of that fish, but there ain't anybody who whips a black marlin in this world that's won an easy fight!"

And a black marlin it was. Not a Pacific blue as were most of the ones caught off Kailua-Kona, nor a striped marlin. It wasn't a big fish, now that I know how much black marlin weigh. It was 378 pounds, the dockmaster said later. I couldn't have cared less.

My arms, legs, and back were sore for a week, and I couldn't get out of bed for days without groaning. But that fish did something to me, and I really am not sure yet whether I am blessed or cursed because of it.

It made me an incurable big-game fisherman, that magnificent black marlin. May God rest its fighting soul.

"The Rockies: Timberline Trout"

... With the two good fish stowed, I disassembled my rod and slid it into its aluminum case. It was almost dusk, and I had about an hour's walk down the mountain to the car. The air, even for early May, was turning cold as I picked up a lightweight jacket from a lichen-covered boulder near the head of the trail and slung my chest waders across one shoulder. Before starting down, I turned to look at the lake again. The feeding had slowed, and only a few small rises dimpled the water. No wind creased the glassy surface that mirrored the green slope slanting up to the bare ridge to the east of the lake. The great horned owl sounded its five-note hoot, and the call echoed and bounced from the dark fringe of spruces and the sides of the hollow bowl surrounding the quiet lake. I could smell the dank, black earth of the lake bank and the odor of freshly caught trout on my hands and jacket. The scent of wet canvas waders was mixed with that of spruce needles—all breathed in with the unbelievably clear air of the high country as I started down the narrow trail. . . .

"Iceland: Land of the Salmon"

... A warm and moist wind, carrying the lung-soothing freshness of the North Atlantic Drift, bathes the green island in August. And in the clear rivers with almost unpronounceable names—the Laxa Adaldal, the Nordhura, the Grimsa, and the Haffjardhara—the great Atlantic salmon leap and churn their way inland to spawn.

Gleaming silver, and fresh from the depths of the sea, the fish gradually change to bronze-purple as they move irresistibly through historic pools with names known for centuries to salmon fishermen long passed on to greater pools and fish which never die.

On pools named The Grastraumur, and runs called the Stekkur, guides like Jonnas Halldorsson, Heimir Sigurdsson, and Thor Thors—many of them owners of the land through which the rivers twist—point out the traditional spots where salmon rest briefly before fighting their way up the next twisting current or plunging waterfall. And for the angler who stands thigh-deep in the cold and clear water while the salmon leap clear and fall back to the surface on their age-old journey, as inflexible as the rise and fall of the ocean tide, it is not difficult to see what brought European fly fishermen, centuries ago and in wooden ships, to fish Iceland.

* * *

We caught beautiful fish, and we talked of the salmon, of flies, reels, and fine fly rods, and of the men who used and loved them. And I released all the fish I caught—simply because I like to see them swim away. They were wonderful days, and I intend to go back. But the high point of the trip was when Thor and I walked upstream together after catching my first Icelandic salmon.

"You know," Thor said, an arm across my shoulders as we slogged up the bank toward the car and a waiting lunch, "the English, years ago, taught us how to catch the salmon with the rods. But," he stopped and looked at his river, "you Americans taught us the sport of it."

"Montauk: Days of the Striper"

When the first chill winds of November shriek past the old lighthouse on Montauk and the seas churn white against the jagged rocks at the base of the eroded cliffs, the big bass of the Atlantic migratory stock reach the peak of the movement around the ancient point.

And it is then—with the occurrence of the full moon—that striped bass fishermen on the East Coast experience what I personally think is the greatest time of the year to fish for these magnificent game fish.

There will be those who say the rocky shores of Rhode Island provide better sport in the spring as the schools pour northward from the breeding grounds of the Hudson River, northern New Jersey, Barnegat, Great Egg Harbor, the mouth of the Mullica River, and even from as far south as the huge spawning area of the Chesapeake. There are others who claim there is no striper fishing that compares to hurling a tin squid or surface plug into the surf off Hatteras or to drifting over the rip and the rocky ledges off Sandy Hook, dragging a freshly dead mossbunker close to the bottom. They all have a point. I have fished them all. I have stood on the wet sloping sandy beach of Martha's Vineyard and felt the striper smash a topwater plug in the gray and curling seas and laughed with the sheer joy of combat as the big bass stripped off my line—my laughter whipped away in the howling winds of fall.

* * *

But there are the lights and the curious faces; the laughter and the heaving of stripers onto the rough dock planking; the hosing down of the boat; the cleaning and storing of gear; and making the boat secure against the night winds. And after that it is a warming and bracing drink, hours of filleting a winter's worth of striped bass for the freezer, the laughter of friends, and the stories of other great days on the water.

And finally, after a hot shower and a change of clothes, there are the fresh fillets of striper cooked by Nelse with his own favorite recipe: boiled in a deep frying pan, simmering in the contents of several cans of stewed tomatoes, laced with salt and pepper and just a few freshly chopped-up onions. Leave it to a Vineyard man to cook striper the right way, while the freezing wind moans around the frame motel room and the schools of striped bass feed throughout the night off Montauk, as they have done for millions of years.

3. A How-To Feature

An example of a solid, well-written feature article by Vic McLeran (Southern Outdoors, March, 1979). If the title hasn't aroused your curiosity, the lead will. The reader is drawn through several paragraphs before even learning the subject—catfish. Not the most popular fish in these days of bassmania, but McLeran goes on to show you exactly why you should be interested.

The article moves right along with lively, effective, often humorous writing. It flows so well that you are almost unaware of the amount of information you are getting. A full range of biological facts about the fish slanted to the fisherman are served up along with details of two distinct styles of catfish fishing. We learn the methods of two successful catfishermen, but these methods are not presented as final solutions, just as what works for those men. Blended in with all this, again so smoothly that you almost don't notice, are safety tips, timing hints, and just plain interesting facts and insights. As if this is not enough, we are given two insets with further and even more detailed information for the aspiring catfisherman. This article not only gets you excited about catfishing, it tells you enough to put the odds of success solidly in your favor.

A secondary, but important aspect of this article is that McLeran deals with a fish that is under-fished. In these populous times such a slant is not only saleable, but a service to the sport of fishing.

By Vic McLeran

In what could loosely be referred to as the pugilistic world of fish and fishermen, his image is no better than that of a worn-out boxer in a small town neighborhood gym.

Perhaps it's not as good.

People view him as tough, but not classy. His human counterparts—if you believe the words of many fishermen—are street fighters, barroom brawlers, back alley thugs. Though his presence is reluctantly acknowledged, few would invite him onto their hooks. He is not, claim his detractors, the kind of fish "nice" anglers associate with.

Thus, he isn't, and likely never will be, a title contender. Which is unfortunate, for if given the chance, he might—just might—swim off with the crown.

Who is this fish? You are about to meet him....

* * *

On its way to the Gulf, the Ochlockonee River snakes gently through south Georgia hills, winding into Florida about 40 miles north of Tallahassee. Fringed with cypress and cabbage palm, the river is dammed near Bloxham to form Lake Talquin, a 4,000-acre impoundment noted for exceptional black bass and striper fishing. At its upper end, where the Ochlockonee enters, an angler is wading the river's mouth. Moving slowly upstream, he flips his bait about a yard above a drift pile and watches as the current swings his monofilament several inches toward the cover.

Out on the lake some 90 feet distant, two bass fishermen are casually working plastic worms and closely observing their boatless counterpart. Momentarily, the wader notices an ever-so-slight twitch of his monofilament and feels a less than vigorous tug. Hurriedly thrusting his rod tip toward the brush to furnish several inches of slack, he waits an instant for the line to draw tight, then sets his hook with gusto and hangs on as the mono shears through dark water on a collision course with the partially submerged bush. Lifting the rod, he turns the fish. Again and again, he pumps it toward open water. Finally, after five minutes of the muscle-straining, seesaw battle, the fish tires and allows itself to be snatched from its domain.

The loser is a four-pound channel catfish.

The winner holds it aloft, so the two nearby anglers can better see his prize.

"Aw, hell, it's just a catfish," mutters one of the bassers. "I though he was wadin' for bass."

The bass worshipers crank up their boat and leave. Their disappointment is a typical reaction, unless, of course, you happen to be somewhat of a rarity among Southern anglers—a catfisherman.

Blame the highly touted black bass for the fact that many "modern" anglers are either overlooking or have completely abandoned a fine game fish—the skillet version of which makes a bass taste like old shoe leather, and the live version which is often still battling long after a similar sized largemouth is in the boat.

There are, however, a few Southern fishermen who, despite its questionable reputation, doggedly pursue catfish—Dixie's seemingly forgotten fighters.

Don Wood of Tallahassee, FL, is such a fisherman. In a state famous for—and obsessed with—black bass, Wood and a few others of his ilk are angling anarchronisms. Why, man, this is *today*. You know, the age of computers and jets and all sorts of electronic gizmos that go bump in the night. Who ever heard of somebody going after catfish when they could be trying to catch bass? That's almost sacrilegious.

Wood doesn't think so.

"You can't imagine all the good catfishing that goes begging due to lack of interest," says Wood, weaving a cord stringer through the four-pounder's jaw. "The rivers of south Georgia and north Florida are chocked full of cats, and there's very little fishing pressure. That's amazing, because regardless of the bait you catch him on, a channel cat—my favorite—is a super scrapper. Maybe not as flashy as the black bass, and you won't get any aerial acrobatics, but ounce-for-ounce, the channel packs more power than any large-mouth. The rest of the catfishes are no slouches, either."

Tying the stringer to his belt, Wood rebaits his hook with a piece of sliced eel and chunks his next cast just upstream from an old cypress stump.

For countless hours during the past 25 years, Wood, the endangered species coordinator for the Florida Game & Fresh Water Fish Commission, has been chunking things: eels, stink bait, blood bait—whatever it takes to attract cats. During that time, he has come to know well these scaleless, bewhiskered dwellers of Southern lakes, reservoirs and rivers. And from his familiarity has evolved respect, and appreciation for the skills necessary to consistently outsmart them.

Don Wood is a catfisherman, and proud of it.

If you were to visit any inland waters in the South—with the possible exception of a flooded gutter in Cut 'n Shoot, Texas—you would be in catfish territory. They're everywhere. Four, it is rumored, were recently ejected from the Omni Hotel in Atlanta after refusing to pay a big room service charge for minnows. The ejectees, says a usually reliable source, claimed the delicacies tasted too "fishy."

A distant relative of the carp, catfish are so named because of the barbels—feelers, actually—which protrude from their faces and resemble cat whiskers. When scrounging around on the bottom, their preferred level, catfish use the barbels to examine and taste meal possibilities. The number of barbels depends on the type (some 2,500 catfish species are known by biologists); the channel cat, for example, sports eight feelers, two above the jaw, four under and one on the tip of each maxillary.

One of the main problems with catching catfish is handling them. If you're not careful, spines in the dorsal and pectoral fins can puncture your skin and release painful—but rarely fatal—venom. So unless an experienced catfisherman shows you how, it's smart to use pliers or wear gloves when de-hooking or stringing them.

Besides the channel, two other varieties popular with catfishermen are blues and flatheads. All grow big; all live in large streams or impoundments, and all are welcome on the dinner table. As is typical of catfishes, the three are basically night feeders, but their eating habits aren't so rigid they'll snub a tender morsel dropped in front of them during daylight hours. Like kids, they'll swallow a snack anytime. Unlike youngsters, catfish are not finicky eaters—they'll suck up just about anything you offer, from worms to small fish to frogs to chicken livers to commercial catfish bait. Their motto, seemingly, is "if it feels good, eat it."

Of the trio, blues are the heavyweights, occasionally attaining a size of 150-pounds-plus. Average weight, however, is two to 15 pounds. Similar in appearance to the channel (both are the only catfish with deep-vee tails), the blue is distinguished by a longer anal fin base.

Comparatively, flatheads are the light-heavyweights, sometimes tipping the scales at more than 100 pounds. Often found below dams of major Southern impoundments, flatheads are a snap to identify—they look like somebody ran over their skulls with a Mack truck. At Possum Kingdom Lake near Mineral Wells, Texas—a clear, rocky reservoir which impounds waters of the Brazos River—divers have reported seeing huge flathead and blue catfish skulking in niches at the bases of submerged cliffs. "One was so immense," says a local diver, "he could have eaten a Volkswagen without bulging his stomach."

In the middleweight division is the channel cat, averaging one to five pounds; a few—those who don't watch their carbohydrate intake—register 25-30 pounds. Of the Big Three, the channel is the scrappiest and most agile. Even little ones give you the feeling you've hooked Moby Dick. Compared to professional football players, channel cats are running backs; the other two are tackles.

Any are worth catching.

"I prefer wading," explains Wood, knee-deep in Lake Talquin, FL, water. "You have much better line control and can approach the fish more quietly than in a boat."

The creatures Wood seeks, he says, normally hold into the current, facing upstream. The logical strategy, then, is to deploy from downstream, behind the fish. Then, notes Wood, your disturbances, such as roiled water or dislodged debris, won't pass in front of a catfish and alert it to the intrusion.

Likely channel catfish refuges, he advises, are in wide, clean rivers with abundant cover. "Nocturnal by nature, channel cats hold in these areas—you know, places with fallen trees, old logs, stumps or drift piles—because they provide shade and protection. Like bass, catfish are fond of 'structure,' " he adds.

"And, oh yes, once you take a catfish from a certain log or drift pile, go back to that same spot a week or so later. You'll probably latch onto another, 'cause whatever attracted one channel cat will eventually lure some relatives."

Waiting patiently, Wood watches his line. Shortly, he reels in and continues upstream. "I usually let the bait lie in one spot for five or six minutes, and if a channel hasn't taken it by then, he's either not home or not hungry."

Approaching an old drift pile, Wood laces a cast which drops the eel chunk several inches past the debris. "I leave a little slack until I see that first tug," he explains, "then I shove the rod tip forward to relax the line a bit more. I stick him after he pulls the line taut. It's similar to fishing for bass with a plastic worm."

No strikes. Wood leaves, hurriedly wading to his next spot. The succeeding two hours—the ones just before dark—are catfishing's prime times, he says.

"Then, since the fish likely haven't fed all day, they're ready to eat, and they're easier to catch than if you wait until after dark," he claims. "At night, when the catfish move out of their cover and into the shallows, they're usually spookier and less prone to be tricked."

In a few minutes, Wood is out of sight, but if you listen closely, you can hear the sporadic plop of his weight as it hits the water and transports the sliced eel to what Woods hopes is a violent encounter with a channel catfish . . .

* * *

It is now two days later and several hundred miles to the north, at a place called Pickwick Landing near Savannah, Tennessee. Here, the catfishermen are, for the most part, non-waders. Their ploy—one popular throughout the South—is fishing the tailwaters just beyond the 113-foot tall Tennessee Valley Authority dam.

At Pickwick and similar impoundments, the choice catfishing times are not in late evening or at night, but rather during early and midday hours—as long as water gushes through the gates, pouring out chopped baitfish and creating an oily buffet for the ravenous channels and blues below.

Equipped with semi-heavy, saltwater-type tackle and a bait container packed with skipjack herring and shad, Don Cannon, Savannah's square-jawed chief of police, is heading upriver, toward the "boils," those large upheavals of water vomited from the turbines. Earlier, he had cautioned some novice boaters not to go too near the turbulence, warning that it could flip a boat and drown its occupants in seconds.

"The larger cats hang around the edges of boils, on the bottom, and scarf up food the current tosses out," Cannon yells above the water's roar. "Some guy took a 105-pounder out last year, and in 1972, they caught a 115-pounder." Cannon knows about heavy catfish. On a recent trip, he boated five weighing 116 pounds.

Fifty or so yards from the dam, Cannon nudges his outboard's throttle so the prop barely turns, explaining, "if I shut it off, the current would sweep me back too fast to properly work the bait."

With momentum furnished by a five-ounce sinker and a stocky arm, Cannon's impaled skipjack sails some 10-yards downstream. The catfisherman leaves his big Penn reel in free-spool, maintaining slight thumb pressure while paying out line about a foot at a time. "You have to keep your line tight," he says, "otherwise, the bait or sinker will hang up on the rocks."

About 60 feet later, Cannon's rod abruptly plunges down, then snaps back as he sets the hook. Almost simultaneously, he kicks the throttle in neutral, clamps his thumb solidly on the spool, engages the reel and begins horsing. The power of the fish—about a three-pounder, he predicts—combined with the terrific force of the current equates with the pulling energy of the Budweiser Clydesdales. It's tough work, this catfishing.

This time, Cannon wins the tug-of-war. The channel, as he guessed, is about a three-pounder. "Imagine how it would have been if the catfish was a real biggie," he says, cranking the motor back up and plodding upstream to start another drift.

"Those bass fishermen back on the lake don't know what they're missing, and that's just fine with me," he allows, right before yet another catfish, a larger one, decides to find out who's the best battler—him or Cannon.

Rigging For Cats

Where you fish dictates the type of catfish tackle to use.

Spinning or spincasting reels spooled with eight to 10-pound test line and light action rods are fine for farm ponds, small lakes or impoundments with relatively clean bottoms. In swift-flowing rivers, tailrace waters or areas which have a reputation for producing large catfish, opt for baitcasting reels, 17 to 20-pound monofilament and stout rods.

In fairly snag-free, calm water Wood recommends the following terminal rigging: "First, place an egg-shaped sliding sinker (one-fourth to one-half ounce, depending on water velocity) on the line, then attach small snap swivel on end and snap on a snelled Eagle Claw No. 1 or 2 hook.

"The major advantage of this rigging is that when the reel is disengaged, a fish can pick up the bait and move away freely, never feeling the unnatural weight of the sinker. The swivel reduces line twist—channel cats roll unmercifully when fighting for freedom—and the snelled hook and snap swivel eliminate a lot of wasted time in removing a deeply imbedded hook. Just unsnap the hook and leave it in the fish until later, and put on a new hook. I prefer small hooks because most of the channel cats you'll catch are in the one to three pound category, and they have a problem taking larger hooks."

Cannon, the swift-water-below-dam man, sees things differently.

"I use a big Penn reel and a saltwater rod; most freshwater tackle just isn't rugged enough for my kind of fishing," he says. "The size of some of these fish, and the velocity of the current require heavy-duty stuff."

Generally, Cannon uses 30-pound line, but switches to 40-pound test when fishing for big cats in boils near dams.

"There's also a dual problem involved when fishing tailrace waters," he says. "First, the current is so swift, you need a real heavy weight to sink your bait to the bottom, and secondly, you have to keep the hooks just off the floor or you'll hang up in the rocks."

(Cannon normally uses two hooks, the latter to nail catfish which strike short.)

Here's how Cannon solves the tailrace rigging dilemma:

"Attach a three-way swivel to the end of the line, and tie to one swivel eye a three to four-inch length of 30-pound monofilament with a five-ounce weight on the end. On the other swivel eye, tie on an 18-inch piece of 30-pound mono with a 2/0 hook on the end. Another 2/0 hook should be knotted on the line about an inch and one-half above the end hook (see illustration).

"Rigged this way, the sinker sits directly on the bottom while the current stretches the hook line downstream, a sew inches above the rocks,"„Cannon explains.

Stomachs of Iron

The stomach of a catfish is open to just about anything that sinks, wiggles, slithers, hops, swims or reeks of blood. Among all-time Southern favorite catfish baits are:

- **Beef milt** (spleen from cow); available from packing houses and butcher shops; cut into finger size portions; most effective in warmer months.
- **Bullheads** (small two or three inch specimens); clip pectoral spines and hook in lip or back; flathead catfish love 'em; also good for other varieties.
- **Catalpa worms** (large black and yellow-green worms); collect them in spring and summer from underneath side of leaves; some anglers turn them wrong-side-out to make them "juicier."
- **Chicken blood;** allowed to coagulate and harden, this is a top stream bait; thickening and toughening with salt and brown sugar improves hook retention qualities.
- **Chicken livers;** excellent for farm pond catfish; allowing to set in sun or "curing" with salt and brown sugar keeps bait on hook better.
- **Crawfish;** fish whole or peel tail and place on hook.
- **Earthworms and night crawlers;** fish several on a hook; sprinkle liberally with anise oil to increase

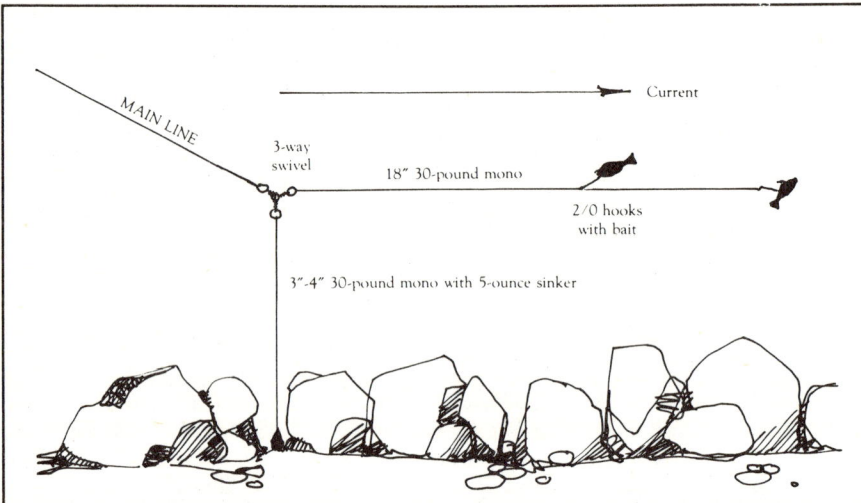

1. — Tennessee catfisherman Don Cannon's rigging method for keeping bait just above rocks when fishing fast waters below dams.

effectiveness; good farm pond bait, especially after rainstorm.

• **Eels;** slice diagonally or cut in chunks; extremely popular in north Florida and south Georgia.

• **Grasshoppers;** particularly good in August and September, when these insects are plentiful in fields near rivers or ponds; use small light wire hook.

• **Hellgrammites** (larval stage of Dobsonfly); ideal creek and river bait where both hellgrammites and channel catfish occur; collect under rocks in a riffle by placing minnow seine directly downstream from riffle and turning over rock—current then washes hellgrammites into net; hook beneath collars; very effective in riffle areas at sundown.

• **Leopard frogs;** fish smaller frogs whole, larger ones should be cut in chunks; good on farm ponds or small lakes.

• **Minnows and baitfish;** fish whole or cut, dead or alive.

• **Prepared stink baits;** these come in a variety of smell and flavors, such as cheese, blood, shad; many anglers use small treble hook with them.

• **River clams;** shuck out meat and allow clams to "sour" in sun for several days; productive river bait in deep holes during summer.

• **Salamanders** (often called spring lizards); found in spring under rotten logs, stumps, rocks and other moist areas; hook through front leg, lips or back; when fishing, raise rod tip occasionally to prevent salamander from hiding under rock.

• **Sand toads** (small, brownish-grey toads about nickel size); found around Southern waterways; dynamite bait in shallow rivers of Texas and Oklahoma.

• **Shad;** fished same as minnows.

• **Shrimp;** thaw frozen shrimp and allow to "ripen" in sun for several hours; use only tail; strong but effective.

4. The Short How-To

Here are two good examples of short how-to articles from Field & Stream (February, 1979 and August, 1978). Some things to note are:
1. The importance of illustration (photos would also work).
2. Each points out common pitfalls or mistakes.
3. Each encourages improvision (encourages the reader to experiment and adapt the idea to his own needs).
4. The prominence of the cost angle (how much the total project will cost, or how the homemade item will compare, in cost and advantages, with the store-bought item).

Build your own camp kitchen

We used to pack all of our cooking and eating utensils in bags and boxes every time we went camping. It was inconvenient in camp, a chore to pack each time, and more often than not we'd find we'd left some essential item at home. I knew there must have been a better way.

Then I built a chuck box, with a few improvements over one I had seen. Some of these add-ons may not appeal to you; others may suggest something else you'll consider desirable:

• A pair of spring-loaded clips on the back to hold a plastic trash bag in place.

• A bracket on one side to hold a small plastic bucket where dirty utensils can be put as they're used.

• Handles on the ends for lifting while the legs are inserted.

• Eye-hooks on the inside for hanging often-used items such as stove lighter, spatula, etc.

• A rack for a roll of paper towels.

• Furring strips on the top to hold the stove firmly in place.

• Magnetic latches on the front door to hold it temporarily shut without using the eye-hooks.

The illustration shows the basics of building your own chuck box. Total cost, including paint and hardware, is only about $20. The overall size shown is what I've found to be most convenient for the equipment I carry and my large, three-burner stove. For smaller stoves and less equipment, a smaller box will do nicely and be easier to carry and set up. But don't make the mistake a friend of mine did. He liked the idea so well that he built a box of his own. He made it big enough to also carry a lantern, a gallon of gas, a few clothes, tools, and the dog's dish. It's fine once it's set up, but it takes two men and a boy to carry it to the truck. And it's so big that he can't reach the stove with the front swung down!

My camp kitchen carries a wide assortment of equipment, supplies, and food, yet is very convenient. All of the kitchen and cooking needs are there at arm's length. The camp stove goes on top and the front swings down to become a handy surface for preparing and serving food. After dinner it holds a wash basin for the clean-up chores.—*Rick Webb*

APPENDIXES 213

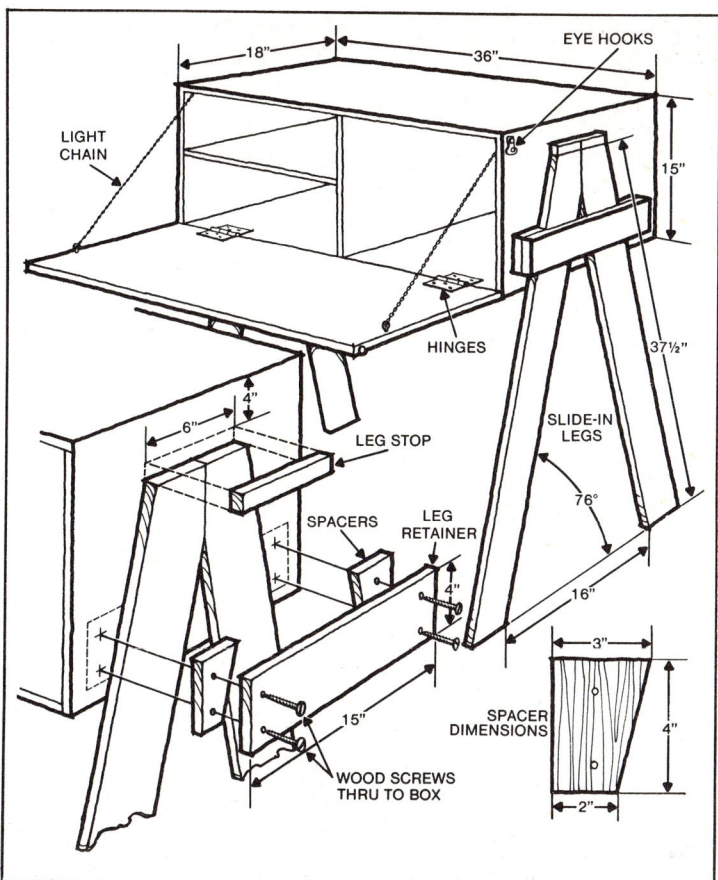

LIST OF MATERIALS

Part	Number Req'd.	Size	Material
Top	1	36 x 18	⅜ Ply
Bottom	1	36 x 17⅝	⅜ Ply
Back	1	36 x 14¼	⅜ Ply
Front	1	36 x 14¼	⅜ Ply
Ends	2	17¼ x 14½	⅜ Ply
Legs	4	4 x 38	⅜ Ply
Leg Spacers	4	4 x 3	⅜ Ply
Leg Retainers	2	4 x 15	⅜ Ply
Vertical Divider	1	14¼ x 17¼	
Shelf	1	17¼ x 17¼	⅜ Ply
Leg Stops	2	½ x ¾ x 6	Pine
Furring Strips	As Req'd.	½ x ¾	Pine
Hinges	2		Brass
Eye Hooks	2		Brass
Gold-plated Chain	2		

Lure yourself from the winter doldrums

This winter, don't just sit around fuming, waiting for fishing season to open. Instead, use some of your pent-up energy (and ingenuity) creating spinning lures out of common-place objects. For example, the lure at upper left in the illustration may not catch any dogfish, but it has caught big trout and smallmouth bass in the upper Hudson River. The two coins, properly shined of course, will definitely give you your money's worth. Old keys (also polished) can unlock some excellent fishing for you. My son caught a 3-pound brownie in the Delaware River on a gold-colored key. Of course, not everything works. The ubiquitous pop-top-can ring was a miserable failure. So were a dogleash snap and a gold-colored window lock that I had lying around. You can't win 'em all, but on the other hand, your failures won't cost very much.—*Coulman Westcott*

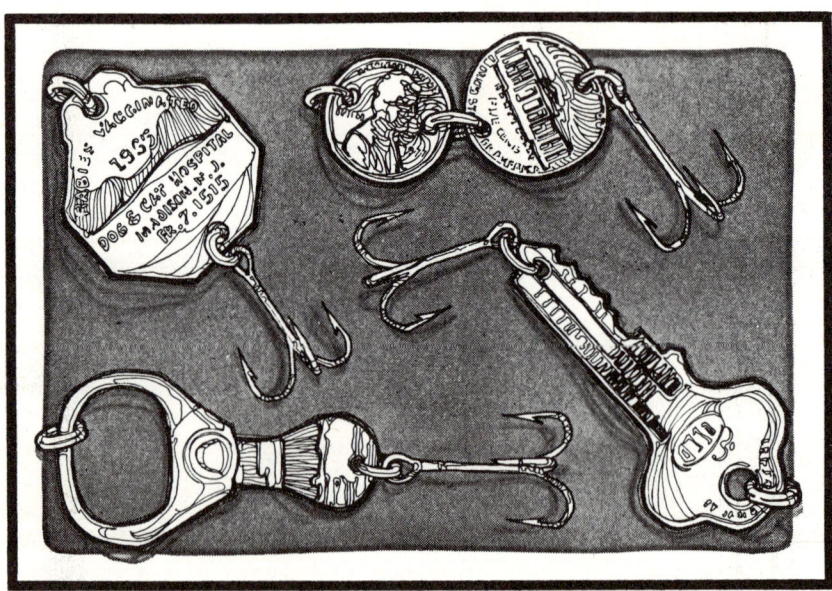

5. Writing for Mood: A Hunting Story

This powerful piece of outdoor writing appeared in Field & Stream in September, 1978. In short simple sentences with no extra words, the author evokes some profound thoughts (the symbiotic relationship of the hunter and his prey, the wider relationship of man and nature, the importance of the outdoor experience in an urban age) in the course of telling a good story.

This sparse but vivid portrait of an "old timer" gives glimpses of another day, and a reluctant glance at the future. Sitton's knowledge and experience are evident throughout. The reader feels what it's like to crouch in a layout boat as the winds howl around the marsh. The evaluation of the decoy in paragraph 27 as well as the familiarity with DU dinner topics make it clear that Sitton does not belong to the group that substitutes talking about for doing.

All in all, a moving and effectively understated outdoor story.

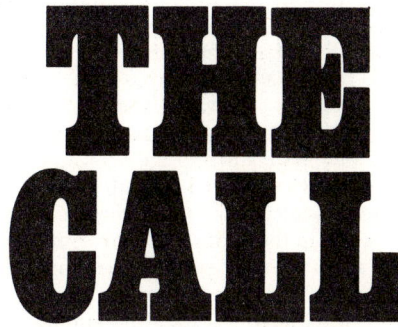

THE CALL

BY GARY SITTON

The letter from Emery Law's wife came in yesterday's mail. It was surrounded by the usual bills and circulars. I read the letter, then went through the commercial trash. When I read her letter the second time, it still said Emery was dead. He was seventy-eight years old when his heart quit. She thought I would want to know.

Emery was past seventy when I met him. He was a bit gruff, sometimes short-tempered, and legendary among the serious waterfowlers of our area. He had spent a lifetime in that particular world where birds and water combine to take ownership of some men's souls.

And in his long time on this earth he remained steadfastly unimpressed by all save the need for protecting the delicate combinations that painted for him a clear, timeless picture of the natural world. Birds, plants, and flowing water, animals, insects, and weather—all running together to make his final truth.

He also remained full of hope because his passion was greater than the sum total of the stupidity and greed encountered in a half-century of tilting at bureaucratic windmills, fighting corporate dragons, and generally fending off the tawdry fools who would have violated his domain.

We spent three seasons hunting ducks together. (Or I spent three seasons hunting ducks with him.) He would generally call me late of a nasty winter night. Because of the time and the weather I always had a pretty good idea who it was before I picked up the phone. While the phone was still ringing, I'd say to my wife, "Bet you a ranch in Texas it's Emery." She would groan and announce there was no chance of my going out in such a hellish storm, knowing as she spoke that I was right and she was wrong.

He never said "hello," never gave

his name. Just, "We have a tide for the morning. Can you go?"

I'd think about my job and the work that always needed doing, and then make the only possible decision: "Yes, I can. What time do you want me to be there?"

"Be at the boats at 3:30. By 5 there won't be enough water in the creek to make Tyler's Hole."

Then he would simply hang up. So I would organize my gear, pack lunch, and go to bed knowing I had maybe three hours to sleep at the very most.

Emery always arrived at the landing before me. Sometimes he spent the night in the shed that served as a locker for the motors, tanks, oars, decoys, raingear, and other equipment so necessary to proper coldwater ducking.

"Come on. We're late. We must get into the marsh before the water is gone."

"Emery, the tide table says we have two hours left before the turning."

"Pay attention. The wind came around about 2 o'clock. It's driving the water out. We have maybe 45 minutes."

I never did figure out how I was supposed to know about the wind changing in my sleep. Or how he knew, but he always did.

Running the little one-man layout boats across the river always spooked me some. It was big water and the black chop under the bows promised that nothing good would come of a mistake or an accident. Certainly, Emery had told me enough times about the men who had died while ducking along that coast. He said some had bad luck, but mostly they lacked proper respect and brought it on themselves.

When we pulled into the appointed place. I would put up the woven grass blinds around the cockpits, cover the motors with burlap, and scatter more grass on the decks, while Emery set out a few decoys. Then we would settle in to wait for shooting time. I'd curl up in the bottom of my boat and pray for sunrise. Emery always sat straight-backed, watching the dark marsh, talking to his dog. I never could figure why he did that, with the wind blowing a steady 30 knots over the ice and nothing at all to see beyond 20 yards. Now I think he was remembering, seeing time.

It was very cold then. But I recall the dampness and discomfort only in a general way, and with a certain fondness. It was good just being there because other people were not. Other people were sleeping warm, resting against the inevitable trial and labor of passing another day in the practical business of living. We were awake to the careless power of a nighttime gale in a duck marsh, preparing to spend the day without thought to getting or spending. Free until tomorrow because we had weather and ducks and guns.

Then the sun would start up. Or the light would just come in the east like frosted, translucent steel. Mark the gunning time. I'd load the old pump then. Emery would load his gun, too, though in the years I hunted with him I saw him shoot exactly one duck. At first, I thought he was being polite, but it wasn't anything like that simple. He just didn't care about the shooting anymore. That part of it was over for him.

The one bird he shot was a drake mallard that I let pass from my side of the set. He finally killed it going away from a clean shot at about 40 yards. The bird was dead in the air. He sent the dog and turned on me. He was plainly angry.

"You got to shoot the birds," he said, talking loud and hard.

So I said, "Hell, Emery, you should have some gunning too."

He gave me the look that old men use when young men demonstrate their lack of wisdom and said, "No. I don't need it. You got to shoot them."

And that was it. He was too old for the shooting, too old to cooperate actively with death, but knowing that the killing—or some of it—had to be done to make the thing full and complete. Without the shooting, it would have been a partial, pitiful, stillborn thing far worse than the circle of living and dying we moved in during our days together.

He always had a pair of calls on a lanyard around his neck, the wood dark and devoid of varnish from long handling. They must have been carried out of habit. I never heard him blow a note. I'd sit there and do my inadequate best to turn the birds to our decoys, sometimes even convincing the more trusting mallards. Once, I actually bent the high-balling pass of a black duck, or so it seemed to me. But Emery was silent.

We spent a lot of days pretty much in this fashion. Then I moved to the other side of the country, and now he's dead and I guess it fits all right, because he had a long run at doing the things that counted for him.

There's not much in the way of ducking where I live now. Some of my friends do well enough shooting over the stock tanks, but that doesn't appeal to me somehow. When I go to the DU dinners, I hear men talking about short seasons, steel shot, and point systems. Some threaten to stop going out altogether, since it's getting to be so much trouble, as if that had anything to do with it. Better, perhaps to drink cocktails with casual acquaintances, buy nice waterfowl prints, and dream of days they'll never spend in duck blinds.

It would be easy to say that Emery's time is gone, and with it a good way of living. I won't do that, because I can sit at my desk and look at an old, scarred black duck decoy. Emery carved it himself, painted it himself. The tarred codline winds around the body with crossing turns on the neck, just as it should. And the hand-cast lead anchor is neatly fitted over the head. There's no chance for the line to foul when you set a block up properly. They'd laugh like loonies down at the Easton show if I showed up with Emery's decoy. All those careful artists with their almost perfect imitations of life.

But they will have to satisfy themselves with the winning of ribbons and money and such. Their carvings will never win a sunrise in December with a hard wind blowing in from the big water and skim ice on Tyler's Hole. This rude old block of mine did that many times, when the heavy, red-legged blacks came to meet the flat clapping of a shotgun. Or perhaps to meet no shooting at all, but only an old man sitting straight-backed in a grassed layout boat, watching the sky, talking to a dog.

So it isn't gone, isn't finished at all. I'll go back there sometime. Not this year, but surely another. I'll borrow a boat and run over to the place where, one bleak day, the tide did not return to the marsh. It never was going to be much of a tide, and a shrieking easterly cancelled it entirely. I shot my birds in the first hour of light and we spent the day sitting in the boats, watching them fly. We didn't talk very much, but late that afternoon he turned to me and asked, "What gun do you have?"

He had seen the gun countless times, but I was ready to discuss anything not having to do with numb feet and the local coffee shortage. "Just an old Winchester. Not fancy. My father gave it to me years ago. I feel at home with it."

He looked out across the blowing marsh for a while. Then he said, "Yes. I used to shoot Parkers. Gave them both to my son when he turned twenty-one. He's an executive now in Chicago. Doesn't gun any more. Doesn't have the time. He has a nice family, though. I tried to teach the grandson to shoot, but he didn't take to it much."

Later, as dusk went toward darkness and we were still waiting for the water to come and float the boats, the ducks began settling into the shallow pools around us for the night. Emery said, "Listen to them. The weather has them afraid. They know there's another blow coming in tonight. They want to be with their own, even though it will do nothing against the storm. Like people. If you want to call ducks, listen. Learn what they are saying right now. They are sounding welcome and promise and fear. They'll say anything to keep from being alone. If you learn to call that way, you can make them come about any time. But I'm not sure you should. You'll have to decide."

That was two or three seasons ago. Once again it is dark outside. My wife is in this house. I can hear my children playing in the other room as I write this story, saying goodbye to Emery Law.

He was wrong about one thing: Being with your own does do something against the storm. And he was right about something else: I never did try to learn that call.

6. RV Writing: A Product Evaluation

"The Sweet and Sour of Diesel Power" (Field & Stream, May, 1978) is a good example of a RV article by Vehicles Editor Bill Kilpatrick.

After an unusual and effective lead, Bill moves into a straightforward, detailed product review. His careful, even-toned evaluation of the respective vehicles shows both a theoretical knowledge of diesel engines and an ability to judge their application in these specific instances. There is constant awareness of both economy and performance criteria. The piece is enlivened with humor and a good-natured but firm grasp of practicalities. And, the author never loses sight of the outdoorsman's unique needs and concerns.

The Sweet and Sour of Diesel Power

By Bill Kilpatrick

One of the private and delicious pleasures of reaching what the French, describing feminine vintage, refer to as "a certain age" is that the discrediting of firmly held convictions is no longer a big deal. As we accumulate both mileage and gray hair, so many bubbles go bust that the deflation of yet another causes hardly a ripple.

Years ago, for example, I locked in on the idea that diesel engines were the stuff of power stations, locomotives, tramp steamers, and Cunard Queens. An offended sense of smell assured me they were used in heavy trucks and buses; and—in taxicabs and small buses—I'd certainly heard them clackety-clacking through European streets. But I never envisioned a day on which I'd find myself cruising around looking for a service station that sold diesel fuel. I figured both my driving habits and yours were too ingrained to put up with the noise, the smell, the lag in acceleration, and the wait-a-minute-or-so start-up procedure. (On the other hand, I never envisioned a world in thrall to the Arabs, either, or—for that matter—to auto mechanics with kidney-shaped swimming pools and Cadillacs.)

I should have realized change was in

the wind when, a couple of years ago, I first drove a posh, zillion-dollar Mercedes powered by a new five-cylinder diesel. It fired up quickly, was quiet, didn't smell, and went like a bat when I mashed down on the accelerator. In all probability, such upgrading in diesel technology didn't sink in because a Mercedes is so far beyond my means that paying attention to its features would be like falling in love with Cheryl Tiegs; don't bother; you can't afford it.

Over a recent month, however, I spent a fair amount of time behind the wheels of two diesel-powered half-ton pickups—one a Dodge, the other a Chevy—and, while I'm not about to stand on street corners passing out tracts and seeking converts, I was and am impressed by both. If you're noodling the idea of buying a new pickup, both are worthy of at least a look-see. (Ford isn't in the light-truck diesel market at the moment, but Detroit's "me too-ism" is notoriously contagious, so an appropriate announcement is only a matter of time.)

Unlike most Motown offerings, the two trucks I drove are as different as night and day; not as diesels per se, but rather in approach and performance. Outside and in, neither appears particularly special. I don't recall whether or not the Chevy bears some sort of lettering or medallion to indicate its uniqueness (if so, I failed to note it), but the tailgate on the Dodge bears the legend "Diesel Power." Otherwise, both look like other new Dodge or Chevy pickups. It's when you start them up and drive off that things take on radically different characteristics.

In general, the disadvantages of a diesel when applied to an automobile or a light truck are summarized above; i.e., it can and does make a bit of a racket (especially at idle or low speeds), it can and does smell (but then I've never been turned on by the smell of gasoline exhaust, either), it does take a minute or so to start up (cold weather requires patience), and—depending upon how the vehicle manufacturer has chosen to go—it can manifest a slight lag between stepping on the accelerator and getting anticipated response. Also, you won't find a diesel fuel pump on every street corner.

The advantages of a diesel include—or are supposed to, anyway—better fuel economy; better emissions control thanks to inherently low carbon monoxide and hydrocarbon output; long engine life; lower maintenance costs; low fuel "blow by" into the crankcase (eliminating the need for a closed crankcase ventilation system), and—in general—lower fuel cost to the consumer.

The principal difference between a diesel engine and a gasoline engine is that in the latter, the fuel/air mixture monitored by the carburetor is ignited by means of a precisely timed electric spark, whereas in the former, the air in each cylinder is highly compressed and thus heated to a degree high enough to explode timed injections of vaporized fuel. When a diesel is cold, glow plugs (heating elements) are needed to heat cylinder air hot enough to burn the fuel, a process accounting for the time interval between turning on the ignition and actually starting the engine. Once the fired-up engine heats to normal operating temperature, the glow plugs automatically shut down. From that point on combustion occurs by means of the hot compressed air.

In the Chevy, turning the ignition key when the engine is cold illuminates an amber dash light displaying words to the effect that the starter should not be cranked until the light goes out. On an 8-degree February morning, this key/light/crank sequence took about 45 seconds, time that might profitably be spent fastening seat belts or checking rear view mirror adjustment, though in my case, that time was spent giving myself hell for dribbling cigar ashes all down the front of a freshly dry-cleaned down jacket.

In the Dodge, you turn the key and push a small red dash button which lights up to indicate that the glow plugs are on the job. When the light goes out, you hear a minor but distinct "clunk" that tells you the starter can now be cranked.

What must be avoided when starting a diesel is the temptation to "prime" the injection system by pumping the accelerator pedal once or twice as one might do when starting a gasoline-powered unit. Doing so puts too much raw fuel in the cylinders, meaning the glow plugs have to contend with a mixture that is too rich. The result of this is not only a labored start, but also enough blue smoke to constitute an ecological threat. I found that both the Dodge and the Chevy started easily and required no idling assistance via my foot or the accelerator. In fact, until you're ready to put the vehicle in motion, it's best to avoid the accelerator altogether.

When a diesel is thoroughly warmed up, no time interval is required between turning the key and cranking the starter. In other words, you can dash in for the Sunday papers, come back out, and start right up.

Driving a diesel is just like driving anything else. No special techniques are called for. But, again depending upon the power route a manufacturer has chosen to take, you may have to pay attention to engine rpm.

The Chevy, for example, is powered by GM's 350-CID V8, essentially the same engine you can order in a new Oldsmobile. It's a powerful package with more than enough torque at the low end of the rpm range, meaning you can stab it and get snappy results. You'll win no impromptu drag races with it, but, coupled with an automatic transmission (as was the case in the truck I drove), it marches from 0 to 50 more or less on a par with its gasoline-powered cousins. At speed on an interstate, say, it's easy to forget all about its being a diesel—you get good response, minimum engine noise, and almost car-like handling.

The Dodge, on the other hand, is all truck, pure and simple. The engine is a 243-CID in-line six built by Mitsubishi. Far from being a neck-snapper, it nevertheless appears to be and feels like an engine that will run forever. What you have to do until you get used to it is ignore the noise (which, in a conventionally powered vehicle would send you whimpering to the nearest mechanic) and wind it right up there, keeping the rpm high through all gear ranges. Otherwise, you'll think you've got a stone, which it most definitely is not. What it is, again, is a truck, geared for work rather than flash; it'll march, but you have to be patient. The unit I drove—an Adventurer SE 150—was equipped with a semi-brutal four-on-the-floor manual transmission, meaning it's not a vehicle the wife is apt to borrow for a grocery run.

As you'd expect, the GM V8 is markedly more thirsty than the Mitsubishi Six. Chevy claims fuel savings of from 20 to 25 percent versus a gasoline engine of similar power rating (120 hp at 3600 rpm). Even so, it's no panacea for the high cost of fuel; quenching its undeniable thirst, I paid 69.9 cents per gallon for diesel fuel on an interstate, 64.9 at a truck stop. The Dodge, the engine of which is SAE-rated at 100 hp at 3700 rpm, is a miser by comparison. Again, you pay for what you get.

What you pay for Chevy's base Fleetside diesel pickup is $6,300. I drove a duked-out Cheyenne loaded with options that bring the total package perilously close to $8,500.

A base Dodge one-half-ton diesel pickup is pegged at $6,400. The Adventurer SE package adds up to about $600, meaning the unit I drove works out to a nice, round $7,000. To give you an idea of what diesel power would set you back, Dodge sells its bottom-of-the-line 150 pickup for around $4,700. That, compared to the $6,400 mentioned above, means specifying the diesel costs in the neighborhood of $1,700.

Is a diesel worth it? Well, that depends. If you've got in mind a workaday vehicle—something that will see reasonably hard service day in and day out—my guess would be yes, it's worth it. You will get more miles to the gallon, and your overall maintenance and service costs should be lower than they would be in a comparably equipped gasoline-powered truck. It should last longer, too, assuming you take care of it. But if you're thinking of a new pickup as a second car, or as something that merely would be handy to have on hand, my guess would be no, it's not worth it.

Guys like ourselves should keep in mind that diesel fuel might be a bit hard to come by in deer country or within reasonable distance of a productive trout stream. And perhaps more if not most important is that as rugged as a diesel is, should you ever need emergency engine work, finding a mechanic able and willing to do it might prove to be a search worthy of the Holy Grail . . . or at least a ten-point buck.

7. Outdoor Food Writing

The following outdoor food article examples are from Field & Stream's Food Editor Sylvia Bashline. All three are good examples of the amount of outdoor (as well as culinary) knowledge and experience called for. Sylvia knows how long it takes to cook a deer heart and that tenderness depends on age and habitat. She knows the basic character of mackerel meat, the differences between Atlantic and Pacific species—and that fishermen are likely to come home with too many of either. Both "Venison Treats" (December, 1978) and "The Mighty Mackerel" (March, 1979) lead in with an interesting historical perspective and stress the achievement of full use of his bag by the sportsman/harvestor. "Wild Mushrooms" (August, 1978) shows the careful treatment some outdoor food subjects need. You have a responsibility to your reader not to lead him into a dangerous area without sufficient information.

Storage and handling instructions are a far more important element of the outdoor, than the conventional, recipe. Proper handling and storage of fish, game and wild plants is critical to the outdoorsman, who sees his food through (often long and far from ideal storage conditions) himself rather than picking up the packaged, finished product at the A&P.

Any recipe you present must be tested to the point that you know it can be dependably duplicated at home or in camp. In the case of camp recipes, harmony, logic and portability of ingredients (are you likely to have that along? Is there a logical seasonal accompaniment?) is important. Bear in mind that food photos (never mind outdoor food photos, which may require special settings or accompaniments) are a tricky business at best (tasting good, and looking good—and dramatic—may be entirely different cases).

VENISON TREATS

BY SYLVIA BASHLINE

Our nation grew up eating venison. From the time we were fledgling colonies, deer meat has played a big part in our diet, just as deer hunting has touched the lives of millions of Americans. The Colonists of yesteryear didn't waste an ounce of this delicious source of protein. However, over the years, many deer hunters have started to think of venison in terms of chops, steaks, and roasts. They tend to forget about the ribs, stew meat, heart, and liver. Sure, you can make burger out of some of the odds and ends (I like a mixture of 2/3 venison to 1/3 fatty pork for my venison burger). But barbecue ribs can certainly be meaty and appetizing, especially when you have bagged a larger-than-average deer.

The liver and heart are traditionally deer-camp fare, often sliced thinly and panfried after a long day's hunt—a sort of celebration of the harvest. The following recipes lift these variety meats out of the ordinary and into the gourmet class. The stew recipe is one of the best I've ever tasted. Cranberries add a special tang. And the next best thing to roast venison is serving it the next day in a mouth-watering meat pie.

Pickled Venison Heart

1 venison heart
2 bay leaves
Salt and pepper
3 parts water/1 part vinegar
1 small onion, sliced

Place heart in a large saucepan. Add enough water to cover the heart; also add a little salt and the bay leaves. Bring to a boil, lower heat, and simmer (covered) until tender. It will take longer than a beef heart, but there is no set time. It depends on the age and habitat of the deer. The last venison heart I cooked simmered for about 4 hours. When it's tender, drain, cool, and then slice thinly. Place the slices in a bowl with the onion and the water/vinegar mixture (enough to cover the meat). Add salt and pepper to taste. Store in refrigerator for several hours. Dry meat with paper toweling before using in sandwiches with mustard or as appetizer material. Place a dab of mustard on a rye cracker; top with a piece of heart and a tiny piece of parsley.

Hunter's Stew

1-1/2 lbs. venison stew meat, cubed
Flour
2 tbsp. cooking oil
1 onion, coarsely chopped
1 clove garlic, minced
1 tsp. salt
1/8 tsp. pepper
2 cups water
3/4 cup dry red wine
1 beef bouillon cube
6 carrots, cut in 2-inch strips
2 stalks celery, cut in 2-inch strips
1 cup fresh (or frozen) cranberries
1 tsp. sugar

1 tbsp. steak sauce
2 tsp. Hungarian paprika
4 juniper berries (optional)
2 whole cloves
1 bay leaf
Cornstarch

Dredge stew meat in seasoned flour and brown in the hot oil in a Dutch oven with onion and garlic. When brown, add wine, water, and bouillon and bring to a boil. Cover and simmer for 1-1/4 hours. Add carrots, celery, cranberries, sugar, steak sauce, paprika, juniper berries, cloves, and bay leaf. Cover and simmer another 45 minutes until vegetables are tender. Thicken to taste with cornstarch mixed with a little cold water. Serves 6. Great with hot biscuits and spinach salad.

Venison Ribs

Marinate ribs for 48 hours in vinegar/water solution (1 part vinegar, 3 parts water) with 2 bay leaves, 2 tbsp. salt, and 1 sliced onion. Refrigerate while marinating.

Dry pieces and put in a shallow baking or roasting pan. Brush with melted butter and roast at 450-degree oven for 30 minutes.

In saucepan, combine following and heat until it comes to a boil:
1 cup chili sauce
1-1/2 cups water
1/4 cup steak sauce
2 tbsp. lemon juice
1/2 tsp. chili powder
1/2 tsp. salt

Turn the oven temperature down to 350 degrees, then cover the meat after liberally coating with the above sauce. Baste the meat at 15-minute intervals with the sauce until the ribs are tender, 1 to 1-1/2 more hours.

Note: If there is any leftover meat, remove it from the bones, trim off all fat, and cut meat into very thin strips. Heat in a frying pan with some catsup and serve in warm hamburger rolls—a delicious barbecue venison sandwich!

THE MIGHTY MACKEREL

Like many of our saltwater species, mackerel go through population cycles. These patterns have been noted since Colonial days. There are many theories about these ups and downs, including pollution, reproduction failure, and lack of food. The reason or combination of reasons will probably not be discovered until more money is earmarked for saltwater fishery research. Our knowledge about these valuable sport and food fish is limited.

Until about 100 years ago, all mackerel sold in this country were salted. The salting was done aboard ship, and most mackerel fanciers didn't get their first taste of the fish flesh until the fishing fleet began to carry ice in the 1800's.

I've worked mainly with Atlantic mackerel, but the Pacific variety has a similar oily flesh that is well suited for broiling, smoking, and salting. Anglers often get carried away when fishing for mackerel and bring home more than they can use in a reasonable time.

Mackerel that will be broiled, baked, or smoked while fresh should be filleted. The skin may be retained. If the fish is to be frozen, remove the skin.

All oily fish suffer from storage. No matter how carefully they are frozen, they should be used in a month or two at the most. Rather than freeze fresh mackerel, I prefer to smoke it first and then freeze it, using double wrapping. (Fish will lose less moisture and flavor if it is stored in a freezer that does not have the frost-free feature. The fan in the frostless models draws moisture from a package of fish no matter how well it is wrapped.) Seal the fish tightly in Saran Wrap first and then wrap it in freezer paper. The package should then be labeled as to species, number of servings, and date.

Our favorite fresh mackerel recipe is broiled—simple but elegant. The roe of the mackerel is also a delicacy, reserved only for the best of friends. And smoked mackerel is an old favorite. If a surplus of mackerel is a problem, canning is a good alternative. Canned mackerel may be used in fish cakes, fish loaf . . . or curried mack.

[Article concludes with recipes for Broiled Mackerel, Curried Mack, Baked Mackerel Glenna, Smoked Mackerel, Mackerel Roe.]

WILD MUSHROOMS

To avoid all wild mushrooms because some are poisonous is to miss one of our finest wild treats. Of course, it is vital to acquire and use a good guide book with pictures and descriptions before you pick a single specimen. Two of the best are mentioned at the end of this article. Forget the old wives tales about shortcuts on how to test for poisonous mushrooms; all of them are worthless. Mushrooms that look as if they'd been nibbled on by mice may well have been eaten by insects that are immune to the poison. A silver spoon held against the flesh of a mushroom indicates absolutely nothing. Varying degrees of unpleasantries can be suffered from mushrooms, all the way from a slight stomach upset to death. Some individuals are allergic even to certain of the edible species, so the first time you serve a new mushroom, eat with moderation. Just as some people are sensitive to milk or eggs, there are those who can not tolerate mushrooms.

The puffball is one of the common mushrooms that my Pennyslvania expert places in the "foolproof four" category. Others are the morel, shaggy mane, and sulphur mushroom. Most people can recognize puffballs without much trouble, especially the giant puffball (*Calvatia gigantea*). The first one I ever ate was presented to me with a flourish by a guest. He was obviously very proud to have discovered such a fine specimen (it was volleyball-sized). Frankly, I didn't know what to do with it, but he quickly took over the kitchen and produced delicious slices of sauteed puffball to awe the rest of the party guests. He sliced the puffball thinly with a bread knife, removed the outer skin and gently cooked it with butter in a frying pan until brown on both sides—about 10 minutes. A splash of white wine was added a few minutes before it was done. Success!

Puffballs are excellent served raw in a salad. Dice a pound of the peeled mushroom into bite-sized pieces, chop up a large celery heart, and cut four hard-boiled eggs into good-sized chunks. Place in a salad bowl with two minced green onions and season with salt and pepper. Make a dressing of four parts olive oil and one part wine vinegar with a pinch of garlic powder. Toss the salad for a couple minutes, then place in the refrigerator for an hour. Serve on lettuce leaves.

Puffballs should be white clear through and firm when cut into. If they have begun to turn yellow and a bit watery, they are past their prime. In most parts of their territory, they appear in August and September. A large puffball will go a long way. To avoid wasting any of it, you may preserve it by peeling, thinly dicing, sauteing in butter, and then packing in jars and freezing.

Most mushrooms dry easily and take up little space on the kitchen shelf. For preserving (both drying and freezing) choose young, firm specimens, wash and dry thoroughly, dice and place in a 180 degree oven (with the door propped open) for 3 to 5 hours. They are done when dry and leathery. Put in a sterile glass jar and store.

Two years ago we moved to an area in Pennsylvania where there are many Amish farms. Shaggy mane mushrooms grow with abandon in their manure-covered fields. What a kick each fall to drive the back lanes with one eye watching the road and the other looking out for the telltale line-up of "little soldiers." Shaggy manes look just like the guidebook pictures and are best picked in the button stage before the gills darken. They are more solid when immature. You know as soon as you get a bagful in the car that you have a treat coming. The aroma is delicious!

Shaggy manes must be used within a day of picking or they will deteriorate into an inky mess. Hold upright under a faucet to wash off the dirt. Dry thoroughly and place in damp toweling in the refrigerator until ready to cook. They can be diced and sauteed in butter like any other mushroom, but our family has a special way of preparing them. I cut them into bite-sized pieces and place in the top of a double boiler with 2 tablespoons of butter and a little salt and pepper, and simmer for 15 minutes over boiling hot water. I then brown 1 tablespoon butter, stir in 1 tablespoon flour, and add the liquid from the cooked mushrooms to make a gravy. Add the mushrooms to the sauce and serve on hot buttered toast.

I enjoy using wild mushrooms with fish and game dishes. The following recipe is great with wild mushrooms, but you can cheat a bit and use the commercial variety if that's all that's available. . . .

8. A Humorous Outdoor Column

This excellent example of outdoor humor writing is from Gene Hill's Field & Stream column, "Hill Country." (February, 1978). A close look will reveal something important to outdoor humor writing beyond the funny angle and deadpan approach Gene uses. The reason the piece hits home is that Gene has artfully tapped the average fly fisherman's secret inferiority complex in the face of the flyfishing mystique. Each mishap and embarrassing ineptitude is part and parcel of the average fisherman's lot.

Fishing terms and allusions ("matching the hatch," "no kill," dace, tippets, backing) are used throughout, without concession to outsiders. Note further the wide variety of incidents of carelessness and just plain bad luck cited in the course of the article. No amount of "pure research" would come up with all this, even if you went to the trouble of rounding up fly fishermen and questioning them. And for the "ranking," Gene had to know not only the order of magnitude of each occurrence but its relative frequency.

As in all other forms of outdoor writing, in order to write outdoor humor convincingly it is not enough to be funny—you must have a hands-on knowledge of your sport. Without this your finest writing efforts won't bring a chuckle.

Low Rod

By Gene Hill

Now that fishing season is just around the bend on the calendar, I have to face the fact anew that my peers with fly rods are many, and united by the common fact that they are not the ones who forced the adoption of "no kill" stretches. Given the natural abilities of the average fly fisherman, "no kill" is an apt way of describing what is likely to happen, no matter where or what. To label that goal as intentional is, to be honest, dishonest.

This year to liven up the (justly deserved) feelings of inadequacy in those of us who describe flies by color ("the brown fly or the gray one?") and who know only three sizes (all right, maybe, and the hell with it if that's what they want), I propose the following competition for the title of . . . Low Rod. Since merely not catching anything would never separate us in ranking, we have to look further for the qualities that distinguish us from each other.

What about a point system? Let's say 20 points for a fly box irretrievably dropped in fast water; 15 points for a fly that comes untied the moment a fish touches it; 10 points for leader knots that come undone; and 10 points for a knot that's too big to pass through the tip guide. At agreed-upon intervals tippets will be checked for wind knots; all those with more than three will get 1 point apiece. No points for being hung up in trees or bushes unless the fly and at least half the leader are sacrificed; then 5 points. Hooks broken on back cast, 2 points. Hooking self in jacket or hat, 1 point; ear, cheek, or neck, 3 points. No points for falling in unless a creditable witness testifies that water depth is less than 18 inches and of virtually no measurable velocity; the points will range from 1 to 5 depending on degree of clumsiness.

When pure ineptitude results in lost pipes, wet sandwiches, or breaking the tip of a one-tip rod, points will range from 5 to 10. Rods broken in screen doors, car doors, or rear windows of station wagons will be 2 or 3 points, depending on circumstances. Rods broken by stepping on them, or by flailing water in anger or frustration, rate somewhat higher.

Reels falling off reel seats, 10 points, unless fish is lost; then 15 points. Line not tied to backing, 10 points. Backing not tied to reel, 10 points. Loss of fish due to either is an extra 5 points.

One-point credits will be given for such things as improper threading of line through guides, upside-down reel, cutting wrong section of leader after attaching fly, tying one clinch knot or blood knot more than three times before it will hold, having wrong reel and line for rod used, and asking someone else to tie leader or fly, or to select fly, streamer, etc. Any normal fisherman should be able to accumulate 5 to 10 1-point items in a single day.

Putting rising fish down with inept cast, careless wading, etc., is to be expected and earns no points whatsoever. Likewise losing fish from not checking leader or hook, or fumbling net procedures.

You cannot win Low Rod if you are found actually matching the hatch—either in size or pattern—unless all concerned agree that this was purely coincidental and occurred without any deliberate intent whatsoever. Catching fish, however, does not absolutely disqualify you, providing you admit it was accidental and the size falls below a keeper. On the other hand, to be fair, catching chubs, dace, or other unwanted coarse fish should be to your credit; hooking and then losing such fish should earn 1 point each time.

A real effort for Low Rod can be made by using flies you tie yourself, providing they fall apart after only a few casts and/or cause audible laughter from at least two other fishermen no more skilled than yourself. This is a real test of character.

In the common case of a tie or near-tie for Low Rod, I think we can use our common sense. Tearing waders or boots more than once an outing on barbed wire, normally only a 1-point incident, can be awarded extra points if the tearee carries no patching material or if his patches refuse to adhere. Having absolutely no yellow or gray flies when that's all the trout are taking, again, though not ordinarily worth more than 1 point, can earn more if this is agreed to be indicative of the Low Rod's span of trout fly knowledge in general. . . .

Needless to say, these are just illustrations or suggestions. Should you choose to adopt such a rating system, you should take into account local conditions and other such variables as you see fit.

If one of your companions wins Low Rod several times and seems unlikely to ever be dethroned, it should be no problem to disqualify him from competition and encourage others to come forward. After all, how many fly boxes does one have to lose before he quits carrying one and resorts to small plastic pill bottles? (The correct answer is four.) And how many expensive rods does he have to step on before he learns to watch where he's putting his felt soles? (The correct answer is two—I hope.)

No doubt some enterprising tackle catalog will have a Low Rod pin like the one that's offered for doubles on woodcock or grouse. Fine. Our society is too advanced to restrict our plaudits for the few born with fine reflexes and coordination. There are those of us who need, desperately, credit just for trying.

9. A Boating/Fishing Article

"Chart Your Way to Better Fishing" (Field & Stream, August, 1978) is an excellent example of a boating article for the fishing audience. F. M. Paulson presents a "boating" subject (charts) from the unique angle of the fish seeker. All the chart symbols and colors are explained in light of their fishing implications. Even the safety aspects are viewed in this manner ("Getting lost is a sad waste of fishing time."). On the other hand, for a pure boating audience the chart explanations would be too elementary.

The direct usefulness of the article follows right through. What could be a formidable subject for the beginner is presented in a way that makes it seem easy as well as useful (it can help you catch more fish). Paulson not only tells you where to obtain charts but how to care for them, even down to the folding and what type of pencil to use. This multitude of very useful tips can only come from someone who is out there using the charts himself.

Chart Your Way to Better Fishing
By F. M. Paulson

There are two unarguable reasons why every boater who fishes charted waters should obtain and employ a nuatical chart. A reliable marine chart can help you avoid danger and return you home safely, and it can help you find and return to better fishing time and again. Fishermen who never leave the sight of land still need charts.

At this time of the year when many of you are trailering your boats to new and unfamiliar vacation waterways, you need one or more charts as well as the usual road maps. There's no substitute for a marine chart for the do-it-yourself fisherman who figures to explore strange waters. A chart costs far less than a guide, even less than an electronic depthfinder. Prices range from $2.00 to $3.50. A chart plus depthfinder is, of course, an ideal way to locate fish-holding water.

Unlike two-dimensional road maps, the modern marine chart provides a third dimension. It reveals water depths and land heights, and contains a goldmine of information useful to fishermen. Chart details reveal the nature of the unseen bottom, noting whether there are rocks, mud, hard sand, etc., present. Charts won't tell you to "fish here," but they provide the habitat information you need to know to find fish. As most fishermen know, some species of fish tend to congregate at certain depths; others are particular about the types of bottom they inhabit. Underwater structures will be noted. Although the chartmakers include them as hazardous objects, wrecks and rockpiles are also proven fish habitat of interest to each and every fisherman.

Charts useful to sport fishermen are better and more available than ever before. The U.S. National Ocean Survey, which produces large-format conventional charts of our inland seas and the U.S. coasts for mariners, also produces an ever-expanding series of charts designed for the convenience of small-craft operators. Their work even includes a series of canoe charts of the Minnesota-Ontario border lakes to serve the paddling fraternity. The National Ocean Survey's small-craft charts are compactly designed for cockpit use. They fold down in accordion style to a folio size about 8 inches wide by 14 inches high. Unlike the larger window-shade-size conventional charts, a small-craft chart can be held in one hand, leaving the other hand for the wheel even when the wind is blowing.

Since it covers parts of two coastal areas as well as an inland waterway, I have pulled small-craft Chart No. 11428 out of my file as an illustration of the many features a nautical chart offers fishermen. Covering the Okeechobee Waterway—St. Lucie Inlet to Fort Myers and Lake Okeechobee, Florida—I used this chart to cruise and fish from Florida's East Coast to the Gulf Coast in a 20-foot outboard.

Two reduction scales are used: 1:40,000 and 1:80,000. In the larger scale insets, 1-1/2 inches (approximately) on the chart is equal to a statute mile of 5,280 feet. In the smaller scale drawings, 3/4 inch (approximately) is equal to a mile. The St. Lucie Inlet and sections of the Caloosahatchee River and Lake Okeechobee are large-scale insets, but the winding, interconnecting canals are shown in smaller scale in order to encompass them in the available space. Land areas are colored yellow. Deep waters are white. Shades of blue typify shallows. Light green color indentifies marsh and grassy areas. Figures on the water designate depths, or soundings, in feet at mean low water. It's important, always, to check the title notes on any chart you use. Sometimes figures are given in fathoms, or 6-foot intervals. Contour lines reveal where water depths change. Among fishing interpretations available, pockets of light blue areas on Lake Okeechobee indicate shallows where you might find bluegill and bass bedding grounds. Offshore shoals marked in pale green tell where to expect grassy islands favored by black bass.

* * *

Getting lost on the water is a sad waste of fishing time. Learning the elements of the U.S. buoyage system, and employing a nautical chart to locate these signposts of the sea conserves time for fishing. The majority of buoys are red or black. As you enter a harbor or head up a channel, the red buoys mark the right side of the channel, while the black mark the left. "Red right returning" is an easy memory aid. All odd-number buoys are black. All even numbers are red. Red and black horizontally striped buoys mark a dangerous object to be avoided. They may be passed on either side. If the top band is black, the preferred channel places the buoy on the left, going upstream. If the top band is red, it's preferable to pass within the buoy on your right going upstream. Black-and-white vertically striped buoys, like a referee's shirt, mark a midchannel or fairway and can be passed close aboard on either side. Shape is of no significance. Among other buoys, cylindrically shaped or can buoys are black, and conically shaped or nun buoys are red. Spar buoys are shaped long and round, and may be used as cans or nuns to mark special areas. Buoys in certain locations may be lighted for night navigation. Green lights are used on black buoys, and red lights on red buoys. White lights may be used on either type or color of buoy.

* * *

On some waters you will find many navigation lights. These may be fixed (lighted all the time), flashing (mostly off, with a short lighted period), occulting (mostly on, with a short blackout period), and various combinations. The first letters on your chart tell you what the light does: Fl, Flashing; F, Fixed; Occ., Occulting. The second letter (or letters) indicates color, and the third set of letters and figures say how often. Fl G 4 sec., for example, tells you that a light gives off a green flash every 4 seconds. Lights are all important to the night fisherman, either to find his way home or to help him locate his fishing area on the water. Boaters who plan only to fish the daylight hours also should acquire some knowledge of lights for that one time when engine trouble keeps you from returning home before dark sets in.

This past spring I used two NOS charts to find my way around the Florida Keys. The small-craft chart had a scale of 1:80,000, and the conventional chart covered a smaller area of the Keys but in the larger scale 1:40,000. (It would be a mistake for you to conclude that one chart is better than the other. For inshore work especially, I recommend that you choose the largest scale possible, and whenever two charts are available, buy both.) The small-craft chart, although printed in a smaller scale, backed up the conventional chart by revealing facilities where gasoline, groceries, hardware, meals, lodging, campsites, and boat rentals were available. None of that information was incorporated in the conventional chart. No matter which type chart you use, make a habit of studying the notes that you will find studded around the perimeter of the chart or printed on the container. Be careful, indeed, that you don't toss out the annotated paper pocket that accompanies any small-craft chart you may buy. If you are using conventional charts, you will need to purchase Chart No. 1, titled, "Nautical Chart Symbols and Abbreviations," for an interpretation of all the symbols employed.

Vacationing fishermen who trailer their boats from inland to coastal waters may have very little knowledge about tides, and often are unaware of the importance of tides in fishing. While you can buy individual publications covering tide tables and current action from the National Ocean Survey at nominal cost, the tide tables you need for local use generally are covered on the folder that accompanies an NOS small-craft chart.

Many fish feed during periods of slack water—the period just before and after the turn of the tide when there is little or no horizontal motion of tidal water. Also shallow flats with their grass beds abound in shrimp and crabs plus other forms of marine life. Large fish often feed in such areas at night. A knowledge of water heights is critical, especially since such areas are often exposed during low tides. Currents, produced by tides or other forces, that flow over bars and shoals stir up natural foods such as shrimp, crabs, and marine worms. And fish are most likely to be feeding when food like this is in suspension. Chumming, or attracting fish by ladling out crushed clams or ground-up fish, is most productive when a strong current is present to carry the chum out away from the boat to attract fish to your baited hooks.

* * *

While an old chart is better than no chart, it's safer and smarter to throw out your old charts and replace them with new ones as they become available. Storms and currents especially cause frequent changes in bottom conditions and the location of obstacles. And that's why you should also seek local knowledge whenever possible to augment what an old or new chart reveals.

I view the marine chart as a standard fishing tool, and while it can be used on a visual basis in ideal weather without employing a compass or binoculars, I place the same priority on the use of compass and binoculars that I do on a good chart. All three are standard fishing tools that complement each other, and can help you become a better fisherman.

Once you have the charts you need, take care of them. Keep them dry. Use soft pencils for markings. Erase carefully. Fold conventional charts into a compact size suitable for storage aboard small craft. Many fishermen store them under seat or bunk cushions. Mark the name that identifies the area the chart covers in one corner for easy reference, and you won't have to fumble through a collection of charts to get the one you want. Don't abuse your chart, but do make use of it. Record the locations of the best fishing spots you discover, and any other information helpful to you in finding your way back to the launch ramp. When your chart wears out or becomes obsolete, buy a new one, but don't forget to transfer your personal notes.

Some government charts, particularly those covering your local waterways, may be available from your marine dealer. He may also have copies of the free National Ocean Survey nautical chart catalogs. All chart catalog prices are available by mail from the following sources:

For charts of the Atlantic, Pacific, U.S. coastal waters, Hudson River to Troy, Atlantic and Gulf Intercoastal Waterways, Great Lakes and connecting waters, write Distribution Center, National Ocean Survey, Riverdale, Maryland 20840.

For charts and maps of Lower Mississippi River (Gulf of Mexico to Ohio River), also St. Francis, White, Big Sunflower, Atchafalaya, and other rivers, write U.S. Army Corps of Engineers, Vicksburg District, P.O. Box 60, Vicksburg, Miss. 39180. . . .

10. An Outdoor PR Article

"Bones in the Bahamas" is an example of outdoor product PR writing, the product in this case being an airplane. The plane is not obtrusive in the story, appearing by name only three times along with specific details such as engine size, type of landing gear, and capacity. Also present—although even more subtly—is the idea that a plane like this can carry you off for one-day excursions to exciting fishing grounds. None of this would be the least bit effective if the story were not strong enough—in action, color, and how-it's-done detail—to stand by itself. If you took out all reference to the Darter Commander, you would still have a credible fishing tale.

This is just one simple form of outdoor PR writing. There are as many ways to promote a product (and as many degrees of sophistication) as there are outdoor products.

Bones In The Bahamas

By Jack Samson

The high scream from my spinning reel told me that the fish I had hooked was moving faster than I had ever known any fish to move. Over 100 yards of six-pound monofilament line spun off the reel in a matter of seconds.

"I don't know," I said to our guide, Francis, who was standing on the after-deck of the bonefishing boat, shading his eyes against the sun. "I've only got maybe another 100 yards."

"He'll turn, mon. Just keep the rod high, with a little more drag," he said softly.

I knew if the "Boney" didn't turn in the next few seconds, I was going to lose him. And I wanted to keep him. I was experiencing something I'd heard about for most of my adult life—a battle with a bonefish, one of the scrappiest gamefish in the world.

A friend and I had been planning the trip for many months. We wanted to try the bonefish flats off the northern tip of Andros Island in the Bahamas. And from the time we brought down our four-place Darter Commander from 7,000 feet to just above the surface of the water off the big island, we knew this was going to be a fishing trip even Hemingway's Old Man would have been proud of.

During that first look at the island, Don eased back on the throttle of the 150-hp Lycoming engine and we squinted in the glare off the white sand that lay just a foot beneath the crystal water. We could see the flats extended for miles in all directions.

We also could see a few bonefishing boats and some Bahama-rigged sailing boats that were scattered on the flats, miles apart. As we increased our power and headed toward the landing strip, I saw a manta ray drift across the flats, casting a shadow that echoed every inch of his 10 foot span.

We touched down just 58 minutes after leaving Fort Lauderdale. The single runway at Andros was smooth concrete and long enough to take an airliner. When we turned off at the first taxi strip, however, we were grateful for the rugged fiberglass landing gear on our Darter Commander. The taxi strips at the field were bulldozed out of the island's bed coral, and they aren't designed for gentleness.

Ten minutes after landing we met our guide who was waiting with his sturdy Bahama bonefishing "pole boat" and we were ready for the big challenge.

Francis told us the best way to catch boneys is to pole the boat slowly and quietly through the shallow water until a school is seen—or even a single bonefish. Wading for them is an effective method too, but after seeing a number of sharks—some up to eight feet long—we considered that suggestion somewhat less than attractive.

There is also the method of "just settin'"—dropping a line over and waiting for a cruising bonefish. But since this particular day was clear and the

surface calm, we decided that poling was our best chance.

In the center of a flat where the water was about two feet deep, Francis baited our hooks with sizable hunks of crab and then began poling our boat.

He told us that bonefish are primarily bottom feeders, much like trout, and when it has its nose down rooting for food, its tail may stick up out of the water. When a tail is sighted—the fish is as good as caught. Or so you would think.

My friend spotted a single fish feeding and cast ahead of it. In a moment the fish took the bait and Don tried to set the hook. The line straightened, then fell slack.

"Too soon," was all that Francis said as he rebaited the hook.

I had a six-joint, ultra-light rod and a tiny spinning reel with about 200 yards of line. I had proven before that big fish can be taken on very light tackle—certainly a boney could be. I wasn't sure, however, that I could turn my fish on the first run in time to have any line left.

That was what I was wondering as I held the rod tip above my head and watched the nylon thread slice the water's surface. I had cast ahead of six boneys that were tailing about 20 yards off the bow.

"He turn, some. He turn," Francis said softly then.

The bonefish was turning, but not quickly, and I could see his arc soon would leave me with no line. Leaning into the rod a little, I held my breath. The reel was still shrieking. The fish's head swung just a little, but he wasn't slowing down at all—and he was about 150 yards out.

Francis ducked his head as the line came about and he grinned. "You got him, mon! That line she don't break."

Suddenly the bonefish slowed and swung in toward the boat. "Better get the line in," Francis warned.

I managed to keep it taut until the fish began a second run about 75 yards out. That run didn't last as long as the first and each run that followed—about a dozen in all—was shorter than the one before.

It took about 45 minutes to land the boney—a small one at roughly five pounds.

But, I'll tell you a little about bonefish—now that I'm an expert (having caught three more that day); they are about the toughest fish I've ever tangled with! They take off like a fox with hounds on his tail and only turn when you really make them turn and they never once quit fighting until the last second—when they die.

My friend took five boneys—the biggest about six and one-half pounds. He was almost as tired as the fish after battling it for nearly an hour.

Francis may have had some secret delight about being able to take boneys with a hand line—I suspect the natives look down on our use of sophisticated equipment and consider us a bit effete. "That's sporty, mon," he commented as he saw me reel in my first on that six-pound line. "That's sporty."

We were well-baked by mid-afternoon and had enough of both fish and pictures to make our day a complete success.

The cockpit of our Darter Commander was pretty warm when we got back to it, but it cooled off quickly once we were in the air. Francis waved as we dipped our wing to him. And then we banked over the small terminal at Andros and began to climb for altitude.

"We should be on the ground at Lauderdale by six," Don said as we took an Omni heading for Florida.

I looked down at the light green water that was shoaling off to dark blue depths.

I only regret one thing. I wish I'd brought a fly rod. I hear boneys put up quite a scrap on the end of a light line.

My friend nodded when I mentioned that. "Next time!" he said.

11. A Man's World No Longer

The outdoor field is a natural (no pun intended) for the woman writer. Women are sharing the outdoor experience with men in ever-increasing numbers—rock climbing, fishing, backpacking, whitewater canoeing, bowhunting. Some of the best shooters on the American Olympic teams are women. Women are deeply involved in the conservation movement, and many of our best outdoor writers today are coming from the distaff side.

Clear in the following extracts from Maggie Nichols' Wild, Wild Women is the deftness, knowledgeability, and ease with which a woman can cover the whole spectrum of outdoor subjects.

On "The Masculine Mystique"

Mention "outdoor woman" and many people—women included—will conjure up visions of large unisex females with chapped lips and heavy shoes who talk in hearty voices and display an irritating lack of sympathy toward anyone who sleeps past daybreak or prefers a cozy bed and warm fire to a night out in the rain. Such unflattering imagery has considerable precedent. For years, bird watchers were caricatured as shelf-bosomed women of uncertain age wearing wool stockings, oxford shoes, rough tweed shirts, and (no doubt) burlap underwear....

But although millions of women, along with men and children, are out camping, fishing, hiking, backpacking, hunting, boating, floating, admiring, and enjoying, many people still think of the outdoors as a place for burly types, especially men. Some of this attitude is pure chauvinist thinking ("Who let you out of the kitchen, wench?") but much of it is merely unconscious, an assumption never questioned or even put into words. This is particularly true of male outdoor writers, who, with no particular bias in mind, tend to write as if all their readers will be men.

The idea of the outdoors as a man's world seems particularly obsolete at a time when female sports figures in everything from gymnastics to race-car driving are gaining recognition. Yet there still remains some masculine bias toward the idea of women in the outdoors, particularly among men raised on sexist ideas....

For example, there was the former editor of an outdoor magazine (since reformed, I've heard) who once told a highly competent woman outdoor writer that the reason he didn't buy any of her work was that no man wanted to read anything a woman had to say about the outdoors. And I recently rode in a car for an hour with an otherwise charming man who spent a good part of the trip telling me that men don't really enjoy the company of women.

But such attitudes belong to another age. Many men themselves have rejected the masculine mystique and are urging women to join them in the outdoors. Family fishing, camping, hiking, boating, or other outdoor vacations are not just some nightmare cooked up to scare old-timers. Lots of men, married and single, are actively looking for feminine companionship under the sun (and stars), and lots of women (single and married) are finding out how good being outdoors can feel. Despite these changes, there are still a number of problems that make it hard for women to enjoy, or even to attempt, the great range of possibilities the outdoors holds. Although modern schools and girls' organizations now teach a number of outdoor activities, this is of little help to women who grew up in less-enlightened times, back when the "open road" was specified for boys and what a fellow was encouraged to take fishing was never a girl. (Even the Girl Scouts was not too helpful on this score when I was a member. In my troop, anyway, most of the badge activity centered around domesticity. My most rugged badge work involved roasting a hot dog on a green stick. Otherwise our instruction tended toward tomato-soup cookery and the creation of tooth-rotting, heart-stopping fudge.)

The worst hurdle for many fledgling outdoor people including men not raised in the rugged tradition is their own fear, either of dirt and discomfort or of being ridiculed for not knowing what to do. It is easy for both beginner and expert to forget that everyone has to be given a chance to learn. No one has ever become good at fishing, shooting, compass reading, canoeing, archery, knot-tying, or anything else without the benefit of some sort of training, some chance to learn from a knowledgeable source—or at the very least, a long uninterrupted period of trial and error. Nothing will send a person back indoors faster than having a fishing rod or a tent peg grabbed from their hands with a helpful comment like "Not that way, you idiot—like THIS!"

Down through the years, many little boys learned outdoor skills at their daddy's knee, when they were small enough to warrant daddy's patience. But many little girls (and many other little boys) were not so lucky. Unfortunately, many would-be teachers refuse to recognize the facts of childhood deprivation, and have no tolerance for grownups who don't know how to build a fire or catch a fish or row a boat. Worse, they don't remember that once they didn't know how to do these things themselves.

This is the real threat of the masculine mystique. The idea that only "real men" belong in the Great Outdoors, and that men who aren't at home out there deserve to be scorned, is not only ridiculous, but damaging as well.

By turning people against the outdoorsman, and thus against the outdoors, it can create indifference to the fate of our waters and wild lands, and strengthen a preference for shopping centers over undeveloped woods. Worse still, it can shut an individual off from a huge area of pleasure, personal fulfillment, and experience.

On Fishing

. . . To some fishing purists, a pickerel on the line is about as welcome as a rat on the bed, but I was thrilled. I even cooked and ate my fish that night, and though it was bony, it tasted as good as anything I'd ever eaten. What's more, the mysterious appeal of fishing had finally been revealed. I had thrown an offering into the void, and the void had answered back.

Such realized dreams of glory are sweet, especially when they occur not only on the simple level of catching fish, but on the higher plane of triumphing over scoffers, impatient experts, and assorted know-it-alls. Just one fish captured in the teeth of adversity, one personal moment of unexpected success, can spark a small fire of devotion—or at least of tolerance—for the fishing sports. Two such experiences can set a person up for life.

* * *

Next to bass, the most popular fish in this country is trout, and in many places, especially in the West, it still is number one. Among certain anglers, in fact, trout is what fishing means. Though Izaak Walton, the great seventeenth-century philosopher of the rod and reel, may have fished for everything from carp to roach (an English fish), it's for his words on trout that he is most remembered. And there is plenty of reason to revere this creature. It's delicious to eat; it's difficult to catch; it's fun to fish for; and it tends to live in the kind of clean, clear, sparkling, calendar-picture settings that give fishing a good name.

On the Shooting Sports

Every time you shoot, you're entering into competition against yourself. Can you get a group of shots closely spaced in the bull's-eye? Can you hit twenty-five clay targets in a row? Better yet, can you keep from collapsing into a heap of twitching nerves after you've hit 22, or 23, or 24? Once you get going you want to keep trying over and over, working to best your last score, to get it all right this time. Like people at a carnival shooting gallery endlessly plunking down coins for more shots at the moving ducks, for more tries at the giant lime-green panda nobody really wants, it's hard to give up.

* * *

Like fanciers of antique cars, many collectors of old guns belong to organizations that not only bring the pieces back to life but re-create those corners of the past that have seized their imagination. For Dr. White and others, that chosen era is the part of the nineteenth century when the beaver trade was flourishing and the mountain men roamed the western wilderness, wild and free. Everything the modern mountain man wears or carries when shooting an antique gun belongs to the time of those long-gone adventurers, men like Jeremiah Johnson and Jed Smith. Even their clothes are accurate, though not really old. The day I met Dr. White, for example, he had a calico shirt and buckskin pants plus a "possibles" bag that he had made himself, sewing everything together by hand with the sort of needle a true nineteenth-century mountain man would have used.

Everything about this sport tends toward ritual. To load a gun like the ones we shot in Utah, you have to pour a measured amount of gunpowder down the barrel, wet a small, round patch of cotton in your mouth, tamp it down on top of the powder with a long rod, drop in the metal ball, and tamp again. All this takes time—you could spend hours happily engaged in a black-powder world without actually taking very many shots. But when you finally do pull the trigger, the reward is not just a good (or bad) shot, but an aura consisting partly of real smoke and fiery flashes as the powder ignites, and partly of fantasies of wagon trains, lines of hostile Indians silhouetted against a cloudless sky, and Walter Brennan chuckling ironically as he prepares to save the day.

On Camping

In the beginning, everyone was a camper. This lasted only as long as it took the naked ape to figure out housing, which proved so much more satisfactory than caves or bare ground that in the course of time it has all but enveloped the earth. Recently, however, an increasing number of well-sheltered moderns have been experiencing a nostalgia for their original state, so on weekends and vacations they abandon their homes and go off with tent, backpack, or recreational vehicle (RV) for those parts of the earth that housing has left alone.

* * *

The best way to experience the adventure of living out is with a tent, but for some this provides a bit more spontaneity than they care to handle: sudden rainstorms, or worse, all-day rains; mealtimes with no kitchen; dirty laundry; darkness; lost flashlights; and, of course, the ground. To many these "problems" are all part of the fun, puzzles to be solved, obstacles requiring the exercise of ingenuity. To others they are simply burdens, and thanks just the same, but they'd rather stay at home. For years the latter attitude probably outweighed the former, particularly among women who saw no reason why exchanging a kitchen stove for a camp stove and lack of running water was much of a treat. With the rise of the recreational vehicle, however, such complaints were pretty much laid to rest. By bridging some of the gap between out and in, the RV industry opened a whole new era in recreation away from home.

* * *

If possible . . . a person's very first camping trip should be arranged to coincide with beautiful weather. Let there be sunny days that soften into star-studded, pine-scented nights, that open into pearly, rose-tinted dawns, that bloom into sunny blue-sky mornings, and so on. Let there be sparkling water to swim in, and soft breezes to temper the air. Let there be a sunset worthy of tears, and a night of crickets, with a touch of mystery. But above all, let there be no rain.

Trail Riding

Despite our lack of trail-ride expertise, the guides had made their peace with us on the long climb up the mountain, and by the time our camp was established, the four of us were like longtime friends. A monstrous amount of gear had accompanied us on the pack horses, but it was off their backs and into its proper place in what seemed like no time, and before the last green-and-gold reflections of the pines had faded from the mirror surface of the drinking-water lake, we were sipping hot coffee laced with cognac and waiting for thick steaks, potatoes, carrots, and onions to cook by the campfire coals. After dinner, while we drank more coffee in the cold air and watched the stars wink through the velvety sky, we swapped stories and laughed at our sore parts. Brick told us then that we were "just like real people," by which we understood him to mean that he'd expected a good deal worse from writers from back East. Somewhere or another, he'd had a bad experience with journalism, which isn't hard to imagine. At any rate, we did not match whatever boorish stereotype he had in mind, and so our mountain visit turned out to be a human adventure as well as an encounter with pure fresh air, crystal skies, and the calls of coyotes under a three-quarter moon.

On Boating

Regardless of craft choice, more and more active paddlers are succumbing to the lure of the rapids—possibly because they are so absolute. You can think ahead, study the situation, work out a game plan—but once you've committed yourself to the action, there's nothing to do but act. It's a time without future; everything in the midst of whitewater is *now*.

* * *

The river where we canoed was narrow and only a few feet deep, a winding stream stained a rich amber from cypress bark, which made the smooth pebbles on the bottom glow like King Solomon's treasure in the sunlit shallows.

Since we were there in midweek, we saw only one other canoe, and we camped in solitude, though not in silence, for the woods were filled with singing birds. It was an easy, leisurely trip, lush with early summer green, and though an Artistotelian ring around the full moon seemed to threaten rain, the weather favored us with two perfect days. We ate more than we should have—and took a midday swim in the cold, jewellike water. When it was over and we drove back to our everyday lives on the Garden State Parkway—guided through the thickening snarls of traffic by CBers with names like the Giant Mouse—it seemed an almost schizophrenic fairy story. How could two such incredibly different worlds exist so close together? Yet they can, and luckily they do.

* * *

What about those other millions who

aren't quite ready, physically or mentally, to trade the abstract burdens of modern life for the all-too-tangible burden of a pack on the back? How do they check out of civilization and book a trip to a place that nature made?

One good way is a river-float trip, the original form of rapid transit, full of the same capricious pace changes that mark the course of travel through man-made canyons, but with none of the rush, crush, dirt, or frustration. None of the time schedules, either, or the sense of destination. On a river, you aren't traveling to get somewhere; you're just traveling. Things come to meet you—towering walls of ancient canyons, rocks twisted by forces beyond imagining, perfect skies enhanced by pure white puffs of cloud, treelined shores and islands with sandy beaches, birds and animals, and a vastness empty of all sound but the voices of the wind and the river.

* * *

All water-related activities have within them the possibility of harm. You would think that creatues so ill-adapted to living in water would keep this in mind. But it's amazing how many people who cannot swim will put their faith in a boat and set to sea. I once watched a group of four adults and about six children cram themselves into a tiny boat with a small motor and take off from the dock in a Key West harbor. The craft was so overloaded that the freeboard was hardly more than an inch, meaning that if the boat hit three-inch waves, water would come pouring in, and it would probably sink. As the family chugged happily away, I saw a pelican riding the surface suddenly disappear, pulled beneath the glassy seas not by magic, but by a pair of jaws. . . .

Looking Good

It's not breaking some commandment of nature to keep your skin in shape in- or outdoors. Two small bottles of lotions are not too much to carry into the wilderness, or on any kind of outdoor trip. Neither is a mirror (metal for the backwoods), although some people feel this has no place on an excursion into nature, where everything should be allowed to hang out in its natural old way. (Usually people who say this have adorable faces with skin like peaches, bee-stung lips, and hair that never needs combing.)

For women who need cosmetics to face the world with confidence and a smile, a small makeup kit isn't too much to carry, either. Just don't overdo it. An eyebrow pencil, a stick of eye shadow, and a lipstick should be enough to correct the flaws. You can stuff all this, along with a small brush or comb and a nail file for clearing away the dirt that has a way of collecting under nails in the outdoors, into a small plastic bag and tuck it into your pocket or someplace where it will be easily accessible.

Side Issues

Although I'm an enthusiastic booster of most of the activities I have covered so far, it would be hypocritical of me to pretend an uncritical love that never lapses into boredom. There are times when fishing holds no charms; when camping seems a disagreeable mistake; when even my much-loved canoeing becomes a hot and uncomfortable drudgery. Since I have these occasional hostilities toward activities I normally enjoy, I can sympathize with people who care nothing for fishing and the rest, and therefore have come to believe that they couldn't possibly care about the outdoors. But though I understand this feeling, I can't agree with it. Unless you have developed a downright hatred for the open air, there's too wide a range of possibilities to give up on nature just because major kinds of outdoor sport don't turn you on.

12. Nature Writing: A Conventional Treatment of a Classic Theme

"Born Again: An Arctic Spring" (International Wildlife March/April 1979) is an excellent illustration of the breadth of nature knowledge required of the outdoor writer today. The author, while sharing his impressions of an Arctic spring, gives the reader a multitude of plant, animal, bird, weather, topographical, etc., detail. Readers that won't blink at sanderlings, saxifrage, wooley lousewort, or boreal forest, to whom lichen and ptarmigan are practically household words, have come to expect this degree of sophistication of nature detail and understanding. (Not to mention the "experts" waiting in the wings for one molting stage, one migration schedule, one feeding pattern to be cited askew.)

Born Again: An Arctic Spring

By Fred Bruemmer

I was tired of winter, tired of white, tired of cold—fed up, restless and rebellious. For months the tundra beyond our camp at Bathurst Inlet in the Canadian Arctic had been an infinity of rolling land mantled by snow, broken here and there by gaunt rock ridges, solemn and silent. It had been that way since October and it would stay that way until May. "*Nuna hiniqpoq*," said the Eskimos with whom I lived. "The land sleeps."

Spring does not arouse this land with a sudden clamor; instead, it arrives discreetly on tiptoe. Most April days are still intensely cold, and vicious storms rage across the tundra, filling the air with stinging snow. In between, there are a few calm and glorious interludes. The sky, a clear robin's-egg blue, turns to cool green near the horizon. The snow is brilliantly aglitter. Each tiny sign of spring is a longed-for miracle, a promise of warmth and color and life.

* * *

On sandy ridges, arctic ground squirrels emerged lean and hungry from hibernation. They dug up rootlets, nipped off emerging shoot and leaves, and crammed their busy little mouths with the sourish crowberries of yesteryear.

By the middle of May, the areas of snow-free land had grown larger. Ptarmigan were courting in the valley, the males still in immaculate white, the females already changing into their brown-gray summer plumage.

On the third of June it rained. Gray, soggy clouds swathed the hills. The snow, so hard in winter that the tracks of our heavy sleds were barely discernible, became mush. Water trickled down the rocks. Lichens and mosses—desiccated and brittle in winter—avidly absorbed the moisture and shimmered with renewed life.

* * *

Meltwater murmured down to tundra lakes and rivers in a shimmering lacework of brooks and rills. Sanderlings and other sandpipers probed the mud for hidden larvae and tiny worms, leaving filigree of three-toed tracks. Golden plovers soared overhead in the intricate gyrations of their courtship flights.

The first flowers had bloomed in late May, tiny rosettes of purple saxifrage, specks of color on sun-warmed ridges. Now, arctic poppies on long slender stems turned their golden blooms toward the sun. Woolly lousewort, wrapped in fur of myriad silvery hairs, opened their purple blossoms. The tiny bells of arctic white heather nodded in the breeze, and the deep-purple flowers of Lapland rhododendron glowed in marshy hollows.

* * *

An arctic fox ran along a ridge, his ragged, white fur already changing into the brindled brown-gray of summer. Grasses and sedges were sprouting, and a delicate green sheen spread over the tundra meadows. Elegant horned larks spiraled toward the sky until they were but specks in the blue, then drifted gently downward on set wings, filling the air with their jubilant, lilting song. From its nest of sticks and dry grasses on a ledge above the icebound river, a rough-legged hawk rose to circle high above us with wild and urgent cries.

We traveled far inland, set up camp on a dry ridge above a tundra lake, made tea and lazed in front of our tent. It was night, calm and infinitely serene. Winter had been sterile, odorless. Now the light breeze carried with it the subtle smell of moist, living earth. A faint golden wash spread over the distant hills. The open water of our lake was deep indigo, the ice in its center a bluish milky-white, candled into myriad silvery rods. From time to time they broke with a tinkling sound, and bits of glistening ice drifted out onto the dark water.

Life for the Eskimos continued in the ancient, seasonal, immutable rhythm of people who still live off the land. They fished for trout. They hunted ptarmigan and ground squirrels. As they waited, patiently, for the caribou to come, I wandered over the tundra, glorying in its space and freedom and life.

The larger lakes were still partly frozen, the ice in their center hemmed by a sable skirt of water. Red-throated loons danced across the surface in their weird nuptial ceremonies, filling the air with wild, maniacal laughter. Nearby, an ermine slithered through a pile of rocks, sinuous and nervy. Its winter coat of white had already changed to a rich chestnut-brown on top and creamy yellow below.

* * *

And now the rhythm of the season was throbbing again. The caribou came. They had left the northern boreal forest months before, marching north, ever north, an immense, irregular host, the cows large with calf in the vanguard. By the time they arrived in our area, the great vital urgency of the spring migration had nearly spent itself, and the animals were content to pasture on the vast and verdant tundra meadows. The Eskimos hunted them day and night.

* * *

At our coast camp, everything had changed. A broad belt of open water rimmed the shore. The sea ice was flooded and rent by dark leads of open water. On rocky islets, eider ducks were brooding their eggs in down-lined nests. Arctic terns hovered above the glittering sea on rapidly beating wings and then plunged like plumed arrows to rise moments later with tiny fish in their beaks.

The seeds of arctic poppy were nearly ripe. The first fledglings emerged and adult birds foraged day and night. The feeling of urgency was nearly palpable, for the seasons of spring and summer are desperately short. The tundra was in the fullness of life. But in a few months, it would be sleeping under snow once again.

13. A Conservation Essay

This article by George Reiger shows just how much you need to know when writing about conservation today. The conservation writer is constantly faced with layers of conflicting theory, fact, and opinion that he must sift through, and already complex and sophisticated issues that he must be conversant with. No matter how personal your approach to the subject becomes, no matter how emotional the issues involved, in the face of almost certain opposition you must know your subject inside and out, pro and con, or you won't be taken seriously. One interesting technical point is the refrain of "9's," an example of finding an angle after walking around the story.

9 x 9 = Moral Decline
By George Reiger

Times change, but what constitutes "times" at present is often just a matter of days. Unwilling to ponder a problem for more than nine minutes or to sit still for more than nine seconds, another generation of Americans has contributed its impatience to a momentum of restlessness that exhausts the "news potential" of an oil spill or a fish kill within nine hours, the understanding and patience of Congress in dealing with land use and clean air within nine days and, the country's capacity to take and maintain positions on minimal standards of environmental health within nine years.

If the American Revolution—which required over nine years to resolve from the day General Gage sent British troops to seize the military stores at Concord to the signing of the Paris Peace Treaty—had been fought by colonists with the intellectual and moral stamina of Americans today, the Revolution would possibly have run out of steam even before our army was driven into winter quarters at Valley Forge.

Nine years ago, several important pieces of environmental legislation were debated by Congress, and one especially significant item—the National Environmental Policy Act of 1969—was passed. However, the ink in the President's signature was barely dry before the forces of inertia and the status quo began nibbling at this landmark legislation, allegedly to make it "more workable"—which would be fine, if true—but more often striving to gut the law so the ten percenters who hadn't yet cut out their piece of the pie could continue with business as usual.

In those early days of concern and debate, scientists and the statistics they supplied were critical to the success of conservationists fighting the good fight in or near the corridors of Congress. In some instances, scientists provided their data with the tacit understanding that conservationists would not involve them in the hurly-burly of courtrooms and hearings.

In most cases, the conservation troops were too happy with the information to question the motives of men unwilling to be linked directly to their research. I suppose many of us accepted the notion that scientists feel their careers lie outside the ordinary events of life which bind the rest of us into the fabric of society.

Scientists may see themselves as oracles of change, or sometimes as victims of its worst repercussions. Yet, by and large, they do not like to admit they play a major role in creating a culture where every one of us (scientists included) now faces the *likelihood* of death from industrially related, if not industrially induced, diseases.

Nine years ago, Boston College and the American Association for the Advancement of Science sponsored a symposium on "Science and the Future of Man." Actually the conference was about the future of science, since the conferees knew something about that subject, while "Man" was simply too nebulous a hook on which to hang their interest, much less their enthusiasm.

Keynote speaker J. Tuzo Wilson, a geophysics professor from the University of Toronto, listed several essential elements which compose the soul of science, but did not point out that two of them—a love of tools and a love of simplicity—are in direct conflict with one another.

Since today's research tools are anything but simple, scientists cannot hope to work as independent thinkers, as they once did when the most innovative thinking was done. Instead, they must hire themselves out to various research institutes which, more often than not, are administered by people less concerned with science than with applied technology which, in turn, contributes to the fame of the institutes and the administrators.

Professor Wilson reminded his audience that progress in science depends on a free exchange of information between colleagues working in the same or related fields. However, neither industry nor government wants its scientists to breathe Word One about what they are doing or have discovered.

Information, far more than money, represents power and prestige for the business and bureaucratic administrators who run the nation. In addition, if, say, the glass specialists at Pittsburgh Plate ever tried to pool their knowledge with the copper specialists at Revere in order to speed up development of solar energy options, the anti-trust division of the Justice Department would be down on those two companies so fast their solar collectors would overheat!

The overriding themes of "Science and the Future of Man" were involvement and cooperation: Scientists should involve themselves more with the law, the humanities, and other scientific disciplines; the universities, business, and government should coordinate their efforts to solve universal problems such as energy needs.

As chemistry professor Franklin A. Long of Cornell University recommended: "Scientists must study the social consequences of science and technology and occasionally be prepared to stand up and be counted."

What then has happened in the nine years since this high-minded conference took place?

Well, for one thing, more environmental legislation has been passed to be followed by increasingly successful counterattacks by the forces of inertia and the status quo. Whereas nine years ago, science was distrusted by some because it was associated with misused technology, today it is distrusted by many more, because its definitions of truth are often contradictory.

We see scientists being used as pawns in a crucial chess game between conservationists and bureaucracy. For every expert we can find to suggest that oil spills are not doing the oceanic environment any good, opponents of conservation can trot out two or three experts to show with charts and slides that oil improves life for all creatures in the sea.

For every expert willing and able to document the dire implications of DDT, PCBs, and Kepone in the environment, industry can find some sincere or venal fool with a PhD willing to eat the stuff to show that such hazardous compounds have no short-term deleterious effects on the human digestive system.

Nine years ago, conflicts in scientific testimony involving environmental issues were uncommon because scientists, feeling the public could not understand or was not interested in technicalities, mostly thrashed their differences out in the relative privacy of scientific journals.

* * *

There was no one from industry to dispute Senator Edmund S. Muskie when he proclaimed during the science symposium that "when the sulfur dioxide content of the air in New York City rises above two-tenths of a part per million, ten to twenty (people) die as a result. In the past five years, sulfur dioxide has reached this level at least once every ten days."

Industry's scientists were unable to dispute such statistics because industry had never sponsored research on the harmful effects of indiscriminately dumped toxins from smoke stacks, sewer outfalls, and tail pipes on human health and well-being.

Even after the fit was in the shan, and at the height of popularity of the environmental movement, industry avoided disputing adverse numbers and instead rushed about dumping millions of tax-deductible dollars onto conservation groups.

Today, many scientists, dismayed by the public's distrust and embarrassed by the spectacle of colleagues calling each other names in public, have begun a retreat from the barricades of moral commitment back to the ivory tower where science can be idealized, pure and uncontaminated by problems in the real world.

In 1969, scientists cheered when attorney Victor J. Yannacone, Jr. told them at the Boston symposium: "Don't just sit there and bitch about the problems; sue somebody!"

Today scientists are inclined to wince at such a raw suggestion, and they tend to avoid the very thing they decided they needed more of nine years ago: Greater involvement with "the future of man."

Like most other Americans, they are depressed by the nation's economy and concerned about job security. The dollar, no longer supported by either gold or silver, is being mass-produced beyond credible limits. Put succinctly, moral commitments can get you fired.

Against this background of anxiety and revised thinking regarding environmental action, zoology professor Paul Colinvaux of Ohio State University has published an ecology overview called *Why Big Fierce Animals Are Rare.*

Contrasts in scientific attitudes over the past nine years can best be revealed by quoting John Platt of the University of Michigan who stated in 1969 that "the age of evolution is at an end, 3 billion years of it—evolution, that is, by *natural* selection. It is now *our* pollution, *our* preservation, *our* breeding, or *our* protection which determines the numbers and kinds of species of animals and plants all over the world. Evolution from now on will be by *human* selection, whether intended or not."

And comparing his words with the opening and closing lines of the first paragraph of Paul Colinvaux's preface: "Ecology is not the science of pollution, nor is it environmental science. Still less is it a science of doom. . . . I take the opportunity to brand as nonsense tales of destroying the atmosphere, killing lakes, and hazarding the world by making it simple."

While it may be scientifically "proper" to attempt to take *ecology* out of the mainstream of public debate and return it to the lofty pedestal it occupied before celebrities began to use the word in connection with breakfast cereals, how realistic or morally correct is this goal?

When Colinvaux discusses eutrophication and water pollution, he writes "If we stop dumping sewage, fertilizers, detergents, and garbage into any polluted lake, its waters will come clean again, by themselves, without any benefit of technology, in a very few years or decades depending on its size and the flow of water. The only way to kill a lake is to fill it in and pave it over."

Unfortunately, such a big biological picture does little to help those many anglers who must fly or drive hundreds of miles for their recreation, or those increasing numbers of people who flee to other states, if not to other nations, for their health and psychic well-being. They are not reassured to know that the area they leave behind may recover within a few decades, if more people, like themselves, move out.

They are especially not reassured because they know that with the United States expecting to add another 30 to 45 million people to its population during the next three decades, not only will it be increasingly difficult to find any place "away from it all," but those sadly polluted lakes Colinvaux talks about will be the next worse thing to being paved over.

Similarly, when Colinvaux discusses the atmosphere's buildup of carbon dioxide, he says that while the vast shock absorber, the ocean, is currently overloaded, things will work out all right over the next few centures:

"In the end (the sea) will soak up all the polluting carbon dioxide from our fossil fuels and pass them to its mud. But meanwhile the shock absorber has more than it can handle, and there is a temporary pile-up of the gas in the atmosphere. The most likely outcome is that the concentration in the atmosphere will nearly double before the oceans begin to catch up and bring carbon dioxide back down to its old proportions.... This will not be catastrophic for life. On the other hand, it will certainly make a difference. The worry is that we do not know what all the effects might be."

Wrong. The worry is that even given such knowledge, there is no longer a durned thing we can do about it. The dioxide has been cast, so to speak, and alarmists can be forgiven if they express concern for life and society as we know it.

Probably the single greatest issue of the past decade, at least in terms of the rhetoric and emotion expended, was the battle over the Alaska Pipeline.

While Colinvaux says he personally disapproved of the Pipeline (one wonders how actively), he implies that the possibility of plant and animal extinctions was a major part of the Alaskan debate. Instead, discussion always revolved about whether we wanted to treat Alaska as we had the rest of the nation, or whether we would attempt to preserve significant portions of that great wilderness so that our children, and theirs as well, might one day know the meaning of the words *alone, self-reliance, humility,* and possibly even God.

How far the high intentions of science have slipped in the nine years since biology professor George Wald of Harvard University declared "now that priests have stopped knowing science, it becomes necessary for scientists to become priests. It is important now that the scientist, in being the man who knows and is deeply concerned with that knowledge, and deeply concerned with the future of the human enterprise, is something of a priest in his outlook. It is perhaps most important that he be disinterested, that he ask nothing for himself."

A cat may have nine lives, but we doubt that a nation does. How many lives can we exhaust in nine years when not even nine hours is a working day and nine months is a year for those who teach and study?

Nine years ago, Professor Wald ended his presentation with this caveat: "We are at a parting of the ways not only for humanity, but for much of life on the earth, all of it now in our custody.... And so these days, all the time, there run through my head those beautiful words in Deuteronomy, chapter 30, verse 19, 'I have set before you life and death, blessing and curse; therefore choose life, that you and your descendants may live.''

Books of Interest From Writer's Digest

The Beginning Writer's Answer Book, edited by Kirk Polking, Jean Chimsky, and Rose Adkins. "What is a query letter?" "If I use a pen name, how can I cash the check?" These are among 567 questions most frequently asked by beginning writers — and expertly answered in this down-to-earth handbook. Cross-indexed. 270 pp. $8.95.

Bylines & Babies, by Elaine Fantle Shimberg. The art of being a successful housewife/writer. 256 pp. $10.95.

The Cartoonist's and Gag Writer's Handbook, by Jack Markow. Longtime cartoonist with thousands of sales, reveals the secrets of successful cartooning — step by step. Richly illustrated. 157 pp. $9.95.

A Complete Guide to Marketing Magazine Articles, by Duane Newcomb. "Anyone who can write a clear sentence can learn to write and sell articles on a consistent basis," says Newcomb (who has published well over 3,000 articles). Here's how. 248 pp. $7.95.

The Confession Writer's Handbook, by Florence K. Palmer. A stylish and informative guide to getting started and getting ahead in the confessions. How to start a confession and carry it through. How to take an insignificant event and make it significant. 171 pp. $7.95.

The Craft of Interviewing, by John Brady. Everything you always wanted to know about asking questions, but were afraid to ask — from an experienced interviewer and editor of *Writer's Digest*. The most comprehensive guide to interviewing on the market. 244 pp. $9.95.

The Creative Writer, edited by Aron Mathieu. This book opens the door to the real world of publishing. Inspiration, techniques, and ideas, plus inside tips from Maugham, Caldwell, Purdy, others. 416 pp. $8.95.

The Greeting Card Writer's Handbook, by H. Joseph Chadwick. A former greeting card editor tells you what editors look for in inspirational verse . . . how to write humor . . . what to write about for conventional, studio and juvenile cards. Extra: a renewable list of greeting card markets. Will be greeted by any freelancer. 268 pp. $8.95.

A Guide to Writing History, by Doris Ricker Marston. How to track down Big Foot — or your family Civil War letters, or your hometown's last century — for publication and profit. A timely handbook for history buffs and writers. 258 pp. $8.50.

Handbook of Short Story Writing, edited by Frank A. Dickson and Sandra Smythe. You provide the pencil, paper, and sweat — and this book will provide the expert guidance. Features include James Hilton on creating a lovable character: R. V. Cassill on plotting a short story. 238 pp. $8.95.

Law and the Writer, edited by Kirk Polking and Leonard S. Meranus. Don't let legal hassles slow down your progress as a writer. Now you can find good counsel on libel, invasion of privacy, fair use, plagiarism, taxes, contracts, social security, and more — all in one volume. 249 pp. $9.95.

Magazine Writing: The Inside Angle, by Art Spikol. Successful editor and writer reveals inside secrets of getting your mss. published. 288 pp. $10.95.

Magazine Writing Today, by Jerome E. Kelley. If you sometimes feel like a mouse in a maze of magazines, with a fat manuscript check at the end of the line, don't fret. Kelley tells you how to get a piece of the action. Covers ideas, research, interviewing, organization, the writing process, and ways to get photos. Plus advice on getting started. 220 pp. $9.95.

Mystery Writer's Handbook, by the Mystery Writers of America. A howtheydunit to the whodunit, newly written and revised by members of the Mystery Writers of America. Includes the four elements essential to the classic mystery. A comprehensive handbook that takes the mystery out of mystery writing. 273 pp. $8.95.

1001 Article Ideas, by Frank A. Dickson. A compendium of ideas plus formulas to generate more of your own! 256 pp. $10.95.

Writing for Regional Publications, by Brian Vachon. How to write for this growing market. 256 pp. $10.95.

One Way to Write Your Novel, by Dick Perry. For Perry, a novel is 200 pages. Or, two pages a day for 100 days. You can start and finish your novel, with the help of this step-by-step guide taking you from blank sheet to polished page. 138 pp. $8.95.

Photographer's Market, edited by Melissa Milar. Contains what you need to know to be a successful freelance photographer. Names, addresses, photo requirements, and payment rates for 3,000 markets. 672 pp. $12.95.

The Poet and the Poem, by Judson Jerome. A rare journey into the night of the poem — the mechanics, the mystery, the craft and sullen art. Written by the most widely read authority on poetry in America, and a major contemporary poet in his own right. 400 pp. $9.95.

Sell Copy, by Webster Kuswa. Tells the secrets of successful business writing. How to write it. How to sell it. How to buy it. 288 pp. $10.95.

Songwriter's Market, edited by William Brohaugh. Lists 1,500 places where you can sell your songs. Included are the people and companies who work daily with songwriters and musicians. Features names and addresses, pay rates and other valuable information you need to sell your work. 480 pp. $10.95.

Stalking the Feature Story, by William Ruehlmann. Besides a nose for news, the newspaper feature writer needs an ear for dialog and an eye for detail. He must also be adept at handling off-the-record remarks, organization, grammar, and the investigative story. Here's the "scoop" on newspaper feature writing. 314 pp. $9.95.

Successful Outdoor Writing, by Jack Samson. Longtime editor of *Field & Stream* covers this market in depth. Illustrated. 288 pp. $11.95.

A Treasury of Tips for Writers, edited by Marvin Weisbord. Everything from Vance Packard's system of organizing notes to tips on how to get research done free, by 86 magazine writers. 174 pp. $7.95.

Writer's Digest. The world's leading magazine for writers. Monthly issues include timely interviews, columns, tips to keep writers informed on where and how to sell their work. One year subscription, $15.

The Writer's Digest Diary. Plan your year in it, note appointments, log manuscript sales, be prepared for the IRS. It will become a permanent annual record of writing activity. Durable cloth cover. 144 pp. $8.95.

Writer's Market, edited by William Brohaugh. The freelancer's bible, containing 4,500 places to sell what you write. Includes the name, address and phone number of the buyer, a description of material wanted and rates of payment. 960 pp. $14.95.

The Writer's Resource Guide, edited by William Brohaugh. Over 2,000 research sources for information on anything you write about. 488 pp. $11.95.

Writer's Yearbook, edited by John Brady. This large annual magazine contains how-to articles, interviews and special features, along with analyses of 500 major markets for writers. 128 pp. $2.50.

Writing and Selling Non-Fiction, by Hayes B. Jacobs. Explores with style and know-how the book market, organization and research, finding new markets, interviewing, humor, agents, writer's fatigue and more. 317 pp. $9.95.

Writing and Selling Science Fiction, compiled by the Science Fiction Writers of America. A comprehensive handbook to an exciting but oft-misunderstood genre. Eleven articles by top-flight sf writers on markets, characters, dialog, "crazy" ideas, world-building, alien-building, money and more. 197 pp. $8.95.

Writing for Children and Teen-agers, by Lee Wyndham. Author of over 50 children's books shares her secrets for selling to this large, lucrative market. Features: the 12-point recipe for plotting, and the Ten Commandments for Writers. 253 pp. $9.95.

Writing Popular Fiction, by Dean R. Koontz. How to write mysteries, suspense, thrillers, science fiction, Gothic romances, adult fantasy, Westerns and erotica. Here's an inside guide to lively fiction, by a lively novelist. 232 pp. $8.95.

Writing the Novel: From Plot to Print, by Lawrence Block. Practical advice on how to write any kind of novel. 256 pp. $10.95.

(1-2 books, add $1.00 postage and handling; 3 or more, additional 25¢ each.
Allow 30 days for delivery. Prices subject to change without notice.)

Writer's Digest Books, Dept. B, 9933 Alliance Road, Cincinnati, Ohio 45242

PN 4784 .O9 S2

PN 4784 .O9 S2

AUTHOR	Samson, Jack	
TITLE	Successful Outdoor Writing	
DATE DUE	BORROWER'S NAME	ROOM NUMBER